HUW HENNESSY

# CYCLING IN
# NORTHUMBRIA

## 21 HAND-PICKED RIDES

Bradt Guides Ltd, UK
Globe Pequot Press Inc, USA

# AUTHOR

**Huw Hennessy** is a lifelong cycling nut, and since childhood has pedalled as much as possible at every opportunity – from Paris to the Loire Valley after finishing his A levels to freewheeling down the Andes when updating the Footprint *Colombia Handbook* a few years ago. Since moving to Devon in 2004, he has cycled all over southwest England, including off-road routes across Dartmoor, Exmoor and Bodmin Moor, as well as family favourites such as the Camel Trail and Pentewan Valley trail. In 2020 he did the Devon Coast-to-Coast cycle route from Ilfracombe to Plymouth, and has completed the Nello (a 100-mile fundraising pedal for cancer charity FORCE) eight times.

Huw is a seasoned travel writer and has written and updated a number of travel guides over many years, including several for Bradt, on St Helena and Mozambique. Most recently, he has written their first two cycling guides: *Cycling in Cornwall & The Isles of Scilly* and *Cycling in East Anglia*.

## DEDICATION
-----------------------------------------------------------------------------------
To my mother

## FEEDBACK REQUEST
-----------------------------------------------------------------------------------
At Bradt Guides we're aware that guidebooks start to go out of date on the day they're published – and that you, our readers, are out there in the field doing research of your own. You'll find out before us when a fine new family-run hotel opens or a favourite restaurant changes hands and goes downhill. So why not tell us about your experiences? Contact us on ✆ 01753 893444 or **e** info@bradtguides. com. We will forward emails to the author who may post updates on the Bradt website at ⊘ bradtguides.com/updates. Alternatively, you can add a review of the book to Amazon, or share your adventures with us on Facebook, Twitter or Instagram (@BradtGuides).

# FOREWORD

*Rob Marshall, komoot*

Northumberland is a wonderful place for a relaxed or adventurous bike ride, and this book shares some of the area's most beautiful routes, coupled with background features on its history, culture and wildlife. Combine this with **komoot** – a convenient route-planning and navigation app that enables users to find, plan and share adventures based on riding type and ability. You can use the komoot smartphone app or & komoot.com, and it syncs with practically any GPS device and wearable.

By scanning the QR code that accompanies each route, you'll gain access to an interactive map and detailed route profile – an inch-by-inch breakdown of the surface type alongside an elevation chart, together with an estimate of how long the route will take you to complete, based on your fitness level. You can also save the route for offline use: komoot turns your smartphone into a navigation device, and when you hit 'start' on the ride the turn-by-turn voice navigation will keep you on track, meaning you can pedal in peace and soak up the views without stopping to check the map at every intersection.

Speaking of pedalling and enjoying the scenery, this Bradt guide gives you a wonderful overview of the places you're cycling through and recommendations for where to eat and sleep. Komoot's 'Highlights' (red dots on the komoot map) can boost this intel with tips from the community – recommendations for things that may not appear in the guidebook, like a hidden picnic spot or a section of road loved by local riders.

Ready to explore more with komoot and Bradt? Create your free account using the voucher code below.

## DOWNLOAD A FREE MAPS BUNDLE TODAY

Download a free maps bundle of your choice by visiting & komoot.com/g.
Simply sign up for a komoot account and enter the voucher code **BRADTNEE**
*Valid until 31.12.2027*

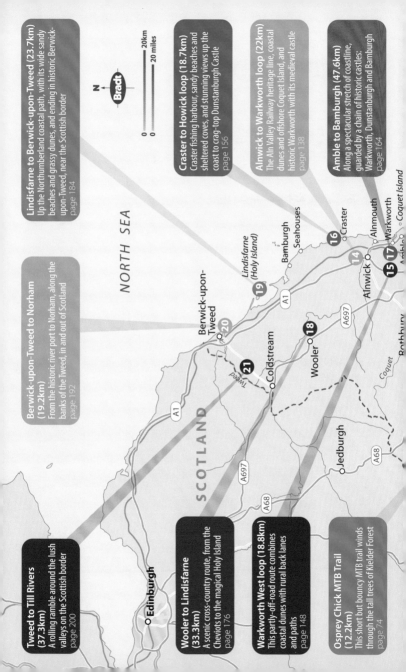

**Lindisfarne to Berwick-upon-Tweed (23.7km)**
Up the Northumberland coastal path, with its wide sandy beaches and grassy dunes, and ending in historic Berwick-upon-Tweed, near the Scottish border
page 184

**Craster to Howick loop (18.7km)**
Craster fishing harbour, sandy beaches and sheltered coves, and stunning views up the coast to crag-top Dunstanburgh Castle
page 156

**Alnwick to Warkworth loop (22km)**
The Aln Valley Railway heritage line, coastal dunes and offshore Coquet Island, and historic Warkworth with its medieval castle
page 138

**Amble to Bamburgh (47.6km)**
Along a spectacular stretch of coastline, guarded by a chain of historic castles: Warkworth, Dunstanburgh and Bamburgh
page 164

**Berwick-upon-Tweed to Norham (19.2km)**
From the historic river port to Norham, along the banks of the Tweed, in and out of Scotland
page 192

**Tweed to Till Rivers (37.3km)**
A rolling ramble around the lush valleys on the Scottish border
page 200

**Wooler to Lindisfarne (33.3km)**
A scenic cross-country route, from the Cheviots to the magical Holy Island
page 176

**Warkworth West loop (18.8km)**
This partly-off-road route combines coastal dunes with rural back lanes and paths
page 148

**Osprey Chick MTB Trail (12.2km)**
This short but bouncy MTB trail winds through the tall trees of Kielder Forest
page 74

NORTH SEA

SCOTLAND

Edinburgh

Jedburgh

Coldstream

Berwick-upon-Tweed

Lindisfarne (Holy Island)

Bamburgh

Seahouses

Craster

Wooler

Alnwick

Alnmouth

Warkworth

Amble ○ Coquet Island

Rothbury

Tweed

Coquet

A1

A697

A68

A697

A68

0    20km
0    20 miles

N

Bradt

16
19
20
21
18
14
15  17

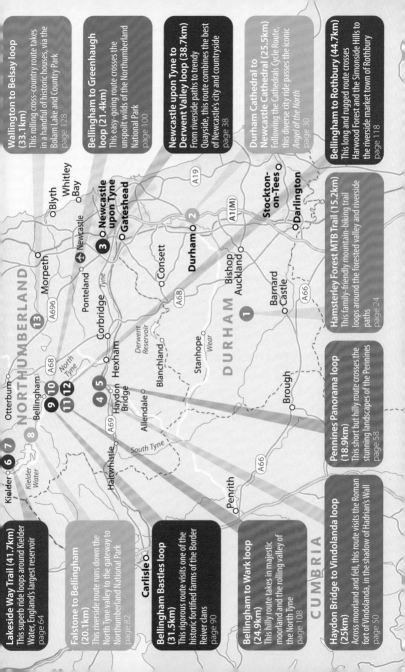

**Wallington to Belsay loop (33.1km)**
This rolling cross-country route takes in a handful of historic houses, via the Bolam Lake and Country Park
page 128

**Bellingham to Greenhaugh loop (21.4km)**
This easy-going route crosses the unspoilt wilds of the Northumberland National Park
page 100

**Newcastle upon Tyne to Derwent Valley loop (38.7km)**
From riverside paths to trendy Quayside, this route combines the best of Newcastle's city and countryside
page 38

**Durham Cathedral to Newcastle Cathedral (25.5km)**
Following the Cathedrals Cycle Route, this diverse city ride passes the iconic *Angel of the North*
page 30

**Bellingham to Rothbury (44.7km)**
This long and rugged route crosses Harwood Forest and the Simonside Hills to the riverside market town of Rothbury
page 118

**Hamsterley Forest MTB Trail (15.2km)**
This family-friendly mountain-biking trail loops around the forested valley and riverside paths
page 24

**Pennines Panorama loop (18.9km)**
This short but hilly route crosses the stunning landscapes of the Pennines
page 58

**Haydon Bridge to Vindolanda loop (25km)**
Across moorland and fell, this route visits the Roman fort of Vindolanda, in the shadow of Hadrian's Wall
page 50

**Bellingham to Wark loop (24.9km)**
This hilly route takes in majestic moorland and the rolling valley of the North Tyne
page 108

**Bellingham Bastles loop (31.5km)**
This rigorous route visits one of the historic fortified farms of the Border Reiver clans
page 90

**Falstone to Bellingham (20.1km)**
This riverside route runs down the North Tyne valley to the gateway to Northumberland National Park
page 82

**Lakeside Way Trail (41.7km)**
This superb ride loops around Kielder Water, England's largest reservoir
page 64

NORTHUMBERLAND

DURHAM

CUMBRIA

Blyth
Whitley Bay
Newcastle upon Tyne
Gateshead
Morpeth
Ponteland
Corbridge
Hexham
Haydon Bridge
Allendale
Haltwhistle
Blanchland
Consett
Stanhope
Brough
Bishop Auckland
Barnard Castle
Darlington
Stockton-on-Tees
Durham
Penrith
Carlisle
Kielder
Kielder Water
Otterburn
Bellingham

Derwent Reservoir
North Tyne
South Tyne
Wear
Tyne

A19
A1(M)
A68
A69
A696
A66
A68

# CONTENTS

**INTRODUCTION** ........................................................10

**CYCLING: THE ESSENTIALS** ........................................ 13

**HOW TO USE THIS BOOK**............................................. 19

 **01** HAMSTERLEY FOREST MTB TRAIL............... 24
**Start/end:** Hamsterley Forest Visitor Centre (loop)
**Distance:** 15.2km **Time:** 1½–2hrs **Difficulty:** ①
**Highlights:** Hamsterley Forest, riverside trails and MTB adventure

 **02** DURHAM CATHEDRAL TO NEWCASTLE
CATHEDRAL ..................................................... 30
**Start/end:** Durham Cathedral/Newcastle Cathedral
**Distance:** 25.5km **Time:** 2–2½hrs **Difficulty:** ②
**Highlights:** Historic cathedrals at Durham and Newcastle, the Angel
of the North and the bridges over the River Tyne

 **03** NEWCASTLE UPON TYNE TO DERWENT
VALLEY LOOP ................................................. 38
**Start/end:** Newcastle Quayside (loop) **Distance:** 38.7km (short
cut 26km) **Time:** 4hrs **Difficulty:** ② **Highlights:** Iconic Tyneside
features including the Tyne Bridge, Millennium Bridge, Baltic Arts
Centre, Sage Gateshead concert hall, Derwent River Park and Gibside

 **04** HAYDON BRIDGE TO VINDOLANDA LOOP .... 50
**Start/end:** Haydon Bridge (loop) **Distance:** 25km **Time:** 3hrs
**Difficulty:** ① **Highlights:** North Pennines AONB and Vindolanda,
historic Roman fort in the shadow of Hadrian's Wall

 **05** PENNINES PANORAMA LOOP ...................... 58
**Start/end:** Haydon Bridge (loop) **Distance:** 18.9km **Time:** 2hrs
**Difficulty:** ② **Highlights:** Stunning Pennines landscape, from a high
ridge with 360-degree views over the Allen and Tyne valleys

**06** **LAKESIDE WAY TRAIL, KIELDER FOREST...... 64**
**Start/end:** Kielder Castle (loop) **Distance:** 41.7km **Time:** 4–4½hrs
**Difficulty:** ② **Highlights:** Kielder Forest, England's largest forest and Kielder Water, the largest artificial lake in northern Europe, fringed with lakeshore artworks

**07** **OSPREY CHICK MTB TRAIL,**
**KIELDER FOREST ............................................74**
**Start/end:** Kielder Castle (loop) **Distance:** 12.2km **Time:** 1½hrs
**Difficulty:** ① **Highlights:** Through the woods and hillsides of Kielder Forest and along the shore of Kielder Water

**08** **FALSTONE TO BELLINGHAM......................... 82**
**Start/end:** Falstone/Bellingham **Distance:** 20.1km **Time:** 2–3hrs
**Difficulty:** ① **Highlights:** Through rolling, heather-clad moorland bordering the Northumberland National Park and along the valley of the inky-dark River North Tyne

**09** **BELLINGHAM BASTLES LOOP...................... 90**
**Start/end:** Bellingham (loop) **Distance:** 31.5km **Time:** 3–4hrs
**Difficulty:** ② **Highlights:** Wild moorland in the Northumberland National Park, meandering streams of the North Tyne Valley, and Border bastles – historic fortified farmhouses

**10** **BELLINGHAM TO GREENHAUGH LOOP.......100**
**Start/end:** Bellingham (loop) **Distance:** 21.4km **Time:** 2–2½hrs
**Difficulty:** ① **Highlights:** The moorland and fells of the Northumberland National Park, the North Tyne Valley, and historic Border Reiver bastles

**11** **BELLINGHAM TO WARK LOOP ....................108**
**Start/end:** Bellingham (loop) **Distance:** 24.9km **Time:** 2½–3hrs
**Difficulty:** ② **Highlights:** Majestic moorland, the undulating North Tyne Valley, and the historic riverside Wark on Tyne

## 12 BELLINGHAM TO ROTHBURY ...................... 118
**Start/end:** Bellingham/Rothbury **Distance:** 44.7km **Time:** 5–6hrs
**Difficulty:** ② **Highlights:** Through the moor and fell, river valleys
and conifer forest of the Northumberland National Park to Rothbury,
with nearby Cragside, historic home of Lord Armstrong

## 13 WALLINGTON TO BELSAY LOOP .................128
**Start/end:** Wallington Hall (loop) **Distance:** 33.1km **Time:** 3–3½hrs
**Difficulty:** ① **Highlights:** Meandering through the Wansbeck and
Blyth valleys via the country estates of Wallington Hall, Capheaton
Hall, Belsay Hall and Castle and Whalton Manor and Gardens

## 14 ALNWICK TO WARKWORTH LOOP ..............138
**Start/end:** Aln Valley Railway (loop) **Distance:** 22km **Time:** 2½hrs
**Difficulty:** ① **Highlights:** The Aln Valley Railway heritage line,
coastal dunes and offshore Coquet Island and lighthouse, and
historic Warkworth with its medieval castle

## 15 WARKWORTH WEST LOOP .........................148
**Start/end:** Warkworth (loop) **Distance:** 18.8km **Time:** 1½–2hrs
**Difficulty:** ② **Highlights:** Medieval Warkworth, rural countryside
and stunning views of the sea, sand dunes and Coquet Island

## 16 CRASTER TO HOWICK LOOP ........................156
**Start/end:** Craster (loop) **Distance:** 18.7km **Time:** 2hrs
**Difficulty:** ① **Highlights:** Craster fishing harbour, sandy beaches
and sheltered coves, and stunning views up the coast to crag-top
Dunstanburgh Castle

## 17 AMBLE TO BAMBURGH...............................164
**Start/end:** Amble/Bamburgh **Distance:** 47.6km **Time:** 5–5½hrs
**Difficulty:** ② **Highlights:** Along one of the UK's most
spectacular stretches of coastline, guarded by a chain of historic
castles: Warkworth, Dunstanburgh and Bamburgh

**WOOLER TO LINDISFARNE** .........................**176**
**Start/end:** Wooler/Lindisfarne **Distance:** 33.3km **Time:** 3–3½hrs
**Difficulty:** ② **Highlights:** Tranquil countryside, from the Cheviot
Hills and moorland to the coast; historic St Cuthbert's Cave and the
Holy Island of Lindisfarne

**LINDISFARNE TO BERWICK-UPON-TWEED...184**
**Start/end:** Lindisfarne/Berwick-upon-Tweed **Distance:** 23.7km
**Time:** 2½hrs **Difficulty:** ② **Highlights:** Up the Northumberland
coastal path, with its wide sandy beaches and grassy dunes, and
ending in historic Berwick-upon-Tweed, near the Scottish border

**BERWICK-UPON-TWEED TO NORHAM** .......**192**
**Start/end:** Berwick-upon-Tweed/Norham **Distance:** 19.2km
**Time:** 2hrs **Difficulty:** ① **Highlights:** Borders history and scenery
taking in the Tweed Valley, Berwick-upon-Tweed, the Union Chain
Bridge and Norham, with the ruins of medieval Norham Castle

**TWEED TO TILL RIVERS LOOP**.....................**200**
**Start/end:** Norham (loop) **Distance:** 37.3km **Time:** 3½hrs
**Difficulty:** ① **Highlights:** The Tweed and Till river valleys with
historic sites from battle-scarred Norham Castle to the Union Chain
Bridge, and a detour to a Neolithic stone circle

**ACCOMMODATION** ..................................................**208**
**CYCLE HIRE AND REPAIRS**.......................................**220**
**FURTHER INFORMATION** ........................................**222**
**ACKNOWLEDGEMENTS** ...........................................**225**
**INDEX** ......................................................................**227**
**INDEX OF ADVERTISERS** .........................................**230**

# INTRODUCTION

As a whole, northeast England is the least densely populated region in the country, but it's packed with scenic and historic wonders to match anywhere in the British Isles and beyond. It boasts a long, sandy coastline, guarded by magnificent historic castles; the dense forests and wild moors of the Northumberland National Park; the undulating hillsides of the Cheviots and North Pennines; Europe's first International Dark Sky Park; and, perhaps best of all for cyclists, its traffic-free roads, quiet bridleways and myriad cycle routes. Even the layout of its uplands seems designed to benefit cyclists, with the reptilian lines of dry stone walls giving unobstructed views of the road ahead (compared to some of the country lanes embedded by tall hedgerows, more typical further south). In short, I cannot imagine how anywhere else in the world could be a better place for cycling.

Before we get on to the rides themselves, though, a brief explanation why this book is *Cycling in Northumbria* and not *Northumberland*. Northumbria usually refers to the area covered by much of northeast England, stemming from the former Anglo-Saxon kingdom of Northumbria. Consequently, locals in Northumberland don't tend to talk about Northumbria as the place where they live (with one or two exceptions, such as the Northumbria Police force – so we're in good

↑ Dry stone walls criss-cross the high moorland overlooking Bellingham (Caitlin Hennessy)

company). Nevertheless, I persuaded my broad-minded publishers that we should use 'Northumbria' because we include several rides in County Durham, Tyne and Tees, even hopping briefly over the border into Scotland. If that still doesn't convince, though, I can only apologise – and take the blame squarely on my own chin.

So, what about the cycling?

From Hamsterley, County Durham, to Paxton, just over the Scottish border in Berwickshire, the 21 rides here span forest, moorland and coastline, including some of the most spectacular landscapes in the UK. They're presented here in a rough south–north sequence, so that if you're thinking of spending some time exploring the whole of northeast England, you could happily hop from one ride to another. There are also certain hotspots, such as Haydon Bridge in the North Pennines, Bellingham on the edge of the Northumberland National Park, Alnwick, midway up the coast, and Norham, on the south bank of the Tweed. As well as being attractions in their own right, these places are handy gateways to a wealth of wonderful rides, including many of those featured in these pages.

Inevitably, of course, there are plenty of other commendable rides out there that didn't make the cut, otherwise a pocket-sized guide would soon turn into a pannier bag-filler. Otherwise, I wish I could have gone down the riverside from Newcastle to South Shields, for instance, and ridden the whole of the Coast & Castles Cycle Route all the way to Edinburgh. Some of the wilder mountain-bike trails, such as in Kidland and Wooler Common, were very tempting (but partly off-limits currently, due to storm damage), and the C2C Coast-to-Coast route, of course… the list goes on. There are also several exciting new cycle routes and cycle-related projects in the pipeline for future reference, such as the new Reivers Trail, which will create a 350km network of traffic-free trails around Kielder Forest and Hadrian's Wall, due for completion by the end of 2023. And Destination Tweed, a long-term project due to open in 2025, which will make a new 180km riverside trail from Moffat in Scotland to Berwick-upon-Tweed. Hopefully, lots of you cyclists out there will give these a go yourselves – please let me know of any good 'uns if you do!

Meanwhile, I hope this lot will keep you going. Happy cycling!

# A WORD FROM CYCLING UK

*Jordan Matthews, Cycling Development Officer for Cycling UK – Northeast England*

Cycling in the northeast of England is often overlooked. Why not head to the Yorkshire Dales, Lake District or North York Moors, or venture further north and explore Scotland? All are excellent places to ride a bike, but what the northeast of England gives you are some hidden gems. Quiet roads, bridleways, forest tracks and cycle paths. You just need to know where to find them.

Huw Hennessy has managed to deliver a great introduction to some of these gems in this route guide. Be it gravel grinding in the forests of Hamsterley and Kielder on Routes 1, 6 and 7; sightseeing past the *Angel of the North* in the city on Route 2, part of the Cycling UK Cathedrals Cycle Route; or being blown away by views of the Northumberland coast on Routes 15, 17, 18 and 19 – there is a ride for everyone. Huw has created some great original routes (or adapted some developed routes by the likes of off-road route campaigner and creator Ted Liddle) to provide a terrific overview of cycling in the area.

Working as a Cycling Development Officer with Cycling UK in the Northeast, being an advocate for cycling and a cyclist myself, any chance to get more people on their bikes in this area is something I will always support.

Cycling UK encourages more people to cycle through its Community Cycling Club (CCC) programme, which has over 200 diverse clubs across England and Scotland (⊘ cyclinguk.org/community-cycle-clubs), and the CCCs in the Northeast ride sections of Huw's routes, week in week out. For example, Teams Wheelers based in Gateshead, Linskill Riders from North Tyneside and Military Veterans Cycling Club all frequent parts of Route 3, spending many happy miles on the adjacent Derwent Walk, while Cycling Minds, based in Hexham, is close to Routes 4 and 5 in the Tyne Valley.

So if you want to discover a bit more about the Northeast community cycling scene, get in touch with the closest CCC and find out about the great ways they are getting more people into cycling. They will, no doubt, add to your Northumbrian cycling adventure.

All you need to do is get out there!

# CYCLING: THE ESSENTIALS

**CHOOSING YOUR BIKE** There's a wide and ever-increasing range of bicycles on the market today, including BMX, cyclo-cross, gravel bikes and fatbikes (great fun on sandy beaches). The routes in this book are suitable for the four most common and popular types (detailed here), and each chapter specifies which of these is the most suitable for that route.

**Road bike** Also known as a racing bike, usually with drop handlebars and made with lightweight material, such as aluminium or carbon fibre. Ideal for speed and for longer distances on road, but with its narrow tyres and less robust frame than a mountain bike it's not so practical off-road on uneven surfaces. Touring bikes are sturdily built road bikes, with racks for carrying panniers.

**Mountain bike (MTB)** Strong frames, with suspension on the front and/or back wheels designed for absorbing the rough and tumble of MTB trails. Their chunky wheels and deeply treaded tyres give good grip on rough terrain off-road, but their weight and wide wheels make them less suitable for long-distance rides.

**Hybrid** With the speed of a road bike and the strength and gearing of a mountain bike, hybrids are extremely popular and versatile, and are the single most useful bike for most of these routes. They're comfortable, sturdy and strong, with lighter frames and thinner wheels than most mountain bikes, and so are better for long distances.

**Gravel bike** Essentially also a cross between a road bike and a mountain bike, the increasingly popular gravel bikes are designed to go faster on all types of terrain. They are lighter and more aerodynamic than conventional mountain bikes, so are also good for longer rides. Most have drop handlebars and some have suspension, and a wide range of wheel widths and tyre treads are available to suit your preferred ride.

**E-bike** Electric bikes are becoming increasingly popular. They come in different types, usually hybrids but also e-mountain bikes and even e-folding bikes too. They're great for getting up hills, and most have an automatic power mode to give you an instant start, or a manual override setting. They're still not getting any cheaper, but as the batteries and motors get better and lighter, they arguably offer better value for money. Depending on variables, such as size of battery, the rider's weight and the terrain ridden, the average charge should last from 30km up to around 150km.

**MAINTENANCE** Keeping your bike in good working order is essential. Before every ride, take a few minutes to do the **M-Check**: a step-by-step assessment of the bike in the shape of the letter **M**. Start from the rear wheel up to the saddle, down to the pedals, up to the handlebars and back down to the front wheel:

**1. Rear wheel:** make sure it is firmly attached to the forks and turning freely. If using quick-release levers, check they are properly locked (facing backwards to avoid snagging on branches, etc). Run through the gears to make sure they're all working correctly.

**2. Spokes:** make sure they are all equally tight; pluck each one to check they sound about the same.

**3. Tyres:** check for possible splits, bulges and tears, and remove any material stuck in the tread which could cause a puncture. Ensure the tyres are inflated to the correct pressure (usually marked somewhere on the tyre wall).

**4. Brakes:** apply the rear and front brake in turn to make sure each grips the wheel firmly under forward pressure. Check there is nothing obstructing the brake pad and that it is not worn or loose.

**5. Saddle:** check that it is firm and that the seat post is not raised above the limit line. If needed, adjust the height and tighten the saddle with an Allen key or spanner. To measure your correct saddle height, you should be able to sit steadily on your bike, with the tips of your toes on the ground and your legs nearly straight.

**6. Chain:** keep it clean and oiled (though not too much oil as this can pick up dirt and debris, which can damage the chain set).

**7. Pedals:** spin them to make sure they rotate freely. Check that the cranks are firm and don't wobble or creak.

**8. Front wheel stem:** check that the handlebars and front wheel do not move independently from side to side. Do this by holding the front wheel between your knees and trying to twist the handlebars (not too hard or that will loosen them). Tighten the stem bolt and handlebar clamp with an Allen key.

**9. Headset:** make sure it is correctly firm. Grip the head tube with one hand and squeeze the front brake with the other, and then try to shake the headset from side to side to make sure there is no loose movement or clicking sounds.

**10. Frame:** check for possible cracks or structural damage; this might occur at the joint between the head tube and the frame, and where the seat post joins the frame.

**11. Front wheel:** apply the same tests as for the rear wheel.

**EQUIPMENT AND ACCESSORIES** For shorter rides, all you really need is a bicycle pump, a bell and a lock.

For longer distances, the following are also useful:

- puncture-repair kit
- lights (if on a long ride)
- toolkit (multi-tool with built-in spanners and Allen keys saves space)
- tyre levers
- disposable gloves (to keep oil off your hands if the chain comes off, etc)
- fluorescent reflectors (ie: arm bands, spoke bars, ankle straps).
- water bottle
- energy snacks (many of the rides have no shops, pubs or cafés en route)

If you have any problems with your bike during a ride, there's a list of local cycle-hire and repair shops on page 220.

**WHAT TO WEAR** As with the equipment, for short rides you don't need much; the only essential item, whether you're going off-road or not, is a **bike helmet**. In addition, for longer rides, the following are also useful:

* sturdy shoes (with cleats for hillier rides)
* loose-fitting clothing (including a lightweight kagoule even in summer, as the weather is unpredictable; bright colours are good for visibility, but be warned: midges love them!)
* gloves
* sunglasses or cycling goggles
* overshoes and gaiters (for muddy mountain biking and/or very wet weather)
* padded cycle shorts (mostly for longer and off-road rides)

**TAKING YOUR BIKE ON PUBLIC TRANSPORT** London North Eastern Railway (✆ 03457 225 225; ⌘ lner.co.uk), is the main train operator covering northeast England, and from London to Glasgow and Edinburgh. Bikes can be taken on trains, with advance booking advisable, but space is limited on busier trains, especially in the holiday seasons. For more details, visit the LNER website, above, and search on 'bicycles'.

For general information about public transport across the UK (including bus, train, coach and ferry), contact Traveline (✆ 0871 200 2233; text/SMS: 84268; ⌘ traveline.info).

Note, though, that one of the few disadvantages about the wonderful wilds of Northumbria is that some of the bike routes in this book are also far from train stations, or even bus routes. So, sorry to say this, especially in view of climate-change concern, but cars are often the best option to get to the start point. However, 14 out of the 21 routes are loops, so at least you will only have to drive to the main start/finish point.

**SAFETY** Cycling is generally a safe and fun form of transport, but is not without its potential risks and hazards. Following these guidelines, based on the Highway and Countryside codes, will make your ride even safer for all:

- Be considerate to other users, taking extra care around those who may be deaf, short-sighted or blind, as well as people in wheelchairs or other mobility vehicles.
- Use your bell when necessary to signal to others you are approaching: don't startle people by speeding past without warning.
- Ride single file on narrow roads and paths.
- Give way to walkers, wheelchair users and horseriders, leaving plenty of room when passing each other in either direction.
- On shared paths and roads, show extra caution if cycling at high speeds.
- Leave gates and property as you find them (and take extra care when crossing fields of livestock: cows can sometimes be aggressively defensive of their newborn calves).
- Take extra care at junctions, bends and entrances, and signal when turning on to another road if other road users are nearby.
- Cyclists must follow the same traffic regulations as other users, including red lights, one-way roads and give-way lines.
- Narrow and high-banked country lanes muffle the sound of approaching vehicles, so listen out for traffic at all times, especially on blind hills and corners.
- Be alert to parked cars on narrow roads in case doors open suddenly in front of you.
- MTB trails often cross other MTB routes, footpaths, forestry roads and bridleways, so always cycle carefully and give way to other users.

Also, be aware that the **Countryside Code** stipulates that footpaths are not legally accessible to cyclists, whereas bridleways and byways are,

## PHONE SIGNAL TIP

As the phone signal is poor in more remote regions, including Northumberland National Park and Kielder Water and Forest Park, there are more BT phone boxes in and around villages to compensate.

and permissive paths have variable access, according to the landowner's voluntary conditions. Happily for cyclists, most of Northumbria is sparsely populated, so there is usually considerably more tolerance than in more crowded regions of the UK, but obviously it is always best to stick to the rules. For more details, visit ⌀ nationaltrail.co.uk/en_GB/countrysidecode/.

**MOUNTAIN BIKING** There are two dedicated mountain-bike trails in this book: in Hamsterley Forest (page 24) and Kielder Forest (page 74). Both routes are well signposted with information and safety warnings. If you'd like more information about the grading system used on MTB trails around the UK, visit ⌀ forestryengland.uk/article/mountain-bike-trail-grades-and-safety.

↑ Climbing up from Embleton Bay, with the dramatic ruins of Dunstanburgh Castle on the horizon (Visit Northumberland)

# HOW TO USE THIS BOOK

These 21 cycle routes comprise a selection of my favourites, gleaned from across the region. Many of them are based on existing National Cycle Network (NCN) routes, as well as sections of the Sandstone Way and other routes devised by the Northumberland National Park. I've added offshoots here and there, such as detours to nearby attractions, and optional short cuts on longer or more challenging rides.

As with Bradt's other cycling guides, the rides are designed for people getting back into cycling, or novice cyclists looking to step up their rides a gear or two. In general, they're intended to be leisure rides – for those who love cycling, but who also want to discover the wonders of this glorious region along the way – rather than Audax time trials for those wanting to better their personal best. The rides range from around 12km up to 47km with a wide selection from across the whole region, from off-road mountain biking in forests and moorland (Routes 1, page 24, 6, page 64, 7, page 74, and 12, page 118) to meandering along the coast from one castle to the next (see Routes 14–19, pages 138, 148, 156, 164, 176 and 184). There are a couple of urban routes too, including the Durham to Newcastle upon Tyne ride on the Cathedrals Cycle Route (Route 2, page 30) and the Newcastle to Gibside route, which highlights some of the architectural gems on the Tyne as well as its proximity to the leafy Derwent Valley (Route 3, page 38). Each ride also comes with a feature box highlighting some of the region's many cultural, historical and natural attractions: from the *Angel of the North* to J M W Turner's landscapes of Norham Castle, from Roman Vindolanda to the birds of the Farne Islands, and more.

## BEST FOR:

**Families**: 1, 6, 7, 14
**History and heritage**: 2, 3, 4, 9, 13, 17, 18, 19, 20, 21
**Off-road adventure**: 1, 5, 6, 7, 9, 12, 18, 19
**Wildlife**: 1, 6, 7, 11, 14, 17, 18, 19

**THE ROUTES** For each ride, an **information panel** details the start and end point, distance in kilometres and approximate time to complete the route (depending on your fitness and number of stops along the way, roughly based on a modest 10km/h). Each route has a **difficulty rating** (① easy or ② moderate) and a **scenic rating** (Ⓐ pleasant/interesting; Ⓑ great; Ⓒ superb), as well as an **overview of terrain** – whether it is on- or off-road, if the path is surfaced, if any major hills are included, etc. I've also listed which bikes are best suited to each ride.

Each also has a QR code link to access a digital map on **komoot**, as explained above. Komoot has its own gradings – Easy, Intermediate and Difficult – based on gradient, total ascent/descent and terrain. All of the route gradings in the book match those on komoot. In addition, I've added advice in a few instances, for example where an Easy-graded ride has a potentially tricky section; or where a Moderate-graded ride is longer than the average, or has a steep hill (ie: Route 12, Bellingham to Rothbury, and Route 17, Amble to Bamburgh). Obviously, if you're on an e-bike, you might find you can downgrade all the difficulty levels, depending on your level of fitness and the performance of the bike itself.

**NCN routes:** the National Cycle Routes covered in each route are listed at the start of the chapter. They won't be mentioned in the directions at every junction as they are generally well signposted throughout, but indications will be given when we first join the NCN route, detour off it, or rejoin it.

At the end of each route chapter, you'll find information about getting to the start point, the nearest tourist office and public toilets, and recommended cafés, pubs and restaurants (including bike-friendly places that have cycle racks and parking space). Finally, note that most car parks in Northumberland are free, so I have only specified the few that do charge (coastal resorts, mostly).

**MAPS** Each chapter includes a map outlining the route and points of interest along the way, plus Ordnance Survey (OS) grid references for the start/end point. We have also teamed up with **komoot**, the route-planning and navigation app, to create a customised digital map for each route. The interactive komoot maps have detailed insights, including an elevation profile, way type and surface information, as well as photos of highlights and signposts at key junctions. You can also use a smartphone to navigate each route, using the komoot app for iOS or Android.

And finally, for those of us who still like paper maps, relevant OS maps available are listed at the beginning of each chapter.

**ACCOMMODATION** See page 208 for a list of suggested hotels, B&Bs, hostels and campsites. Covering a reasonable price range, most of these are on or close to one or more cycle routes, and many have lockable, indoor cycle-storage facilities. Some of the routes are far from the towns and villages where you'll find most hotels, inns and B&Bs, but even the remotest corners often have nearby holiday cottages and cyclist-friendly campsites, with glamping pods, safari tents, yurts, shepherd's huts and even tree-houses among the growing range of accommodation options on offer. The **Camping and Caravanning Club** (⊘ campingandcaravanningclub. co.uk) has several dozen campsites across northeast England, including an excellent site in Bellingham near Routes 8–12. Holiday lettings agents, such as **Original Cottages** (⊘ originalcottages.co.uk), have hundreds of properties all across the region. We have also included the nearest tourist information office within each chapter, which has details of local accommodation; some may also offer an on-site booking service.

**EATING OUT** A selection of places to eat on or near each route is given at the end of each chapter. I have tried to pick independent eateries, and places that I have either tried myself or had recommended to me. Most will have somewhere suitable for locking up bikes either on the premises or nearby, and will include a range of gluten-free, vegetarian and vegan options (though this seems to be quite standard nowadays).

Price codes are based on the cost of a main course and soft drink/beer/ glass of wine:

**£** up to £12      **££** £12–20      **£££** £20+

**CYCLE-HIRE SHOPS** At the back of the book (page 220) is a list of local cycle-hire and bike shops, marking which routes they are closest to. This includes four that are right on the route: at Hamsterley Forest (Route 1, page 24), Newcastle upon Tyne (Route 3, page 38), Kielder Water and Forest Park (Routes 6 and 7, pages 64 and 74) and Wallington Hall (Route 13, page 128). Most of these shops have a range of adult and children's bikes for hire, as well as toddler seats, tagalongs and trailers (for children and pets!). They're usually hybrid bikes, but some will also have e-bikes, mountain bikes, and bikes adapted for wheelchair users. Hire charge usually includes essential equipment, such as helmet, pump and lock. Some companies will drop off and collect hired bikes, usually up to a range of about 10km.

↑ The traffic-free roads of the lush Tweed Valley (Norham Bike Yard)

# 1 HAMSTERLEY FOREST MTB TRAIL

| | |
|---|---|
| **START/FINISH** | Hamsterley Forest Visitor Centre |
| **DISTANCE/TIME** | 15.2km/1½–2hrs |
| **DIFFICULTY/TERRAIN** | ① Blue-graded MTB route on gravel trails and forestry roads, mostly undulating but with a few steep descents; suitable for cyclists with some MTB experience and skills, no special fitness level needed |
| **SCENIC RATING** | ⑧ Through the North Pennines' forested valleys; ideal, traffic-free route, with nature trails and animal sculptures |
| **SUITABLE FOR** | Basic MTB |
| **NCN ROUTE** | NCN70 |
| **MAPS** | OS Explorer 308 (1:25 000) |
| **KOMOOT REF** | 952647720 |

**H**amsterley is County Durham's largest forest, covering more than 2,000ha (two-thirds the size of Durham city) in the North Pennines. The family-friendly forest includes a range of MTB trails to suit different abilities; our loop route follows the moderate-graded Blue Trail, with no technical MTB features but with plenty of twists and turns, ups and downs. (For more information about the MTB Trail Grading System, see ⊘ cyclinguk.org/article/cycling-guide/mtb-trail-grading-guide.) It's well signposted throughout, starting alongside Bedburn Beck, winding back up the valley and, finally, returning to the visitor centre, with an information office, café and toilets.

Be aware that this is a working forest, so keep alert for timber lorries, other vehicles and machinery; warning signs indicate active works or possible diversions.

## THE ROUTE

Leaving the ❶ **visitor centre**, turn right on to Forest Drive and then left after around 100m, leading shortly to a gravel path. Cross a bridge over ❷ **Bedburn Beck** and then turn right after around 50m, signposted Grove Link. The trail zigzags left sharply uphill after the stream, then levels out, continuing under the trees. Now we're above the stream, the hillside drops away sharply to the left (take care).

← A shady trail beneath Hamsterley Forest's rows of tall evergreen trees (Caitlin Hennessy)

Carry on ahead at a crossroads after a few hundred metres, but be alert for walkers and other cyclists, with the MTB Red Trail crossing our path here too. It's very pretty here under the tall slender trees, with the bubbling brook down in the valley below.

Turn left at a junction about 100m after the crossroads, soon winding downhill now, all the way to the stream on your right. Continue along the side of the valley, mostly level but with some ups and downs until, after around 12km, the trail crosses over Bedburn Beck again, then turning left back on to Forest Drive, leading to ❸ **Grove House**.

Now with Bedburn Beck running alongside the trail to our left, continue straight ahead (with green arrows marking the Spurlswood Walk), and mostly level. Gradually, though, we start climbing for a few hundred metres until we reach the crest of a hill and then drop down over the stream again, leading to a narrow bridge and ford to ❹ **Blackling Hole**, with a car park and nearby footpath signposted to ❺ **Spurlswood Beck** waterfall.

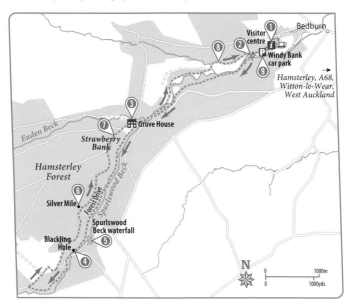

Follow the blue arrows across the car park, climbing gently uphill back into the forest. Winding sharp right as we climb, we enter a clearing of open moorland. Carry on straight at a fork after about 100m across the clearing, and in another 100m or so the trail winds uphill moderately. Carry on climbing, with occasional glimpses through the trees back to the open moorland on your left. Turn right at the crossroads at the top of the hill, marked Blue Trail.

We soon begin to wind downhill again, generally running parallel to our way out to Blackling Hole earlier on, coming out into an area overlooking younger trees, with splendid long views ahead across the valley.

After another few hundred metres, still winding gradually downhill, the trail comes to a T-junction, signposted ➏ **Silver Mile**. There's a wide clearing of felled trees here, as well as a tangle of storm-felled trees on the right from 2021's Storm Arwen, contrasting more tranquil views of moorland on the hillside beyond. Turn right here, still descending and winding left and right.

Turn right again after around 1km at another T-junction, following the edge of the forest on your left. The trail starts dropping down steeply now, going straight ahead at a crossroads signposted ➐ **Strawberry Bank**.

↑ Crossing a clearing of young saplings, above Blackling Hole (Huw Hennessy)

## HISTORY OF HAMSTERLEY FOREST

Today, Hamsterley Forest is a major Forestry England plantation, with more than 50,000 trees planted annually, producing some 20,000 tonnes of timber each year. The forest has a rich mix of trees, mostly conifers (predominantly Sitka spruces) but also redwood, monkey puzzle and Scots pine.

Prior to World War I, however, the area comprised two farms, mostly for grazing sheep. Before that, the heather-clad moorland was used by the Surtees family, one of County Durham's oldest and wealthiest landowners, for shooting grouse. In 1919, though, with the UK government needing to rebuild its forests and reduce post-war unemployment, the new Forestry Act installed so-called 'Instructional Centres' across the country, including at Hamsterley. Labourers were housed on site in wooden barracks, and set to work planting thousands of trees in return for bed, board and pocket money.

With the onset of World War II, unemployment levels fell and the forestry camps were closed. Hamsterley Forest didn't remain silent for long, however, with the barracks re-used as a POW camp for German and Italian prisoners, who were also put to work in further planting.

Today, the camps have long gone; instead, some 180,000 visitors are welcomed to Hamsterley Forest every year. Not least many cyclists, attracted to one of the best mountain-biking centres in northeast England.

Eventually, the trail reaches the bottom of the hill and back on a wider road – turning sharp right and beneath high-voltage cables (high overhead – no need to duck!).

Now back on the valley floor, by Euden Beck, the trail winds to the right and then sharp left as we pass **Grove House** again on our right, and on to Forest Drive. After about 2km on the road, turn left back on to a trail climbing moderately uphill, parallel to the paved road. After about 100m the trail turns to gravel and another 100m beyond that we come to a ❽ **right fork** – with sculpted squirrel and rabbit and information displays for young nature detectives. Continue downhill and take another right-hand turning after another 100m or so, still zigzagging downhill under the mixed-leaf woods.

After another 100m or so we return to Forest Drive, past ❾ **Windy Bank car park** and turn left up and around to the ❶ **visitor centre**. Note that the road straight ahead is actually the visitor centre exit, so you need to enter via the road that loops behind the building (or dismount at the junction and walk to the café, if you have run out of steam by now!).

## THE ESSENTIALS

**GETTING THERE** By car, Hamsterley Forest is off the A68 in Bedburn, 9km northwest of West Auckland. Unfortunately, there is no public transport nearby.

**FACILITIES** There are public toilets at the visitor centre.

### WHERE TO EAT

✖ **The Cross Keys** Hamsterley DL13 3PX; ✆ 01388 488457; ⎙ crosskeyshamsterley.co.uk. Highly rated for its gastropub cuisine, this popular local offers a range of pub classics, including steak pie, fish'n'chips & burgers, as well as several veggie & gluten-free options; booking advisable. ££

✖ **Forest Café, Hamsterley Forest Visitor Centre** Bedburn DL13 3NL; ✆ 07969 014530; ⎙ Hamsterley Forest Cafe. This casual café, right at the start and end of the Blue Trail, serves a range of hot & cold snacks (including vegan & gluten-free dishes), sandwiches, ice creams & soft drinks; with outdoor tables too, so you can keep an eye on your bike. ££

✖ **The Well Café** 46 East Green, West Auckland DL14 9HJ; ✆ 01388 834005; ⎙ thewellatwest.co.uk. This volunteer-run café serves great homemade sandwiches, soup, cakes & pastries; also runs a food bank for the local community; railings opposite where you can lock up your bike (open Tue–Fri daytime). £

### FURTHER INFORMATION

ℹ **Hamsterley Forest Visitor Centre** Bedburn DL13 3NL; ✆ 01388 488312; ⎙ forestryengland.uk/hamsterley-forest. The information office next to the café has staff on hand for local information, including visitor activities and events; trail maps are also available.

# 2 DURHAM CATHEDRAL TO NEWCASTLE CATHEDRAL

| | |
|---|---|
| **START/FINISH** | Durham Cathedral/Newcastle Cathedral |
| **DISTANCE/TIME** | 25.5km/2–2½hrs |
| **DIFFICULTY/TERRAIN** | ② All on road or cycle path, with some busy roads and junctions; mostly undulating the whole way, including a final downhill stretch to the Tyne; suitable for experienced cyclists |
| **SCENIC RATING** | ⑧ From historic Durham Cathedral to Newcastle's medieval St Nicholas Cathedral, via the *Angel of the North*, with great views over the Tyne Valley |
| **SUITABLE FOR** | Road bike, hybrid |
| **NCN ROUTE** | NCN725 and NCN14 |
| **MAPS** | OS Landranger 88 (1:50 000) |
| **KOMOOT REF** | 984495102 |

↑ Durham Cathedral, on its rocky outcrop above the River Wear (Iordanis/S)

P art of the Cathedrals Cycle Route which spans all 42 of England's cathedrals, this urban route from Durham to Newcastle offers a fascinating gateway to Tyne and Wear. Starting from historic Durham Cathedral, we head north, past Sir Antony Gormley's iconic statue of the *Angel of the North*. Passing a former World War II refugee camp and around Saltwell Park, we descend through Gateshead suburbs and over the Tyne to Newcastle, revitalised heartland of the Northeast and home to Geordies' beloved Toon: Newcastle United FC.

## THE ROUTE

Start from ❶ **Palace Green** in the shadow of Durham Cathedral, one of the oldest cathedrals in England (founded in 1093), perched on a hilltop overlooking the River Wear. Head down Owengate on the northeast corner; we're in the historic heart of the city and this narrow, cobbled lane usually has plenty of visitors milling around, so take care and walk if necessary.

Cross Market Place and down Saddler Street. As you come to the bridge across the A690, turn sharp left on to Walker Gate (signposted NCN14 and NCN70) then cross the road and turn left again on to a cycle path over the bridge, with beautiful views of the cathedral towering over the River Wear on the left.

Across the river, follow the cycle lane to the right, up Framwellgate Peth, and carrying straight on uphill under the railway bridge. Continue up the tree-lined road, past Wharton Park on your left and playing fields on your right. Follow the cycle path northwards, turning left off Framwellgate Peth and right on to North End, taking the first exit on the roundabout on to Southfield Way.

Continue for about 1km (the cycle path criss-crossing one side of the road to another) till you reach another roundabout with the ❷ **A167**, which we join and follow northwards for most of the way to Newcastle. The NCN725 cycle path continues the whole way, either alongside the road, or on cycle lanes on the road itself. They are well marked, but keep alert for traffic and give parked cars a clear berth. And as you pedal past fields and modern suburbs, note that you are following roughly the same route – in reverse – that early Christian monks took more than 1,100 years ago when they carried the remains of St Cuthbert from his home on Lindisfarne to his final resting place at Durham Cathedral (see box, page 181; we'll pick up other sections of St Cuthbert's Way on subsequent routes further north).

Follow the A167 for a long, straight stretch, moderately downhill for the most part, with the cycle path on the right and leading around three roundabouts at Pity Me, Plawsworth and Chester Moor. At the next roundabout after around 7km, coming into ❸ **Chester-le-Street**, take a left-hand fork down Durham Road, crossing over on the pedestrian/cycle path crossing.

Carry on straight ahead through Chester-le-Street's main shopping high street; the cycle lane is on the main road here, so keep alert for traffic and parked cars. The road starts climbing uphill mildly from here for a while, up to around **Birtley**. Today, it is best known as the home of Durham County cricket ground, tucked behind the shops on our right. It was also the temporary home for St Cuthbert, at the nearby site of St Mary and St Cuthbert Church, before being transferred to Durham Cathedral.

Continue straight on through Chester-le-Street, rejoining the A167 at a roundabout on North Road after around 10km. About 1km later, we pass under a former railway bridge, which is now part of the C2C Coast-to-Coast route (see page 222). Another 1km later, as we pass a string of industrial estates and warehouses, note a long, low red-brick complex on your left, just before Birtley Leisure Centre. This former World War II barracks housed Belgian refugees who were employed in arms manufacture; today, its more commonplace use is as a storage warehouse. As we approach the suburb of Birtley now, you may shortly catch your first glimpse of the ❹ *Angel of the North*, Sir Antony Gormley's most famous statue, towering over the rooftops on your left.

The road starts climbing slowly now for a short stretch after Birtley. Here the cycle path detours left under the A1(M), which at the time of writing is being expanded; follow signs according to works in progress.

Coming out the other side of the A1(M) flyover, we reach the *Angel of the North*, welcoming us to northeast England. The cycle path passes right by the statue; its vast 54m wingspan and blank face oblivious to the roaring traffic at its feet. Continuing up the Durham Road again, turn left after a few hundred metres on to the Angel Cycleway, diverting away from a busy stretch of the A167 (and off the NCN725). Instead, we wind through quiet and leafy suburbs, with sweeping views over the Tyne Valley before we plunge into the city streets of Gateshead.

After about 1km, at the end of the Angel Cycleway, turn left up Salcombe Gardens, then right at the T-junction, up Chowdene Bank. Take the next left on to St Andrew's Drive, following it up to another T-junction in about 500m, where we turn left on to Saltwell Road South, staying on this long

## THE *ANGEL OF THE NORTH*

Built symbolically on top of a former mine and overlooking the A1(M) outside Gateshead, Sir Antony Gormley's statue is now hailed as the most famous sculpture in the UK and possibly the largest angel statue in the world (made of enough steel to build four Chieftain tanks). When it was erected in 1988, however, the statue was pounced on by critics, who warned that it would cause accidents (from rubber-necking drivers), attract lightning strikes and even hamper television reception. Gormley himself took some persuading to make it, with his initial response to the proposal being 'I don't do roundabout art.'

Today, however, its trouble-free survival has rebutted the nay-sayers, and the *Angel of the North* has become the icon for northeast England, viewed daily by an estimated 90,000 motorists. As Gormley explained it, the angel's iron body represents the region's mining past, while its winged image symbolises the ongoing transition to an information age, as well as a focus for our future hopes and aspirations. Not to be weighed down by such profundity, however, pranksters have shown their teasing fondness for the statue over the years, putting a Santa hat on its head one Christmas, and even dressing it up in a Newcastle FC football shirt.

road for just over 1km until we pass the **Nine Pins pub** on the left, then take the next right on to East Park Road.

The road winds around to the left, along the perimeter of ❺ **Saltwell Park**. This is a great green space, based around Saltwell Towers Gothic mansion, and with a vibrant community hub, ReCoCo (⌀ recoverycoco. com), which runs a burgeoning cycling collective. There's also a café in Saltwell Towers, if you wanted to wet your whistle before we reach our destination, shortly. The entrance is on the left at the top of East Park Road, on the crossroads with Saltwell View/Enfield Road.

Otherwise, continue straight ahead on to Avenue Road for just under 1km, turning right at the crossroads with Bewick Road, then turning left at the T-junction just up the road to rejoin the NCN725. Heading downhill

↑ The *Angel of the North* (Viktor Kovalenko/S)

again now, continue straight ahead, past Gateshead Civic Centre and Gateshead Interchange station on your left. Finally reaching the River Tyne, continue up West Street into Wellington Street and High Level Road to cross over the ❻ **High Level Bridge**, with the Swing Bridge and the Tyne Bridge to the right. The High Level Bridge is twin-tiered for trains above and buses and taxis below, with separate pathways – between age-encrusted girders – for pedestrians and cyclists (giving way to other users, as always).

Through the web of bridges there are great views along the Tyne in either direction. And coming off the bridge on to St Nicholas Street, suddenly there is the cathedral, ahead of you on the brow of the hill: instantly distinctive, with its rare, open-sided lantern spire. The medieval ❼ **Cathedral Church of St Nicholas** also boasts some impressive stained-glass windows, as well as an excellent café (see below), so it's the ideal stop for some well-earned refreshment at the end of our ride (cycle racks outside the east entrance).

↑ The fairy-tale mansion of Saltwell Towers (DavidGraham86/S)

# THE ESSENTIALS

**GETTING THERE** By car, Durham is 4km southwest of the A1(M), on the A690; by train, it's just over 3 hours from London, King's Cross, on LNER (⊘ lner.co.uk), or just over 2 hours from Edinburgh on LNER/ CrossCountry (⊘ crosscountrytrains.co.uk) lines.

**FACILITIES** There are public toilets on the corner of Palace Green and Owengate, Durham; at Saltwell Park; and at St Nicholas Cathedral, Newcastle upon Tyne.

## WHERE TO EAT

✕ **Flat White Kitchen** 21a Elvet Bridge, Durham DH1 3NU; ⊘ 0191 384 0725; ⊘ flatwhitekitchen.com. Just up the road from Durham Cathedral, this superb little café has a long-standing local following, serving b/fasts & brunches; with delicious homemade cakes, scones & sandwiches; coffee, tea, hot chocolate, & smoothies. £

✕ **The Centurion Central Station** Newcastle NE9 5AX; ⊘ 0191 261 6611; ⊘ centurion -newcastle.com. Housed in Central Station's former 1st-class lounge, with magnificent tiling and frescoes adorning its walls, this perennially popular pub serves b/fasts, pizzas, burgers, pasta dishes & tapas; and its bar stocks a good selection of beers, cask ales, cider & wines. ££

✕ **Café 16** Newcastle Cathedral, 42–44 Mosley St, Newcastle upon Tyne NE1 1DF; ⊘ 01670 462595; ⊘ oswinproject.org.uk. This warm & welcoming café based in the cathedral refectory is run by prison leavers as part of the Oswin Project; it's open for b/fast & lunch, also serving sourdough sandwiches, soups, panini, cakes & pastries, with the baked produce made inside HMP Northumberland. £

## FURTHER INFORMATION

ℹ️ **Durham World Heritage Site** 7 Owengate, Durham DH1 3HB; ⊘ 0191 334 3805; ⊘ durhamworldheritagesite.com. This information office is right at the start of our route, with staff available for information about the city (plus cycle-friendly tips on its website).

# 3 NEWCASTLE UPON TYNE TO DERWENT VALLEY LOOP

| | |
|---|---|
| **START/FINISH** | The Cycle Hub, Newcastle Quayside |
| **DISTANCE/TIME** | 38.7km/4hrs (short-cut alternative, approx. 26km, see below) |
| **DIFFICULTY/TERRAIN** | ② One of the longest routes, with some long climbs and busy roads, moderated by the pleasant and easy riverside trails; overall, best suited for fit and experienced cyclists |
| **SCENIC RATING** | ⑧ Mix of riverside trails, country parks, industrial heritage and modern urban architecture |
| **SUITABLE FOR** | Gravel bike, hybrid or road bike |
| **NCN ROUTE** | NCN72 (Hadrian's Cycleway) and NCN14 |
| **MAPS** | OS Explorer 316 (1:25 000) |
| **KOMOOT REF** | 957179917 |

From Newcastle's vibrant Quayside, this diverse route follows the Tyne upstream along the traffic-free riverside path, passing under all seven of the city-centre bridges. Soon out of the city, we start climbing the lush valleys of the Tyne and Derwent, then wind back through Derwent Country Park, via Gibside and along the south bank of the Tyne to Gateshead. All in all, it's a great combination that sets metropolitan Newcastle and Gateshead into context as gateways to the rolling countryside flanking this industrial conurbation.

Note that for the first part of the route, from Newcastle Quayside until we cross the river at Newburn, we follow the NCN72 (also called Hadrian's Cycleway), returning via the NCN14, Keelman's Way.

## THE ROUTE

Start from the ❶ **Cycle Hub** in lower Ouseburn, one of Newcastle's up-and-coming trendy neighbourhoods. Apart from its hip bars, cafés and restaurants, it's also on Hadrian's Cycleway, the long-distance cycling and walking trail, which we follow along the south bank of the Tyne. Cross the mouth of the Ouseburn tributary and follow the riverside cycle path. The regenerated Quayside is lined with colourful artworks, street cafés

← Newcastle's cycle-friendly riverside path and the iconic Tyne Bridge with the Sage Gateshead and Millennium Bridge behind (Rich Kenworthy/NewcastleGateshead Initiative)

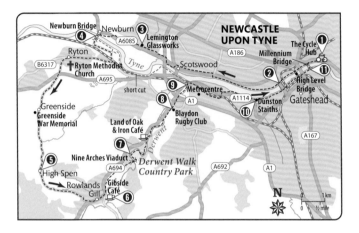

and picnic benches, buzzing both night and day with city workers and visitors alike (so go carefully here, with pedestrians and other cyclists coming and going).

After a few hundred metres we pass three of Newcastle's most iconic buildings, on the opposite bank of the river: first, the Baltic Centre for Contemporary Art, housed in the converted, red-brick Baltic Flour Mill; then the graceful modern arch of Gateshead Millennium footbridge, which can be raised – like an eyebrow – for passing ships. Finally, just beyond the footbridge is the Sage Gateshead, Norman Foster's stunning concert hall, all gleaming glass and steel.

Shortly after passing these modern monuments, we cross under the famous Tyne Bridge, probably Newcastle's most familiar site, built in 1928 by Dorman Long, the Teesside company that also made the similar but larger Sydney Harbour Bridge four years later. Adjacent are the colourful red-and-white Swing Bridge and the twin-tiered, rail-and-road High Level Bridge.

Just beyond the last railway bridge we pass the Quayside pub on the right and shortly after that we go under two more railway bridges: the King Edward VII and Queen Elizabeth II bridges. And finally, the ❷ **New Redheugh Bridge**, a high modern concrete span carrying the A184. So, in less than 1.5km, we've passed all seven of Newcastle's city-centre bridges: this may have given you a pain in the neck to look at eventually, but they're all solid symbols of the city's world-famous engineering prowess, past and present.

Looking ahead now instead of up, though, we're beginning to leave the city centre, with the river widening, fringed with shady trees and lined with modern apartments and offices. After a couple of kilometres, at a broad bend in the river, notice the long wooden piers on the opposite bank: Dunston Staiths, which we pass close by on the return leg (see below).

About 1.5km later, shortly after passing a row of modern red-brick offices, the path winds right away from the river and climbs up to continue left alongside the A695/Scotswood Road. The cycle lane is on the road here but, if you're not keen on traffic, the pavement is easily wide enough here for cyclists and pedestrians; however, give way to other users.

In about 400m, cross over the road at the cycleway traffic lights, still signposted Hadrian's Way. Across the road, turn left and continue briefly alongside the A695/Scotswood Road, before taking a right fork after about 200m, up a pathway through a leafy tunnel of trees, blanketing us nicely from the traffic below. Carry on straight ahead when you come out of the trees and into a strip of parkland. After about 200m, take a left fork, signposted Gateshead.

Shortly after the left fork, we come to a crossroads before a green iron bridge: don't cross the bridge, but take the turning slightly to the right. And at the next fork, as we start descending towards the river again, carry on straight ahead.

As we wind downhill, turn right briefly and then left across the road at traffic lights, just before a roundabout back on the Scotswood Road. Turn right and carry on across a side road, still on the cycle path (look out for traffic here). These last few kilometres away from the river and past industrial estates have been fiddly and hardly picturesque – sorry! But the NCN72 signage is clear, the path is wide enough for cyclists and pedestrians, and we'll soon be out in the countryside.

Take a right fork just after we go under the A1 and before the modern Lemington Bridge, with its decorative white street lights, over a small tributary. We don't cross that bridge, but turn right in front of it, via traffic lights and then left, running parallel to Lemington Gut tributary.

After a couple of hundred metres, turn right up Neptune Road and then veer left uphill (rejoining the NCN72), passing between a school on your left and a housing estate on your right. The path levels out now, going through another tunnel of trees. As you come out of the trees, pass a Lidl supermarket and a squat brick chimney on your left. This rather incongruous-looking conical chimney, dating from 1787, is all that remains of the ❸ **Lemington glassworks**. Originally with four chimneys, the glassworks was a major industry in the former mining village, now a residential suburb of Newcastle.

Shortly after passing Lidl we come to a junction: take the left fork, signposted NCN72. Finally, after all these fiddly junctions, we're coming to a long, straight, traffic-free run, a nice chance to stretch your legs if you fancy a burst of speed. It's straight on from here for just under 2km, on the gravelly path under the trees, until we reach ❹ **Newburn Bridge** on our left, with a wrought-iron sign on the right.

Cross over the bridge – and look out for boats on the Tyne here, as there are several rowing clubs either side of the road on the opposite bank. Carry on straight ahead, along Newburn Bridge Road. The road winds gently downhill here at first, to the left and then right, past industrial workshops, until you cross a railway line. Climb steeply up from here to a T-junction, with traffic lights where we turn right, joining the B6317. There is a cycle path on the road, but take care as some cars speed up the hill towards Ryton.

As you approach the brow of the hill, passing the @ The Castle playschool on your left, the cycle path rejoins the pavement, possibly providing some relief from the traffic. Coming into Ryton, after a few hundred metres, turn left on to Woodside Lane/B6315, the next road but one after **Ryton Methodist Church**. Thankfully, we're on a quieter road now, through tree-lined fields. We're also climbing gently uphill again here (though this middle section has some long climbs, which could become tiring).

Carry on up Woodside Lane until we come to a T-junction, crossing the A695. The cycle path leads to a footbridge, just to the right of this busy junction, with a winding ramp as well as steps. Cross the bridge and continue left along Woodside Lane, signposted Rowlands Gill and Greenside: the cycle path first runs along the right-hand side and then joins the road itself. Keep going, still gently climbing, straight up towards ❺ **High Spen** (the clue is in the name: it's the high point of the route here, you might be relieved to know).

We're out in the countryside now, too, with glimpsed views of the Derwent and Tyne valleys all around: very lush, rolling and green, wooded mostly, past horse paddocks, grazing sheep and cows. Coming uphill into **Greenside**, we reach a T-junction with traffic lights, where we turn right on to Lead Road, followed soon after by a left-hand turn, in front of the **war memorial**, on to Spen Lane. We're still on the B6315, and follow it for nearly 7km, until we come to Rowlands Gill, near Derwent Country Park, which we cross on our way back up to Gateshead and Newcastle.

Shortly after you leave Greenside, cross over the road to join the cycle path running parallel, starting to wind downhill again now, gently at first but then winding quite steeply left and right, before climbing up again, reaching High Spen, a former mining village, between the Tyne to the north and Derwent to the south.

After that long, slow climb, we're rewarded now with a similarly long, lovely descent, with views opening up of the lush green Derwent Valley below. Still on the B6315 (Smailes Lane and Strathmore Road), the road winds left and right through Highfield. Turn left at the T-junction on the outskirts of **Rowlands Gill**, on to Station Road. We join the A694 briefly, but it's only a two-lane road here, so not too busy. We're heading northeast now, back towards the Tyne, and with the River Derwent on our right.

If you feel in need of refreshment at this midway point, just around the bend is the National Trust's ❻ **Gibside**, a Georgian hall, with a **café** (see below) amid woodlands and ornamental gardens. To get there, take the next right-hand turn on to Stirling Lane, then right at the T-junction on to Burnopfield Road and Busty Bank, with the entrance on the left just after crossing the River Derwent. To return to our route, turn right back on to Burnopfield Road and follow the cycle path (NCN14) to the entrance on the right to ❼ **Derwent Walk Country Park**. We stay on the NCN14 northwards for around 4km through this park, following the route of a former railway line to the Tyne (see box, opposite).

The way through the park is on a gravel track under the trees at first; there are some side-paths joining the track too, so look out for others. After a few hundred metres, we come out into the open and cross the **Nine Arches Viaduct**. If you can crane your neck over the high stone walls, there are glorious views either side of the Derwent Valley, with the river visible below the tree canopy.

Just after the viaduct, take the turning on the left. This loops alongside the river, but if you're in a hurry carry straight on here instead to rejoin the path when it loops back again. Cross over the river on a little stone bridge, as you loop back around: it's a narrow and shallow stream here, very different from the big, industrialised Tyne coming up ahead. After the bridge, turn right at a T-junction in the path, now following alongside the river on your right.

Shortly after passing the **Land of Oak and Iron café** (🧭 landofoakandiron. org.uk) on the left, urban conglomeration begins to intrude on our leafy idyll as we approach Gateshead. The cycle path continues, though, still following the river on your right, and with the A694 on the left.

In a couple of kilometres, after passing ❽ **Blaydon Rugby Club** on your right, go under a bridge, for the Hexham Road (B6317), and a few hundred metres later, as the river winds right, continue straight ahead under the A1. We rejoin the left bank of the river on the other side, with the vast sprawl of the **Metrocentre** beyond the right bank, with its superstores and shopping mall.

Around 700m later, the path winds right under the A114, then turns right on to the railway bridge over the Derwent, now at its ❾ **confluence** with the broad Tyne. Follow the path alongside the railway line for another 1.5km, under a roundabout and passing the Metrocentre again, now closer on our right. Coming to a crossroads with Cross Lane, about 400m after the Metrocentre, turn left at the traffic lights, and under the railway bridge. Follow the path to the right, winding past houses and shops until we reach ❿ **Dunston Staiths**, which we saw from a distance on the opposite bank of the Tyne. This vast wooden pier, thought to be the largest wooden

# DERWENT WALK COUNTRY PARK

This riverside park, which our route runs through on the way back to Newcastle, is a prime example of how Tyne and Wear has been and is transforming itself from an industrial hub to an environmentally friendly modern conurbation. From 1867 until it closed in 1961, the Derwent Valley Railway ran through the valley, transporting passengers, as well as coal, bricks and timber to be loaded on to ships at the Derwenthaugh Staithes, now a yacht marina. The railway was pioneering in its time, with four viaducts, including the Nine Arches Viaduct, built because the landowner (the Earl of Strathmore) refused permission for it to go through the Gibside Estate.

Following the closure of the Derwenthaugh Coke Works, however, over the last two decades Gateshead Council has converted the site into a huge green space, approximately the size of 146 football pitches. Today, the park stretches down the Derwent Valley for 18km, from riverside Swalwell in the north to Consett in the south, with footpaths, nature trails and the NCN14 and NCN72 cycle routes, which form part of this ride. Now attracting a rich variety of wildlife, including birds such as sparrowhawks, woodpeckers and nuthatches, as well as shy mammals including roe deer, foxes and badgers, the valley has recovered many of its former natural habitats, with a mix of woodlands, meadows, riverbanks and wetlands. For more information, visit the Land of Oak and Iron heritage centre (⌖landofoakandiron.org.uk), whose café we pass by on our way through the park.

↑ Autumn colours at a weir across the River Derwent in Derwent Walk Country Park (Washington Imaging/A)

structure in Europe, is another symbol of the Tyne's industrial heritage, though sadly closed now following several arson attacks. Nevertheless, it's worth a stop here to take it in; the mudbanks in front of the pier also offer great birdwatching opportunities, with avocets, curlews and other waders often seen here at low tide.

Carry on straight after Dunston Staiths. We're back on the riverside path now, past modern art installations and ongoing urban regeneration work, including more of the Quayside path that makes exploring the north bank of the Tyne such a pleasure.

As we approach Gateshead Quayside, turn right up Bridge Street by the Swing Bridge, going under the A167 (over Tyne Bridge), continuing along South Shore Road. With the graceful ⓫ **Millennium Bridge** just ahead of you now, take a left fork sloping down by HMS Calliope naval unit, to reach the Baltic Centre for Contemporary Art. There are a few bike racks in front of the entrance to this massive brick building, if you fancy some leisurely art appreciation to ease your leg muscles (not to mention your sit bones!). Otherwise, cross over the Millennium Bridge – with a separate side lane for cyclists and pedestrians – then turn right back on to the Quayside, only a couple of minutes' ride back

↑ The disused pier at Dunston Staiths (coxy58/S)

to the ❶ **Cycle Hub** where we started. There's a café here, as well as a bike repair shop and the Saddle Skedaddle cycling holiday operator (see page 220).

**SHORT-CUT ALTERNATIVE** If you're not keen on hills and just want a shorter ride out and back along the Tyne (see komoot map 958192672), you could turn left after ❹ **Newburn Bridge** instead of going straight on, and follow NCN14 (Keelmen's Way) along the south bank, rejoining the main route at the mouth of the River Derwent where it joins the Tyne ❽. This short cut is all level and only 5.5km, compared to approximately 18km on the longer loop via Gibside.

## THE ESSENTIALS

**GETTING THERE** By bike, the Cycle Hub is around 10 minutes' ride from Newcastle Central Station: turning left along Neville Street, left down Marlborough Crescent and Forth Banks to the Quayside, then left again along the riverbank. By train, Newcastle is around 3¼ hours from London, King's Cross, on LNER; or just under 1½ hours from Edinburgh. By car, Newcastle is just off the A1, about 5½ hours via the M1 from London, or around 2½ hours from Edinburgh on the A1.

**FACILITIES** There are toilets for customers at the Cycle Hub's café; likewise at other cafés on Newcastle Quayside and along the route.

### WHERE TO EAT

✖ **Market Place Café** Gibside NT, nr Rowlands Gill, Tyne & Wear NE16 6BG; ☎ 01207 541820; ⬦ nationaltrust.org.uk/gibside. Housed within the grounds of the National Trust's Georgian Gibside Hall, this café serves hot & cold snacks, soups, sandwiches, cakes & pastries, with indoor tables as well as outside in the cobblestoned courtyard. Note that at the time of writing, all visitors have to pay the entry fee,

even if only using the café; however, Gibside is planning a new 'Green Corridor' project which might change this policy, so it's worth enquiring if you plan to stop off here. **£**

✖ **Kaltur Wine Bar** 8 High Bridge, Newcastle upon Tyne NE1 1EN; ☎ 0191 447 4464; ⬦ kalturrestaurant.co.uk. This Spanish bar & restaurant 10mins' walk up from the Tyne Bridge has an enticing menu of authentic tapas dishes for lunch & dinner, as well as paella (chicken or vegetarian, min 2 people, Sun–Thu), and an extensive list of Spanish wines. It's a snug & lively place and very popular too, so worth booking ahead, especially for the paella. **££**

**The Cookhouse** Foundry Lane, Ouseburn Newcastle upon Tyne NE6 1LH; 0191 276 1093; cookhouse.org. This highly regarded restaurant in hip Ouseburn has an uber-cool & arty vibe, with stripped-brick walls and exposed beams. It also serves superb food to match, focusing on British cuisine, using locally sourced produce & with a contemporary twist. Open Tue–Sun for lunch & dinner, also b/fast/brunch Sat–Sun. **££**

## FURTHER INFORMATION

**NewcastleGateshead**; newcastlegateshead.com. The official tourist office for all things related to Newcastle and Gateshead, this website covers everything from where to stay & eat to what to do, what's on & more. As with an increasing number of cities, there's no physical tourist office for visitors, but they do have a live chatline as well as 24/7 live feeds on their social media pages (Facebook, Twitter and Instagram).

# The award-winning Slow Travel series from Bradt Guides

Over 20 regional guides across Britain.
See the full list at bradtguides.com/slowtravel.

# 4 HAYDON BRIDGE TO VINDOLANDA LOOP

| | |
|---|---|
| **START/FINISH** | Haydon Bridge |
| **DISTANCE/TIME** | 25km/3hrs |
| **DIFFICULTY/TERRAIN** | ① Not a long route; climbing for much of the first half uphill, but downhill for most of the return half to Haydon Bridge; mostly on quiet country roads and farm tracks |
| **SCENIC RATING** | © Open moorland of the North Pennines; plus Vindolanda, a historic Roman fort in the shadow of Hadrian's Wall |
| **SUITABLE FOR** | Hybrid or gravel bike |
| **NCN ROUTE** | NCN72 and NCN68 |
| **MAPS** | OS Explorer 43 (1:25 000) |
| **KOMOOT REF** | 926173138 |

This loop, from Haydon Bridge and back, winds through a peaceful stretch of the Tyne Valley in a designated Area of Outstanding Natural Beauty (AONB) between the North Pennines and Northumberland National Park. Climbing uphill from Haydon Bridge, we cross moorland and fell, past the Roman fort of Vindolanda guarding nearby Hadrian's Wall, before returning along a high ridge overlooking the rolling valley.

Apart from one stretch along a rubbly farm track, the route is all on quiet back lanes, with no busy junctions. Although most of this route is hilly, it's good to know that the return half is largely downhill. As such though, it's quite a challenging ride, suitable for fit and reasonably experienced cyclists. We pass a couple of refreshment options, at The Sill and Vindolanda (see below), but otherwise there are no shops or pubs en route.

## THE ROUTE

Start from ❶ **The Bridge** Visitor Information Centre, next to Haydon Bridge station (with a car park behind).

Turn right on to Church Street, over the railway crossing and up North Bank past Haydon Bridge High School on your left. Steep hill warning! Plan ahead and change down a gear or two, as we wind steeply uphill for a few hundred metres. As we rise rapidly above the town, impressive views open up, looking over the rooftops of the honey-coloured stone cottages to the sweeping Tyne Valley beyond. While you get your breath

← The River South Tyne at Haydon Bridge (Kevin Eaves/S)

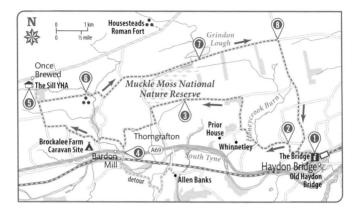

back after this tough start, it may be some comfort to know that most of the return journey, soon after Vindolanda, is downhill, freewheeling back into Haydon Bridge.

Turn left at the junction near the crest of the hill, signposted Chesterwood. Carry on up this narrow country lane, with increasingly broad, open views over dry stone walls to the valley beyond. Winding uphill to the right, finally we reach the brow of the hill, where we turn left at a ❷ **T-junction** on to Heugh House Lane.

About 100m after the T-junction we come to a fork, where we turn left, signposted **Prior House** and **Whinnetley**. We're coming to a nice downhill run now, gentle at first then steep and with a sharp right-hand bend halfway down (take care not to overshoot and go straight on). The road may be a bit pot-holey here too, so go carefully; at the bottom of the hill, cross an old stone bridge across Honeycrook Burn, still signposted Prior House and Whinnetley.

Wind left, then turn sharp right a few hundred metres further on (not straight on, which is a no-through road), climbing again steadily through this peaceful countryside, with a few grazing sheep and pecking crows for company. Before I come over all bucolic and poetic, though, we go under a line of tall electricity pylons straddling the road. A noisy crowd of starlings were perched halfway up one pylon when I passed by here recently; their cheerful chatter seemed to echo through the high wires.

After continuing up this straight stretch for about 1km, we come to another T-junction: turn left here on to an unpaved farm track, which runs straight on, westwards between the fields. It's mostly downhill, though quite rough and bumpy in parts, so go carefully.

Eventually, after several kilometres, we reach a T-junction with a paved road, and on our right is ❸ **Muckle Moss National Nature Reserve**, a heathland area of shrubs and protected peat bog (which attracts hen harriers and golden plovers, in case you're on the lookout). Turn left here and follow the road downhill, bending sharp right at the bottom and continuing straight ahead for a few hundred metres, winding through **Thorngrafton**, a tiny farming hamlet.

↑ Grindon Lough (neil denham/A)

## VINDOLANDA

The first Roman fort at Vindolanda was built in around AD85, around 40 years before Hadrian's Wall itself was built, some 1.5km to the north. It formed part of a defensive chain, called the Stanegate Road, which stretched across the northern border from Corbridge, east of Hexham, to Carlisle in Cumbria. Subsequent forts were erected here over 400 years, with an extensive community housed within its 5m-high walls, including officers' residences, temples, workshops, bathhouses, wells and stores.

Ongoing excavation works continue at the site, and have resulted in some of the most important Roman finds ever discovered. The most famous are the remarkably preserved Vindolanda Writing Tablets: these delicate, tissue-thin wooden sheets survived nearly 2,000 years underground, and are considered the oldest surviving handwritten documents in the UK. The tablets contain spidery ink messages written in Latin by the Roman residents of Vindolanda, relating military issues but also more mundane matters such as birthday invitations and requests for beer and underpants! The tablets were returned on loan from the British Museum and are now on display in Vindolanda's own museum, protected in hermetically sealed glass cabinets. Some of the oldest

Hold on tight after Thorngrafton, as the road bends right and sweeps downhill for a nice long run, ending up almost at the valley floor again, with the faint hiss of traffic from the A69 just ahead. Not quite, though, as we come to a T-junction after around 500m, where we turn right and back uphill again (joining the NCN72 and NCN68). Eventually, though, the hill levels out and we wind left on to a straight road, undulating between rows of stone cottages at Westwood.

At the next crossroads, turn left towards ❹ **Bardon Mill**. If you're planning to do the detour to Allen Banks (see page 61), continue straight on here, and through the riverside village of Bardon Mill. If not, after around 200m, turn right on to Park Lane, heading westwards again along the side of the valley. Follow Park Lane for around 1km until we come to another T-junction, where we turn right, now heading northwards,

archaeological finds have been particularly fruitful at Vindolanda, as remains were compressed deep beneath layers of turf and clay, free of the oxygen and bacteria which normally corrode ancient artefacts.

signposted Vindolanda and the wonderfully named **Once Brewed**, just to the north on **Hadrian's Wall**.

About 800m up the road is the turning on the right to **Vindolanda**. First, though, a short detour further on leads to ❺ **The Sill** (⌀thesill.org. uk). The National Landscape Discovery Centre is run by Northumberland National Park, and its array of attractions include a grass rooftop walk, and geology displays about the Carboniferous rocky ridge after which The Sill is named and on top of which the Romans built nearby Hadrian's Wall. To get there, continue for around another 800m, and the entrance is on the left.

Returning to the turn-off to Vindolanda, by a long row of conifers, after 1km we come to the entrance to ❻ **Vindolanda** on the right. The fortified complex (⌀vindolanda.com) is one of the best-preserved Roman

↑ An aerial view of Vindolanda (makasana photo/S)

sites on their British northern frontier (see box, page 54). There's a museum here as well as lectures and tours of the site, which is still being excavated.

Leaving Vindolanda, continue to the right and start descending steeply, with the hillsides rising dramatically up either side of the valley. After some 300m we cross Bradley Burn through a ford (usually dry in the summer), after which we climb steeply upwards again. If you pause in a lay-by on the left near the brow of the hill to get your breath back, there are superb views over Vindolanda below. Carry on to the top of the hill, and turn left at the T-junction.

Winding right at the top of the hill, signposted Newbrough, the road leads on to an east–west ridge, with stunning views over the valleys to north and south. As we pass a small lake, ❼ **Grindon Lough**, on our left, you may also spot **Housesteads Roman fort**, on Hadrian's Wall itself, on the horizon beyond. We also revisit **Muckle Moss** again, on our right, the nature reserve we passed earlier on, near Thorngrafton.

After around 7km of a glorious downhill spree along the ridge, we come to a ❽ **crossroads** where we turn right, finally leaving the NCN72 (which carries on eastwards to Newcastle; see page 38). For these final few kilometres, carry on straight ahead and southwards back to Haydon Bridge – still downhill, apart from one short sharp climb in the middle.

Eventually, as we glimpse the rooftops of the town below, we reach the fork in the road where we turned left towards Chesterwood. Here we wind left and descend – steeply for the last few hundred metres – back over the level crossing and turn left into the station car park.

## THE ESSENTIALS

**GETTING THERE** By train, Haydon Bridge is just under 1 hour from Newcastle, on Northern Railway (⊘ northernrailway.co.uk), with direct connections to other cities in the UK including Edinburgh, York and London. By car, it is 50km west of Newcastle or just over 50km east of Carlisle, both via the A69.

**FACILITIES** There are public toilets at the Bridge Community Centre at the start of the ride, as well as customer toilets at The Sill and Vindolanda en route.

## WHERE TO EAT

✖ **Anchor Hotel** John Martin Street, Haydon Bridge NE47 6AB; ✆ 01434 688121; ⌂ anchorhotelathaydonbridge.org.uk. On the south bank of the Tyne, overlooking Haydon Bridge, this long-standing pub-hotel has a colourful history of diverse roles, including as a courthouse (with the car park and garden located on the site of the former gallows); its menu features daily specials, focusing on classic British cuisine & local produce, with its Sun roasts particularly recommended. Eat either in its cosy snug bar by the log fire, or out on its sunny riverside terrace. **££**

✖ **Once Brewed Coffee & Bakehouse** The Sill, Once Brewed NE47 7AN; ✆ 01434 341200; ⌂ thesill.org.uk. This proudly local café at the National Landscape Discovery Centre (free entry) sources 80% of its food & drink from the area, serving all-day b/fasts, lunches, sandwiches, soups, cakes & pastries, hot & cold drinks, wine and beer. Located on the first floor of this modern eco-building, it has superb views over Northumberland National Park and Hadrian's Wall. There are cycle racks at the front entrance, as well as secure cycle storage (hire charge). **£**

✖ **Queen's Hall Café** Beaumont St, Hexham NE46 3LZ; ✆ 07722 078733. Worth making a special trip to visit some 10km from Haydon Bridge, this smashing café, attached to Queen's Hall Art Centre, does great b/fasts & freshly made snacks, savoury scones, deli sandwiches, jacket potatoes, soups & toasties, cakes & tray bakes, & marvellous milkshakes (closed Sun–Mon). **£**

## FURTHER INFORMATION

ℹ **Haydon Bridge Visitor Information Centre** Church St, Haydon Bridge NE47 6JQ; ✆ 01434 688658; ⌂ haydon-bridge. co.uk/visitors-tourist.php. Right next to the train station, this multi-use, volunteer-run community centre, library, café and tourist office is also the hub for several bike rides in the Tyne Valley and North Pennines, including this one and the following Route 5, Pennines Panorama Loop (see page 58). Open 09.00–noon Mon, 13.00–16.00 Tue–Wed, 16.00–18.30 Thu (summer only), 16.00–18.30 Fri & 09.30–12.30 Sat.

# 5 PENNINES PANORAMA LOOP

| | |
|---|---|
| **START/FINISH** | Haydon Bridge |
| **DISTANCE/TIME** | 18.9km/2hrs |
| **DIFFICULTY/TERRAIN** | ② A short route but hilly throughout, including a few steep climbs and downhill stretches too; mostly on quiet back roads, as well as a few kilometres on rough farm trails; in all, best suited for reasonably fit, confident cyclists |
| **SCENIC RATING** | © Stunning Pennines landscape, from a high ridge with 360-degree views over the Allen and Tyne valleys |
| **SUITABLE FOR** | MTB, gravel bike or hybrid |
| **NCN ROUTE** | NCN68 and NCN72 (on the north side of the valley) |
| **MAPS** | OS Explorer 43 (1:25 000) |
| **KOMOOT REF** | 909318843 |

↑ The tarn in Morralee Wood at Allen Banks (Dave Head/S)

T his short but rigorous ride climbs up from Haydon Bridge to a ridge overlooking the South Tyne Valley, winding through Pennines moorland and past Stublick Chimney, a monument of the region's mining heritage. Returning to Haydon Bridge, we take an exhilarating cross-country route through fields and woodland trails.

The only refreshment option we pass en route is Carts Bog Inn (see below), but there are plenty of eateries and shops in Haydon Bridge.

## THE ROUTE

Start from ❶ **The Bridge** Visitor Information Centre, next to Haydon Bridge station (with a car park behind). Turn left up Church Street and cross **Old Haydon Bridge** (footbridge; give way to pedestrians) over the South Tyne River.

On the other side, turn right on to Shaftoe Road (passing Oddfellows Café, see below), and first right again down Land Ends Road, a narrow lane opposite Haydonians Community Club. The lane runs alongside the river on the right for a short while, then begins to climb upwards, inland.

Follow the road uphill, under the A69, winding left and right until you come to a left-hand turn after a few hundred metres: no sign but with a bench on the left-hand corner. Continue uphill here, finally levelling out in front of **West Land Ends Farm**, with some lovely views back over the valley below to reward your efforts.

Passing the farm, the uphill climb starts again, gently at first then steeply up to a small copse, ❷ **Black Byre Plantation**, where we turn right at a T-junction. As you come out of the trees, note a TV mast atop Morralee Fell to the west, a useful landmark that we pass later on. Turn right at the crossroads approximately 1km ahead before going downhill and up again to the ❸ **top of the hill** – finally. Turn left and cross the open moorland of **Morralee Fell**. (Or right downhill from here for the detour to **Allen Banks**, approximately 2.8km; see box page 61, and komoot map 909678290.)

Pass the TV mast on your right after around 100m. A few hundred metres beyond that, turn left at a T-junction and then straight on at the next junction, with the road winding to the left. After all the climbing we're on a relatively level stretch now for a while: out in wide-open moorland, criss-crossed by the Pennines' distinctive dry stone walls, with just a few sheep grazing in fields and occasional woodlands fringing the fells.

About 1km after that left bend in the road we come to a right-hand turn; it's not signposted but it's a right-angled turn just in front of a small conifer plantation. After about another 1km, with the road undulating between woods, we take a sharp right turn at a T-junction with the A686. We're only on this A-road for approximately 100m but cycle carefully, alert for traffic speeding uphill here. Turn left after the **Carts Bog Inn** (see below), on to the B6305. We're climbing slightly uphill again here, but the road then levels out as it winds eastwards along the valley. We're coming to a high ridge here, similar to the one above Vindolanda (see Route 4, page 50), with superb views over the Pennines moorland to the north and south.

Pass **Langley Dam** reservoir on the left and, shortly after that, go straight across the staggered crossroads with the B6295. The road is climbing slowly but steadily now for a while, until after around 600m, we come to a line of trees and a telecoms mast on the left, with a grassy path opposite

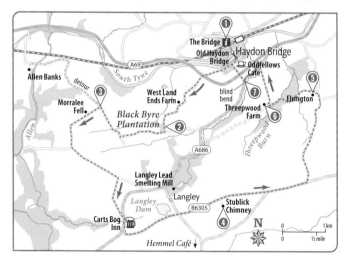

## ALLEN BANKS AND STAWARD GORGE

Running through a deep gorge to the southwest of Haydon Bridge are the twin natural attractions of Allen Banks and Staward Gorge. This National Trust site is prized for having the largest area of ancient semi-natural woodland in Northumbria, 'semi-natural' because much of the woodland that thrives here today was planted by Susan Davidson, granddaughter of the Earl of Strathmore, whose family owned the former Allensgreen Estate. Marked trails wind along the steep-sided Allen Valley, which is rich with a wide variety of wildlife, particularly fungi and flora. The woods are beautiful in the late spring, when bluebells carpet the ground, as well as ramsons (aka wild garlic). It's also a great birdwatching spot, with dippers and kingfishers among the 70+ species seen here.

There's a pay-and-display car park at the main entrance, near Ridley Hall (OS ref: NY 79591 64296), with maps of the four walking trails. The walk to Staward Gorge itself is a demanding 9km hike, but for a shorter taster the 3.5km Walks Wood trail follows the side of the valley under the trees and down to a beach on a bend in the river.

Although cycling is not permitted in the gorge itself, it's easy to get here by bike via short detours from either of our adjacent Routes 4 and 5: it's approximately 3.6km from Bardon Mill and across the South Tyne on Route 4 (see page 54, before waypoint 4; komoot map 961953532), or approximately 2.8km steep downhill and up again off Route 5 (see page 59, from waypoint 3; komoot map 909678290). Or to get here by road, it's 5km west of Haydon Bridge.

For more details, visit ⊘ nationaltrust.org.uk/allen-banks-and-staward-gorge.

on the right leading to ❹ **Stublick Chimney**. This impressive, 100m-tall brick chimney was used by the **Langley Lead Smelting Mill**, and erected in this isolated spot in 1859 because of the toxic lead fumes. The local lead industry thrived until closure in the late 19th century, outdone by rival competitors and the replacement of lead by less dangerous aluminium. Today, the chimney is an English Heritage listed monument, and the site also provides beautiful moorland views all around.

Continue along the B6305 after the chimney, with the B6304 joining the road from the right after approximately 1.5km. Shortly after that we turn left on to a farm track (public way), leading through a gate into a field of inquisitive cattle and sheep so go carefully, also as the track is quite rough here. Follow the track downhill for around 2km, through several fields, heading north back to Haydon Bridge.

Finally, we rejoin the paved road briefly at ❺ **Elrington**, and cross a bridge over a former railway line. Follow the road around to your left, passing Elrington Farm on your left, then back on to another farm track (public way) through a couple of gates. The track really becomes a rubbly roller-coaster ride now: steep downhill across a couple of streams, including Threepwood Burn, then wiggling uphill through woodlands. After around 1km we emerge, shaken if not stirred, thankfully back on to a paved road at ❻ **Threepwood Farm**, with views of Haydon Bridge visible now in the valley not far below.

Pass the farm on your left and on to a long straight downhill stretch for nearly 1km. Tempting as it may be, don't overdo it here, as we turn sharp left at a T-junction at the bottom and on to the A686. Wind uphill to the left for about 600m before turning right (take care with oncoming traffic around a blind bend) coming into Haydon Bridge. Go back under the A69, past the cemetery on your left and the Haydonians Club again, on your right. Finally, turn left back over the footbridge, up Church Street, and right back into the station car park. Rattled, rolled and all done!

## THE ESSENTIALS

**GETTING THERE** By train, Haydon Bridge is just under 1 hour from Newcastle, on Northern Railway (⊘ northernrailway.co.uk), with direct connections to other cities in the UK including Edinburgh, York and London. By car, it is 50km west of Newcastle or just over 50km east of Carlisle, both via the A69.

**FACILITIES** There are public toilets at the Bridge Community Centre at the start of the ride, and customer toilets at Carts Bog Inn en route (below).

## WHERE TO EAT

✖ **Carts Bog Inn** Langley, Hexham NE47 5NW; ✆ 01434 684338; 🖥 cartsbog.co.uk. This family-run gastropub, in an 18th-century former coaching inn midway around our route, has a simple but diverse menu of pub classics with one or two international favourites added to the mix, from Moroccan tagine to chilli con carne, but best known for its Guinness-braised beef Bog Pie. It is strongly focused on local produce, including from the owners' nearby farm. Advance booking is advisable. **££**

✖ **The Hemmel Café** Allenheads NE47 9HJ; ✆ 01434 685568; 🖥 thehemmel.cafe. Tucked away, deep in idyllic North Pennines countryside south of Haydon Bridge, this café is worth going out of the way for (also as it's right on the C2C Coast-to-Coast cycle route). With a beautiful garden, library, lounge & children's play area, its menu ranges from all-day b/fasts (with gluten-free & veggie options) to panini, salads & afternoon teas, with their own scrumptious freshly made cakes & scones. **££**

✖ **Oddfellows Café** Shaftoe St, Haydon Bridge NE47 6BQ; ✆ 01434 671449. Overlooking the town's old footbridge across the Tyne, near the end of our route, this friendly little café serves an interesting mix of light lunches, brunches (eg: smoked salmon & avocado on sourdough bread), freshly baked cakes & dim sum dishes, with great coffee and tea; it also has secure cycle storage. Open daytime only; closed Tue. **£**

## FURTHER INFORMATION

ℹ️ **Haydon Bridge Visitor Information Centre** Church St, Haydon Bridge NE47 6JQ; ✆ 01434 688658; 🖥 haydon-bridge.co.uk/visitors-tourist.php. Right next to the train station, this multi-purpose, volunteer-run hub is the town's community centre, library, café and tourist office. Open 09.00–noon Mon, 13.00–16.00 Tue–Wed, 16.00–18.30 Thu (summer only), 16.00–18.30 Fri & 09.30–12.30 Sat.

# 6 LAKESIDE WAY TRAIL, KIELDER FOREST

| | |
|---|---|
| **START/FINISH** | Kielder Castle |
| **DISTANCE/TIME** | 41.7km/4–4½hrs |
| **DIFFICULTY/TERRAIN** | ② This traffic-free trail is one of our longer routes; hilly throughout, including some steep climbs, descents and sharp bends; mostly on loose gravel, with some paved sections; best suited for reasonably fit and experienced cyclists |
| **SCENIC RATING** | © Lakeside panoramas fringed by dense pine forests |
| **SUITABLE FOR** | MTB, gravel bike or robust hybrid (knobbly tyres a must!) |
| **NCN ROUTE** | NCN10 (along the south shore, between the dam and Kielder Waterside) |
| **MAPS** | OS Explorer 42 (1:25 000) |
| **KOMOOT REF** | 911437581 |

↑ Kielder Viaduct (Michael Conrad/S)

This superb off-road trail loops around the largest manmade reservoir in northern Europe, surrounded by the dense Kielder Forest, England's largest forest.

Starting from the top of the lake, we go clockwise down the northern shore. Alternatively, you could go anticlockwise, but there are more facilities along the south side, when you might be more in need of refreshment; also, as it's a loop route, there are various other points along the way where you could start, with car parks noted below.

Most of the trail runs close to the shore, fringed with reeds, bracken and heather, or beneath the tall trees, with glowing sphagnum moss carpeting the forest floor. Besides the stunning scenery, intriguing art installations are dotted around the waterside and forest, as well as bird hides and lookout points. Although it's called Lakeside Way and there are plenty of breath-taking views over the water, there are also inland stretches, around inlets and side-channels.

Note that swimming is not allowed in the reservoir; the water is very cold and deep in parts. Also, it might be surprising to learn that the trail is mostly hilly throughout, with signs warning of occasional steep descents. Take care on loose gravel and sand; if you're using cleats, keep one foot free for balance on these tricky stretches.

Finally, before setting off, check at Kielder Visitor Centre about possible trail closures due to forestry works and potential storm damage.

## THE ROUTE

Start from **❶ Kielder Castle Visitor Centre** in the northwestern corner of the lake, with Hide car park (pay-and-display) across the road opposite. Turn left and follow signs to the North Shore and the Over Viaduct.

The paved road winds uphill to a junction where we turn left and immediately right, on to the path, signposted Lakeside Way North Shore. Go through a tunnel of low trees then left across **❷ Kielder Viaduct**, over

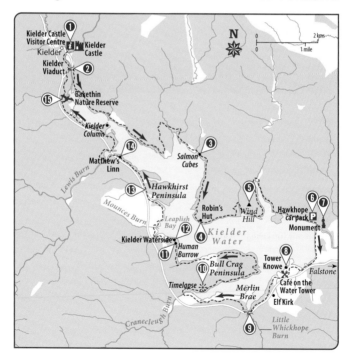

the River North Tyne, the main source feeding the reservoir. The viaduct walls are only about 1m high and it's a long drop to the river below, so keep a firm grip if you have small children with you: they may be at eye level with the wrought-iron panels set into the walls, featuring animals, plants, trains and even a bunch of grapes (referencing wine production by the Romans, perhaps?).

Turn right at the fork going uphill shortly after the viaduct, with a wooden signpost to the Lakeside Way North Shore. At the top, get ready for a long downhill stretch for several kilometres, overlooking the shore. It's great fun but, before careering off, prepare ahead for a sharp right-hand bend at the foot of the hill after about 3km. We cross a stream here, and loop back towards the lake, passing a weir at a narrow neck with the opposite bank.

The downhill spree carries on after the stream, running close to the shore, then after a couple of kilometres winding inland and around to the right again, crossing another stream, Plashetts Burn. About 1.5km later, going downhill and near the waterside again, we come to a row of giant blocks on the right: ❸ *Salmon Cubes*, one of a collection of art installations around the lakeside. These large blocks are decorated with designs inspired by salmon, which swim down through Kielder Water to the mouth of the Tyne every year. One of the cubes, *Scales*, is covered with mirrored tin sheets, which reflect the light and jangle in the wind; you'll probably hear it before you see it. Some of the other artworks are visible on this route, but a guide to the whole set, with a walking trail map, is available from Kielder Castle Visitor Centre (see below).

Soon after the *Salmon Cubes*, the path winds right around a headland jutting out into the lake and, after about another 2.5km, at the tip of this headland, we come to ❹ **Robin's Hut**: an open-sided wooden shelter overlooking the lake and the opposite shore. This is one of the most popular lookouts on Kielder Water, with wonderful views to the north and south. If you stop to have a look for yourself, the story of why it's lined up with Freya's Cabin, another shelter across the shore, is written inside. (I won't spoil the treat by telling the story here: it'll be much nicer to find out *in situ*!)

Continuing around the headland for about 1km beyond Robin's Hut, we catch our first glimpse of Kielder Dam spanning the south end of the lake. The low straight wall seems almost within arm's reach from here, but sorry to dangle that carrot before you, as we now come to the end of the headland and wind to the left, around the foot of ❺ **Wind Hill** and up a deep inlet, with more frequent and steeper ups and downs.

Finally, we return to the lakeside after around another 2.5km. The track levels out and follows the waterside for the next 1.5km until we reach ❻ **Hawkhope car park** by the dam, with picnic benches and toilets. If you're staying overnight at Kielder Water, you might want to come back here after dark as it's a Dark Sky Discovery Site: one of a number of designated locations that are particularly light-free after dark and thus ideal for some stargazing (see box, opposite).

Opposite the car park, to the left of the road over the dam, a commemorative ❼ **monument** marks the opening of Kielder Water by Her Majesty Queen Elizabeth II on 26 May 1982. As you cycle across the dam, you can look far up the reservoir. Its wiggly shape means that there is nowhere on the shore from which you can see its full length, but this is one of the best long views, often with sailing boats bobbing about, from the nearby sailing club which we're about to pass. Looking over the dam to your left is also interesting, with the overflow weir below running down into the North Tyne. Northumbrian Water, which manages Kielder Water, pumps around 30 million litres of water per day into local rivers during threatened droughts: an unimaginable volume to most of us, but to put it into context, that's the equivalent of nearly 15 Olympic swimming pools a day. The whole of Kielder Water contains 200 billion litres of water, making it the largest manmade reservoir in northern Europe.

Meanwhile… once across the dam, cross over to the right, behind the small car park, to continue the trail, back on to gravel and – for now – on the level. After about 1km, pass ❽ **Tower Knowe** on your right: one of Kielder's other main visitor hubs, with a sailing club, toilets, café and information.

Soon after Tower Knowe, note a left-hand turning up to **Elf Kirk**, another Dark Sky Discovery Site. The path descends steeply after that

# KIELDER – DARK SKY PARK

Located far from sources of light pollution, deep in the heart of Northumberland, Kielder Forest and the surrounding Northumberland National Park comprise the first **International Dark Sky Park** to be designated in England by the International Dark Sky Association and the largest in Europe (⊘ darksky.org/our-work/conservation/idsp/parks/northumberland/). Several sites around Kielder are listed Dark Sky Discovery Sites, including Kielder Castle, Hawkhope, Falstone, Elf Kirk and Kielder Observatory.

The Dark Sky Park has been recognised as England's best place for stargazing, and the second-largest area of protected night sky in Europe. Kielder Observatory, a short drive from Kielder Water, is a world-class site for viewing the heavens above. As a charity dedicated to attracting a wider audience to astronomy, it holds around 700 events every year, including 'Young Explorer' evenings and school visits. Housing the telescopes on the hilltop site are two turrets and an observation deck. There's also the grandly titled Gillian Dickinson Astro-Imaging Academy, used for astrophotography (with some stunning photographs on display in its gallery). With limited visitor space available, the popular events are often booked weeks ahead; for more information, visit ⊘ kielderobservatory.org.

Alternatively, if you just want to gaze at the stars from one of the sites listed above, the recommended times are during a new moon, when the sky is darkest, or just after nightfall on a clear night before the moon rises. Warm clothing and hot drinks are advisable; and let somebody know where you are going and when you plan to be back. A telescope will help too, but the Milky Way, shooting stars and billions of other astral bodies can be visible with the naked eye.

turning to Elf Kirk, with a sharp turning across a ❾ **bridge** over Little Whickhope Burn at the bottom, after about 800m, so go carefully here.

Zigzag uphill from the bridge and carry straight on across a couple of road junctions, cutting inland across the neck of a headland, **Merlin Brae**, home to a waterski club. Continue along the level trail for a couple of kilometres before descending again, across another stream, Cranecleugh Burn.

Winding up the other side of the stream, follow the path sharply around to the right and on to the large **Bull Crag Peninsula**. After around 500m, we come to another art installation/lookout point: ❿ *Timelapse*, a square-sided wooden shelter offering a panoramic pit stop overlooking the inlet, if you're in need of a break. From here, the path hugs close to the shore for about 6km around the peninsula, with gorgeous open views across the water.

Coming back to the main shore, turn right and continue along the level path for another 600m or so, coming to a slipway. Just beyond, turn sharp left, opposite a lifebuoy on the right, and follow the NCN10 signs, cutting uphill across the headland. (Or a short detour straight on leads to a truly immersive art installation: ⓫ *Human Burrow*, built into the hillside, with animal sounds played in a cork-lined grotto.)

Within about 100m, we come to ⓬ **Kielder Waterside**, a holiday resort (see page 211) with a wide range of facilities including café, restaurant, bike hire (The Bike Place, see page 220) and toilets. Going through the site – slowly, looking out for children and vehicles – turn right on to the

↑ The *Timelapse* shelter overlooking Kielder Water (Caitlin Hennessy)

main road, then first left through the car park, following the Lakeside Way signpost.

About 100m beyond the car park we rejoin the trail proper, winding uphill to the left. Cross a bridge over Mounces Burn then down to the waterside, past Rushy Knowe Wood and through three gates between fields. Around 200,000 trees were planted here in 2019, in the first phase of a Forestry England project to diversify the woodland, with 12 broadleaved species and nine conifers planted so far, and more to follow in 2025. When I passed by in late 2022, I saw only small saplings on the edge of the plantation, but it extends uphill inland to merge with the main forest. There are particularly beautiful views from this open hillside – especially if you're lucky enough to be out on a sunny morning, with the rising sun sparkling over the water.

Shortly beyond Rushy Knowe we cross a small bridge and then turn left at a T-junction, just before the Hawkhirst Scout Activity Centre on the right, on ⓫ **Hawkhirst Peninsula**.

Some 300m later we come to a sign on the left, pointing straight on to Lakeside Way, South Shore and Kielder Castle (7km from here). Carry straight on here, cutting across the peninsula and passing a side road to the scout centre, mentioned above. About another 300m beyond that, take the right fork, around a locked gate and on to a level, paved path, running parallel to the main road. The trail turns back shortly to gravel and runs alongside the waterside again. After about another 1km we come to ⓮ **Matthew's Linn**, a lookout point next to Lewis Burn with car park and toilets.

Carry on straight ahead, keeping alert as the path crosses the road into the car park, and now heading up towards **Bakethin Reservoir**, the long narrow branch at the head of the lake, with a nature reserve. Hold on tight first, though, as we descend a sharp downhill stretch, winding under the road and across an impressive modern bridge over Lewis Burn. There are more stunning views across the lake from here: safer to look once you've negotiated the descent and climb up again from the bridge!

Go back under the road and continue winding up and down, to the left/northwards for about 1km. Shortly after passing a jetty on the right, turn left at a T-junction and within about 50m turn right, by a Lakeside Way signpost. If you're interested in adding another art installation to your collection, though, a short footpath leads right at the T-junction to another artwork, ***Kielder Column*** (a spiral sandstone pillar), and a lookout point by the narrow neck of Bakethin Reservoir.

From here the path winds downhill to the water's edge and after a couple of kilometres we come to ⑮ **Bakethin Nature Reserve**, an area spanning the northwest shore of the reservoir comprising mixed woodland, grassland and wetland habitats; a haven for waterfowl, with lichens and mosses carpeting the forest floor. A path on the right leads to two bird hides (on foot only, but you can wheel your bike: it's only about 100m long), with one for Lake Views and the other for Forest Views. An abundance of species are commonly spotted here, including kingfishers, herons and ospreys, Kielder's latest wildlife success story (see box, page 78).

And talking of wildlife, about 200m further down on the main path is an impressive log bench carved with the shapes of otters and a spreadeagled bird – possibly an osprey. From here, continue for approximately 1km up through the trees, coming to the tree-tunnel by the viaduct where we started, then turning left up the tunnel and then right up the road back to ❶ **Kielder Castle**.

## THE ESSENTIALS

**GETTING THERE** By car (as there is no public transport), Kielder Water and Forest Park is just under 62km northeast of Carlisle via the A7 and B6357, or 84km northwest of Newcastle via the A69 and A68.

**FACILITIES** Public toilets, refreshments and information points are available at various locations around the lake, including Kielder Castle, Tower Knowe and Kielder Waterside.

### WHERE TO EAT

✘ **The Anglers' Arms** Kielder NE48 1ER;
𝒹 01434 250230; ☉ anglersarms.business.

site. Handily located opposite Kielder Castle, this pub is as popular with locals as it is with visitors. The menu has classic favourites including burgers, steaks, curry & fish'n'chips, as well as several veggie, vegan & gluten-free options such as quinoa chilli. The bar stocks a range of local ales. **£**

✕ **Forest Bar & Kitchen** Kielder Waterside, Falstone NE48 1BT; 🕾 01434 25100; 🖰 kielderwaterside.com. In the heart of this extensive holiday village (see page 211), this family-friendly restaurant with great waterfront views is open for lunch & dinner, with a comprehensive menu ranging from light-bite snacks & sandwiches to burgers, curries, pizzas, pasta dishes & several veggie options (**££**). The adjacent Hide Café is open daily until 11.15 for b/fasts, snacks & freshly made cakes & pastries (**£**).

✕ **Café on the Water Tower** Knowe NE48 1BX; 🕾 01434 240923; 🖰 visitkielder.com. Halfway around our lakeside ride, this bright & breezy modern café has indoor seating & outdoor terrace, serving sweet & savoury pastries, sandwiches, cakes & scones, & hot & cold drinks. Handy for a quick refuel en route. **£**

## FURTHER INFORMATION

**Kielder Castle Visitor Centre** Kielder NE48 1ER; 🕾 01434 250209; 🖰 forestryengland. uk/kielder-castle. Staff at Kielder's main visitor centre provide tips & advice with route maps, leaflets and timetables of activities organised all year round. Note that, at the time of writing, Kielder Castle was undergoing redevelopment work – for the latest information, see 🖰 visitkielder.com/visit/know-before-you-go. For the latest updates about route closures in Kielder Forest, due to Storm Arwen (2021) or other potential storm damage, visit 🖰 forestryengland.uk/article/kielder-water-and-forest-park-storm-arwen-recovery-update.

# 7 OSPREY CHICK MTB TRAIL, KIELDER FOREST

| | |
|---|---|
| **START/FINISH** | Kielder Castle |
| **DISTANCE/TIME** | 12.2km/1½hrs |
| **DIFFICULTY/TERRAIN** | ① Mostly off-road on gravel-and-earth trails, over rocks and knobbly roots, and with a few MTB features (ie: berms, humps and drops); suitable for reasonably fit cyclists, including families, with some mountain-biking experience |
| **SCENIC RATING** | © Through the woods and hillsides of Kielder Forest and along the shore of Kielder Water |
| **SUITABLE FOR** | MTB, robust hybrid or gravel bike (with knobbly tyres) |
| **NCN ROUTE** | NCN10 |
| **MAPS** | OS Explorer 42 (1:25 000) |
| **KOMOOT REF** | 911452888 |

This short but fun mountain-biking route follows the Osprey Chick MTB Trail as it winds, bounces and zips through Kielder Water and Forest Park. Bordering Northumberland National Park, Kielder is the largest forest in England, covering 600km², an area larger than Birmingham. From Kielder Castle, climb up on to the trail, with stunning views over the treetops, then zigzag down to the shore of Kielder Water, the largest manmade reservoir in northern Europe.

At the start of the trail, there's a short MTB circuit where you can practise your skills and check that your bike is all in good working order. The trail is a moderate Blue-graded MTB route, suitable for cyclists with some on- and off-road experience, riding mountain bikes, robust gravel bikes or robust hybrid bikes. Moderate as the route is, wearing a cycle helmet, gloves and stout shoes is strongly advised.

The route is well signposted throughout, including information boards with emergency contact numbers. Keep alert for vehicles on the forestry roads, and give way to horses and walkers. The trails are single-track, so be aware of other cyclists, in front and behind.

## THE ROUTE

Start at ❶ **Kielder Castle** at the north end of Kielder Water, with visitor centre, bike hire (see page 220) and car park. Turn right, uphill, following the sign for the Osprey Trail (which includes the Osprey Chick route),

← An osprey in full flight (Mark Medcalf/S)

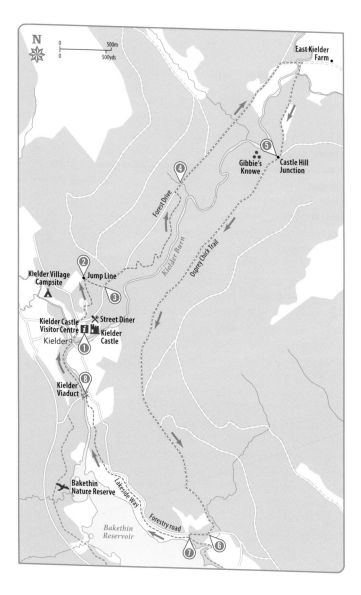

opposite the car park. There's an information board here too, about the Osprey and other MTB trails that start from here (graded Green – easy, Red – difficult, and Black – severe!).

The path soon begins to wind gradually uphill between the tall, densely packed trees – predominantly Sitka spruce and other conifers. We're heading roughly northwards at first, between Kielder Burn and Ravenshill Moor. After about 100m, on the right, is the ❷ **Jump Line**. This nifty little circuit has a few berms (banked turns), humps and drops to help MTB learners practise their skills before the real thing coming up. It's also useful exercise to help you warm up and test brakes, gears and steering. It's only about 200m long, and not steep or difficult: slaloming between the trees, and bouncing over low humps and knobbly roots. The single-track path winds downhill to the right, then turns right again to rejoin the main trail.

Continue uphill, past Jump Line again, before coming to a T-junction after around 50m where we turn right. In another 200m, we come to another T-junction, turning left on to ❸ **Forest Drive**, the wide forestry road (keep alert here for timber trucks and other working vehicles).

Still climbing for a little longer, turn right after about 200m back on to a rough, single-tracked trail. Now we begin winding downhill through the trees, negotiating a few more berms, bumps and dips. It's exhilarating but also peaceful: zipping through the forest with moss, fungi and bracken all around, and hardly a sound to be heard.

This section of the trail twists and turns, mostly downhill, for about 1km, before climbing left gradually and back on to Forest Drive, where we turn right. The road levels off, giving us a pause for breath before the next round of off-road action. After about another 1km, cross a little bridge over a ❹ **stream** (a side-channel of Kielder Burn), then climb again and go straight on at a crossroads. The forest is opening up more now, with views emerging over the treetops to the bare moorlands beyond.

Follow Forest Drive bending around to the right about 700m after the stream. We're coming out of the trees here, with the fields of **East Kielder Farm** on our left. But around 200m further ahead, cross Kielder Burn again and, just after that, turn right back into the forest, around a gated entrance on to a wide, gravel forestry road.

## KIELDER'S OSPREYS

Kielder Water and Forest Park boasts an impressive array of native wildlife, including red squirrels, deer, goshawks and a wealth of wildfowl. Its star conservation success story in recent years, though, is the osprey. This large, fish-eating raptor disappeared from Northumberland for about 200 years. In 2009, however, a pair of ospreys successfully bred in Kielder. Every year since then, with help from Forestry England which built nesting platforms around the forest, ospreys have returned, with the population increasing to seven breeding pairs in 2021.

Northumberland Wildlife Trust runs a viewing point and wildlife cabin at Tower Knowe Visitor Centre, on the southwest shore of Kielder Water, opened in 2022. Regular osprey-watching events are held here and there are also osprey-watching cruises on the Osprey ferry from Kielder Waterside (⌀ wildintrigue. co.uk/mini-expeds/osprey-watching-cruise/).

The best times of year to see ospreys hunting over the water are between late March and early September. They use all parts of the reservoir, but favourite sites include the water on either side of the dam, and between Bull Crag Peninsula and Leaplish Bay. The birds regularly hunt just after dawn and again in the early evening, but may be seen at any time of the day.

The work to protect and monitor ospreys at Kielder is funded by the Osprey Watch programme, with donations gratefully welcomed via ⌀ kielderospreys. wordpress.com/donate.

↑ The Osprey ferry sets off from Kielder Waterside to view the resident ospreys (Hazel Plater/S)

We're on another gradual uphill stretch now, with views to the west over the treetops down to Kielder Burn at the bottom of the valley. High up the other side are bare-topped fells on the Scottish border, including Deadwater Fell (with satellite masts on its summit). At 569m, this is one of the highest points in Kielder.

So, carry on straight ahead at **⑤ Castle Hill Junction** at the top of the hill after a couple of hundred metres, with a signpost to **Gibbie's Knowe**, the nearby remains of an Iron Age settlement. It's a raised earthwork on a hill overlooking Kielder Burn just ahead on the right; there's no access through the forest, but you might catch a glimpse between the trees as you pass by.

We head downhill now, still on the wide forest trail but with trees closing in around us. At the foot of the hill, though, a couple of kilometres after Castle Hill Junction, a tangle of uprooted trees lines a clearance either side of the trail: stark evidence of the powerful winter storms that hit much of Northumbria in recent years, including Storm Arwen in 2021. Forestry England is working hard to repair affected roads and trails, so look out for warning signs (and see below for Forestry England contact details). Continue straight ahead past the clearance, descending again and winding left, approaching Kielder Water. In a few hundred metres, pass the sharp left-hand turn for the main Osprey route (it's about twice as long as the Chick, but also Blue-graded).

This last downhill stretch is great fun, but it's on loose gravel with some sharp bends, so take care. After about 1.5km, we reach another **⑥ forestry road** where we turn right, then shortly after that turn left on to a smaller path (signposted Osprey Trail and Kielder Village) and then sharp right on to **⑦ Lakeside Way**, heading gently uphill, under telegraph lines, and back towards Kielder Castle. We get our first close-up glimpses now of Kielder Water through the trees close ahead on the left.

Continue straight ahead at the next junction, signposted towards Kielder Village and Kielder Castle. Keep going along the level waterside path for a couple of kilometres, then turn left across **⑧ Kielder Viaduct**, over the River North Tyne. After the viaduct, turn right up Lakeside Way, continuing for about another 500m, with the river on your right, until you come to

a T-junction. Turn left on to the road, then right up the hill and back to ❶ **Kielder Castle** on your right (with the car park ahead on the left).

## THE ESSENTIALS

**GETTING THERE** By car (as there is no public transport), Kielder Water and Forest Park is just under 62km northeast of Carlisle via the A7 and B6357, or 84km northwest of Newcastle via the A69 and A68.

**FACILITIES** Public toilets and information points are available at Kielder Castle.

### WHERE TO EAT

✖ **Street Diner** Kielder Castle, Kielder NE48 1ER; ✆ 01434 250209; ⌂ visitkielder.com. This take-away counter in the castle courtyard does freshly made pizzas, burgers, b/fast butties & other sandwiches, & hot & cold drinks. It's nothing fancy but handy for a quick bite if you're doing our Kielder rides (see Route 6, page 64). £

✖ **The Pheasant Inn** Shilling Pot, Stannersburn NE48 1DD; ✆ 01434 240382; ⌂ thepheasantinn.com. This family-run inn, a tastefully refurbished 17th-century farmhouse, is a short drive from Kielder, near Falstone. Inside it's cosy, with exposed stone walls, oak beams & open fireplaces; the regularly changing menu is based on seasonal local produce, often

↑ A winter sunrise at Kielder Water (Tim Saxon/S)

including slow-roast Northumbrian lamb, dressed crab & fresh fish from North Shields Fish Quay. A choice of vegetarian dishes is also available, & the bar stocks an impressive range of ales, malt whiskies & wines. All in all, great food & drink: booking advisable. ££

✕ **The Blackcock Inn** Falstone, NE48 1AA; ☏ 01434 240200; ⊘ theblackcockinnat falstone.com. Only about 1.5km down the road from Kielder Water, this family-run 16th-century coaching inn has a welcoming bar with log fire & adjoining pool room. Its eclectic menu covers Sun roasts to 'Falstone Footlong' hot dogs, steaks, burgers & vegetarian risotto, while the bar offers a range of local cask ales & even a gin menu. The beer garden is popular on sunny days, especially with passing cyclists. Closed Mon–Tue. ££

## FURTHER INFORMATION

**Kielder Castle Visitor Centre** Kielder NE48 1ER; ☏ 01434 250209; ⊘ forestryengland. uk/kielder-castle. Kielder's main visitor centre provides tips & advice with route maps, leaflets and details of organised activities. At the time of writing, Kielder Castle was undergoing redevelopment work – for the latest information, see ⊘ visitkielder.com/visit/know-before-you-go. For updates about route closures in Kielder Forest due to storm damage, visit ⊘ forestryengland.uk/article/kielder-water-and-forest-park-storm-arwen-recovery-update

# 8 FALSTONE TO BELLINGHAM

| | |
|---|---|
| **START/FINISH** | Falstone/Bellingham |
| **DISTANCE/TIME** | 20.1km/2–3hrs (including detour to Dally Castle) |
| **DIFFICULTY/TERRAIN** | ① On quiet, undulating country lanes with a few short, steep climbs but no major road junctions; suitable for reasonably fit cyclists, including families |
| **SCENIC RATING** | ⑧ Through rolling, heather-clad moorland bordering the Northumberland National Park and along the valley of the inky-dark River North Tyne |
| **SUITABLE FOR** | Hybrid, gravel bike or road bike |
| **NCN ROUTE** | NCN10 and NCN68 |
| **MAPS** | OS Explorer 42 (1:25 000) |
| **KOMOOT REF** | 970997060 |

This tranquil ride undulates between burns trickling through the moorlands of the Northumberland National Park and the wooded banks of the River North Tyne. Starting in Falstone, in the shadow of Kielder Water dam, we go eastwards through the North Tyne Valley to the bustling little market town of Bellingham, a gateway to the national park and also a popular stop-off for cyclists and walkers on the Pennine Way.

The route follows quiet country roads, with no major junctions. For the most part it's only moderately hilly, but with two or three short steep climbs. It is based on a popular ride known as the Bellingham Salmon, named after the annual salmon run down to the mouth of the Tyne (see box, page 86) which makes the North Tyne the top salmon-fishing river in England. The route makes a handy link from Kielder to Bellingham, if you've already done our two Kielder rides (see pages 64 and 74).

With a good selection of places to stay and eat out, Bellingham is the base for four more of our routes (see pages 90, 100, 108 and 118), exploring the North Tyne Valley, Northumberland National Park and further eastwards to Rothbury. Some of the rides interconnect so, as most of them should take only around 2–3 hours, more energetic types could do two in a day – or more!

Bellingham dates back to the 12th century, with the building of a castle by the de Bellingham family. The castle was subsequently demolished, and its stones were

← The dam across Kielder Water, upstream from Falstone (Dave Head/S)

recycled during the Industrial Revolution when the town had a sizeable ironworks and railway, both now long gone. The oldest building still standing in Bellingham now is St Cuthbert's Church, founded in 1180, but today mostly dating from the 17th century. Tucked behind the Black Bull Hotel on Bellingham High Street, the church's most notable feature is its unusual vaulted stone roof, possibly the only one of its kind in England.

## THE ROUTE

Start from **Falstone**, a little village by a bend in the River North Tyne, a short way downstream from Kielder Dam at the foot of Kielder Water.

Before we set off, though, you might be interested in visiting a memorial to the North Tyne communities that were submerged when Kielder Water dam was built in 1982, flooding the higher valley. A 5-minute walk from the village (follow signs from Falstone Tea Rooms, past the United Reform church) leads to *Stell*, made in 2006 by artist Colin Wilbourn, standing on the edge of a field by the riverbank. The stone sculpture is of a sheep pen ('stell' is the local name for a livestock pen), reimagined in the form of two sofas, decorated with wrought-iron antimacassar covers and cushions. On the floor between the sofas is a concrete rug patterned with a map of the reservoir and the river valley before it was flooded.

Now, on with the ride: from the ❶ **car park** behind **Falstone Tea Rooms** (see below) turn left and left again, in front of the Blackstone Inn. The road dips under a former railway bridge then climbs to the right, signposted National Byway. It then levels out, passing the old station (now holiday

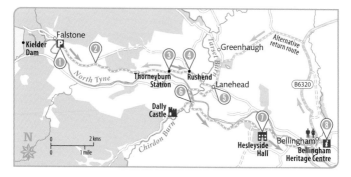

cottages), and opens out into wide, rolling moorland, with the fringes of Kielder Forest behind us. It's all very idyllic and rural, past fields of goats, ponies and horses, and with the inky but sparkling waters of the North Tyne glimpsed occasionally between the trees on the right.

The country lane rolls along the valley, over side-streams flowing into the North Tyne. After about 2km, with a line of tall conifers on our right, we pass a side-turning on the left. This is an ❷ **alternative route**: a rough and hilly track across the moorland, suitable for mountain bikes or gravel bikes. It runs parallel to the road for around 4.5km, rejoining our main route later on at Lanehead.

We're sticking to the smooth paved road straight ahead here, though. In about another 4km, after coming down close to the riverside, a left–right–left zigzag takes us between a pair of old level-crossing gates, at the former ❸ **Thorneyburn Station**. This remote stop was on the Border Counties Railway, a line running between Newcastle and Carlisle which closed in 1956. After the level crossing, go through a gate into a field of sheep and cattle, then down across a stream and **steeply** up the other side. At the top of the hill, going over a cattle-grid, wind right by the hamlet of

↑ Artist Colin Wilbourn's *Stell* sheep pen, near Falstone (Huw Hennessy)

## SALMON OF THE TYNE

The River Tyne is widely considered the best fishing grounds for salmon and sea trout in England and Wales. With the confluence of the North and South Tyne at Warden Bank, near Hexham, the river is dyed inky black by the moorland peat through which it flows. This dark colour gives the fish added confidence and also allows anglers to go fishing by day as well as night.

Every autumn, around 32,000 fish make a remarkable migration up the Tyne to their spawning grounds, a figure that is increasing every year. In 1960, however, not one single salmon was recorded as having been caught on the river, which had become uninhabitable from centuries of industrial waste pollution. In response, better sewage treatment and declining heavy industry on Tyneside led to cleaner waters and revived fish populations. In addition, salmon hatcheries were opened on the North Tyne in 1979 to compensate for the construction of Kielder Water and its dam, which obstructed tributaries that were vital spawning grounds for the salmon.

Today, numbers of Atlantic salmon have recovered in abundance on the Tyne, but the river is still the only one in England in which the fish is not 'at risk', according to a recent study by the Environmental Agency.

For more information, visit ⏣ tyneriverstrust.org.

↑ Wild salmon leaping up a waterfall on the River Tyne at Hexham (angus reid/S)

❹ **Rushend**. From here, descend to cross Tarset Burn (a tributary of the North Tyne), then up to Lanehead, a hamlet on the brow of the hill, with glorious, sweeping views south over the North Tyne Valley.

Turn right at the T-junction in ❺ **Lanehead**, winding downhill, across an old railway bridge, followed by another bridge back over Tarset Burn and finally, at the foot of the hill, cross the North Tyne. Turn left after the bridge to follow the river; after a few hundred metres, though, just before the road winds left over another stream, go straight on, down a ❻ **narrow lane** which leads to **Dally Castle**. It's a short detour (around 3km return) to the ruins of a 13th-century motte-and-bailey stone fortress, on a bare hillside overlooking the moorland. Historical records relate that the former Chirdon Manor was gifted by King Alexander II of Scotland to his sister Margaret in 1230. There's not much left today, with just the foundation walls perched on a small hilltop on the right. It's a pleasant spot if you fancy a break, though, before coming shortly into Bellingham.

Returning to the main road, turn right across the bridge over Chirdon Burn and wind right along the valley. The road is more level now for a while, with the North Tyne flowing wide and gently on our left. About 7km after Dally, there's a nice downhill run passing the entrance to ❼ **Hesleyside Hall**, the ancestral home of the Border Reiver Charlton family since 1343. Today, it's a luxury hotel, in spacious grounds designed by Lancelot 'Capability' Brown; there are also glamping huts (see page 209). You can't see the house from the entrance but, as you continue around the perimeter of the grounds, its imposing façade appears between an avenue of trees.

Winding mostly uphill again from Hesleyside, after a couple of kilometres we go through a straight avenue lined with tall plane trees and up to a T-junction, with a war memorial chapel opposite. Turn left here, on to the B6320, and downhill into **Bellingham**, a few hundred metres from here. Cross the bridge over the River North Tyne once again (one-way, priority for oncoming traffic; but with a cycle lane on the right).

Coming into Bellingham, the road winds right and left up through the High Street. Turn right next to the post office on the corner, and

after around 200m you'll come to ❽ **Bellingham Heritage Centre** on the right. This excellent, multi-purpose information centre, museum and gift shop also has the **Tea on the Train** café opposite (see below), and free car park adjacent.

**ALTERNATIVE RETURN ROUTE** If you're returning to Falstone rather than staying at Bellingham, either retrace our route or, for a slightly different way back, see komoot map 965702054. This is roughly the same length as the way here but, heading north from Bellingham on the B6320, turn left just before Greenhaugh (a pretty village with a great pub, the Hollybush Inn, see page 99), and rejoin the outbound route at Lanehead.

## THE ESSENTIALS

**GETTING THERE** By road, Bellingham is 53km west of Newcastle upon Tyne, via the A69, A68 and B6320. The nearest train station is at Hexham, 27km south of Bellingham, with direct trains from Newcastle and connecting 680 bus service; average journey time around 1¾ hours.

↑ Hesleyside Hall (Huw Hennessy)

**FACILITIES** There are public toilets next to Falstone car park at the start of the ride, and in Bellingham opposite the Bellingham Heritage Centre at the finish.

## WHERE TO EAT

✖ **Riverdale Hall Hotel** Bellingham NE48 2JT; ✆ 01434 220254; ⬧ riverdalehallhotel. co.uk. Bellingham's smartest hotel has a gourmet restaurant led by chef Iben Cocker with her 30 years' working experience at the hotel. The contemporary British menu is strong on local produce, including salmon & trout from the River North Tyne, Northumbrian lamb & Kielder venison; they also do excellent-value Sun lunches, including vegetarian options. It's a large restaurant but with cosy nooks creating an intimate ambience (& the hotel swimming pool is open to diners). ££

✖ **Falstone Tea Rooms** Falstone NE48 1AA; ✆ 01434 240459; ◼ Falstone Tea Rooms.

This highly recommended café in Falstone's converted old schoolhouse serves b/fasts, light lunches, soups, sandwiches, freshly made cakes & pastries, teas, coffee & soft drinks. £

✖ **Tea on the Train** Station Yard, Bellingham NE48 2DG; ✆ 01434 221151; ◼ Tea on the Train Bellingham. This delightful café is based inside converted old railway carriages standing at the platform of Bellingham's former train station, next to the town's Heritage Centre (museum & visitor information centre). It serves homemade cakes, soups, sandwiches & afternoon teas: a wonderfully nostalgic experience in this traditional town brimming with history. £

## FURTHER INFORMATION

◼ **Bellingham Heritage Centre** Station Yard, Woodburn Rd, Bellingham NE48 2DG; ✆ 01434 220050; ⬧ bellingham-heritage.org. uk. This multi-purpose visitor information centre & museum has friendly and knowledgeable

staff, with masses of useful local information and tips. Its excellent local museum has an impressive collection of tableaux focusing on the region's diverse heritage of mining, farming and countryside crafts.

# 9 BELLINGHAM BASTLES LOOP

| | |
|---|---|
| **START/FINISH** | Bellingham |
| **DISTANCE/TIME** | 31.5km/3–4hrs (including 5.2km detour to Black Middens Bastle) |
| **DIFFICULTY/TERRAIN** | ② Mostly on quiet lanes, and an off-road stretch on a rubbly track; hilly throughout, including a few steep climbs and descents |
| **SCENIC RATING** | © Wild moorland in the Northumberland National Park, meandering streams of the North Tyne Valley, and Border bastles – historic fortified farmhouses |
| **SUITABLE FOR** | Gravel bike, hybrid or road bike (with knobbly tyres) |
| **NCN ROUTE** | NCN10 and NCN68 |
| **MAPS** | OS Explorer 42 (1:25 000) |
| **KOMOOT REF** | 971330653 |

↑ The ruins of Low Cleughs Bastle (Dave Head/S)

his loop route explores the moors and valleys of the Northumberland National Park. Starting from Bellingham, we follow the River North Tyne meandering up the valley, crossing streams – or burns, as they are called here. As England's prime salmon-fishing river, the Tyne is hugely popular with anglers, so you're likely to see some along the way (the fishing season runs from the beginning of February to the end of October). We cross the river below Lanehead, then climb up and across stunning moorlands, with panoramas stretching 360 degrees across the valley to the bare-topped fells. En route, we see a couple of historic bastles: farms that were fortified against raiders who roamed the borders during centuries of Anglo-Scottish conflict (see Border Reivers box, page 95).

It's one of our longer routes and moderately challenging, with hills from start to finish. Most of the climbing is mid-route, but it's happily downhill for most of the way back to Bellingham. You're unlikely to encounter much traffic along the way, which is mostly on quiet country lanes and farm tracks. The last few kilometres back to Bellingham are on the B6320, but this two-lane road is not generally busy either. (And note that the first part of the route, from Bellingham as far as Lanehead, is on the NCN10 – the Reivers Cycle Route – which is well signposted throughout.)

Overall, this ride is suitable for reasonably fit and experienced cyclists.

## THE ROUTE

Start from Bellingham, at the ❶ **Heritage Centre** on the edge of town. Turn left out the car park and left again at the T-junction on the main road (B6320) through the town centre. Continue through the town and across the bridge over the North Tyne; it's single-lane, one-way only across the narrow bridge, but there's a separate cycle lane on the left-hand side of the road.

Around 200m after the bridge, just before a Commonwealth War Graves cemetery on the left, turn right – take care, as there's blind bend in the road ahead.

Climb gently uphill. Follow the road straight at first, through a shady tunnel of plane trees, then meandering gently up the valley with the North Tyne lazily flowing between wooded banks on our right. After a couple of kilometres, winding right and then downhill, pass the grounds of ❷ **Hesleyside Hall** on your left. The early-18th-century house is

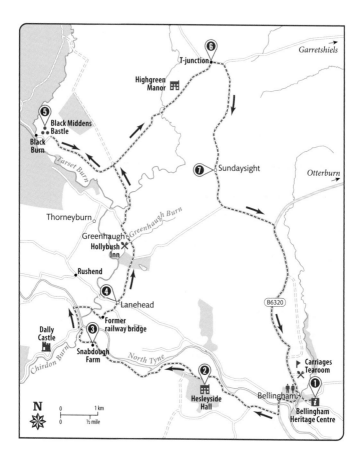

mostly hidden from view inside the grounds, designed by Lancelot 'Capability' Brown, but it appears briefly between a formal avenue of trees. The Charlton family has lived in Hesleyside since the 14th century and is one of the area's many Border Reiver families. Today, the estate is home to a luxury hotel and glamping site (see page 209).

After Hesleyside Hall, the road continues undulating alongside the river until, after another 3km, we come to ❸ **Snabdough Farm** on our left.

With its defensive barred windows and massive stone walls (2.5m thick in places), it was one of the historic bastles that are dotted around the area (see Border Reivers box, page 95). Now a working farm, the fortified core of the building dates from the late 15th or early 16th centuries. After Snabdough, the road zigzags left and right, across a bridge over Chirdon Burn, and then winds right (past a road on the left leading to **Dally Castle**; see page 87). We've had it pretty easy so far, but get ready now for some proper hills!

A few hundred metres after passing the Dally Castle turning, turn right at a T-junction, signposted Lanehead and Greenhaugh, and across a bridge over the North Tyne. Climbing up now, and away from the river, we cross over another couple of bridges (over Tarset Burn and a **former railway bridge**) until we reach ❹ **Lanehead**: a hamlet clustered around the brow of the hill.

Carry straight on through Lanehead, past the Crackin' View guesthouse (see page 210) and Tarset village hall on your left. As one of Northumberland's designated Dark Sky Discovery Sites (see page 69), there's a stargazing display board next to the hall. We're on a high ridge here, so it's a good time to pause, gather breath after the climb, and look left as we reach the top of the hill. There really are some cracking views from here, over the moorland and towards Kielder Forest beyond the valley below.

Continuing straight on, about 1km after Lanehead we start to wind downhill, gently at first then steeply, into **Greenhaugh**. If you can resist freewheeling all the way into this pretty little village, on your left just before crossing the bridge over Greenhaugh Burn is the **Horsebox Gallery** (🅵 The Horsebox Gallery). Local

↑ The Horsebox Gallery, housing the smallest art exhibition in Northumbria! (Huw Hennessy)

artist David Lucas exhibits his watercolour landscapes in a converted vintage horsebox and there are picnic chairs arranged under the trees, so it makes an arty pit stop. Otherwise, continue downhill over the bridge and into Greenhaugh, a quiet little village right on the edge of Northumberland National Park. There are no shops here, but the **Hollybush Inn**, on the left in the centre of the village, is open all day for breakfast and evening meals (see below).

Leaving Greenhaugh, turn right at the first junction around 400m out of the village, signposted to the Black Midden Bastles (also High Green and Combe) where we're heading now on our detour. It's only about 2.5km each way to these historic ruins, but it's a hilly route including one steep (17%) descent, with the same climb back up. However, the well-preserved site, as well as its stunning setting, mean it's well worth the effort if you don't mind the roller-coaster ride to get there.

We're climbing up on to open moorland now, with sheep grazing on the gently rolling hillsides. It's not all uphill effort, though, with a steep drop down to the river a few hundred metres after that turning, followed by an equally steep climb. Finally, we make another descent, coming to a crossroads where we turn left.

At the foot of the final descent, just before a ford over Black Burn on the right, we come to the entrance to ❺ **Black Middens Bastle** on the right, with a small car park by the roadside. After climbing over a stile, it's a short walk uphill to the solid, squat two-storey stone building, which dates from the late 16th or early 17th centuries. The owners kept their livestock on the ground floor, with living quarters for the family above. Defensively built, with walls 1 metre thick or more, and standing on an open hillside, it makes a good defensive vantage point, with long views across the moorland and west to vast Kielder Forest. There are other bastles around here too, with a walking trail linking them (see box, opposite).

Returning to the crossroads at the top of the hill where we started this detour, carry on straight ahead. It's an undulating road, more up than down now for the next few kilometres until we turn right at the next T-junction, heading south back towards Bellingham. Climbing uphill after crossing a cattle-grid (through fields of sheep and cattle), we pass the grand Highgreen Manor on the left. With its grey-tiled conical towers, it may look like a mini-Balmoral Castle to casual passers-by, which makes sense as it was built in 1894 in a Scottish baronial style. You might also note a wooden signpost on the right as you pass the entrance to the manor, its three fingerposts pointing different ways and enigmatically marked 'Anglican (engine shed/shooting but [sic] rebuild)', 'Catholic (private

## THE BORDER REIVERS

For several centuries, during Tudor and Elizabethan times, the areas bordering England and Scotland, including Northumberland, were riven with lawlessness from marauding clans known as Reivers, or raiders. The roots of the Border Reivers' life of raiding could possibly be traced back to Norman times, when parts of northeast England were considered so far from the seat of power in the south that they were allowed a level of independence or 'liberty'.

Local landowners and farmers fortified their homes against the violent raids, building the castle-like bastles, such as those visited on this ride, as well as the characteristic fortified tower houses known as pele towers. The raids were not necessarily English clans attacking Scotland or vice versa, however, for the Reivers' prime allegiance was to their own clan rather than to the English or Scottish crowns. Feuds sometimes involved Reivers supporting their fellow clan members regardless of which country they were in, as the clans often had family members on both sides of the border. Border Reiver surnames included many that were common in both England and Scotland, such as Armstrong, Charlton, Elliot and Robson, and many of which are still common today.

With the Anglo-Scottish wars gripping both countries throughout this period, and their borderlines being ill-defined and disputed, the violence throughout the Borders region was constant and bloody. In addition, the Reivers' feuds were often related to land ownership, grazing rights and livestock, provoking outright warfare which often continued for generations.

The Tarset Bastle Trail is a walking route from Greenhaugh to seven local bastle remains, including the Black Middens Bastle. For details, visit ⊘ tarset. co.uk/visiting/bastletrail.cfm.

family chapel)' and 'Protestant (Presbyterian hill sermon)'. Highgreen Manor runs residential courses in art, writing and yoga (⌂ highgreen -arts.co.uk), which may explain this mystery. Or it might be connected to the border region's early history of Anglo-Scottish conflict – apologies, but this writer's investigative efforts have drawn a complete blank! (Any answers welcome to **e** info@bradtguides.com.)

Continue inexorably uphill past Highgreen, winding around to the left about another 1km, to reach a ❻ **T-junction** in the heart of wild,

↑ Black Middens Bastle (Dave Head/S)

empty moorland. Turn right here, signposted Garretshiels, with the road at last levelling out and, 400m later turn right again, signposted 'Sundaysight 1¾ miles'. We're on a rough, gravelly farm track now, interspersed with grassy central strips and patches of tarmac to give your wheels – and buttock muscles – some relief. It is mostly downhill now, though, through beautiful moorland all around: great swathes of heather and windswept grass, dotted with a few uninterested sheep here and there. After around 3km, still mostly downhill, we reach

❼ **Sundaysight**, a tiny hamlet with a cottage on the left and farm on the right.

From Sundaysight, we're back on paved road again, though still quite pot-holed in places. And we're still surrounded by the moorland, with particularly stunning views to the right, looking west towards Kielder Forest. It feels so wild and empty up here, almost as if we're on another planet… or perhaps, the same planet as it used to be and seems to have remained so.

About 1km after Sundaysight we come to a T-junction/lay-by, where we turn left, signposted Elsdon and Otterburn: a smooth paved road (no more pot-holes!) with a nice downhill run for about 1km until we reach another T-junction, where we turn right on to the B6320, signposted Bellingham and Hexham. Keep alert for traffic on this main road to Bellingham, as it may be busier – for Northumberland that is – but probably not much.

The road is gently undulating again for a short while, but with one or two steep downhill sections. Resist the temptation to shoot down hell-for-leather, particularly after around 3km where there is a sharp right bend.

Continue winding downhill all the way for the last few kilometres into Bellingham, passing the pristine freeways of Bellingham Golf Club on your left. As the road bends right into the High Street, pass Fountain Cottage Café on the right – Bellingham's most cycle-friendly waterhole (see below). To return to the start, however, carry on for another 200m, turn left in front of the post office, follow signs for **Bellingham Heritage Centre** and turn right into the car park after another 600m.

## THE ESSENTIALS

**GETTING THERE** By road, Bellingham is 53km west of Newcastle upon Tyne, via the A69, A68 and B6320. The nearest train station is at Hexham, 27km south of Bellingham, with direct trains from Newcastle and connecting 680 bus service; average journey time around 1¾ hours.

**FACILITIES** There are public toilets in Bellingham, opposite the Bellingham Heritage Centre at the start/finish, and customer toilets at the Hollybush Inn, Greenhaugh.

## WHERE TO EAT

✗ **Fountain Cottage Café** Bellingham NE48 2DE; ✆ 01434 239224, 07753 239224; ⌂ fountain-cottage.com. Based in a former Victorian workhouse at the top end of Bellingham High St & decorated with local art & quirky curios (ie: table lamps made from wood-planes), this excellent café (with B&B; see page 213) has a tempting array of treats, including steak & wine nights, afternoon tea with scrumptious cakes, local ales from the First & Last Brewery, & ice cream from the local Morwick Dairy. Its pleasant front garden is a favourite with cyclists (who get a 10% discount off B&B rates & café menu). Highly popular, advance booking advisable. **££**

✗ **Hollybush Inn** Greenhaugh NE48 1PW; ✆ 01434 240391; ⌂ hollybushinn.net. This superb traditional village inn offers a warm welcome to passing cyclists (they're happy for you to wheel your bike through the bar to the beer garden if you don't want to leave it out front). With its roaring log fire & snug bar it's open daily for b/fast, or a full dinner menu including burgers & fish'n'chips. A chef's special is the mighty Reiver Pie, packed with chicken, haggis & black pudding; vegetarian dishes are also available. **££**

✗ **Carriages Tearoom** Bellingham Golf Club, Boggle Hole, Bellingham NE48 2DT; ✆ 07719 387154 ⌂ carriages-tearoom.co.uk. Based at Bellingham Golf Club, which we pass at the end of our ride, this café is open to non-members, serving b/fast, light lunches & afternoon teas, with freshly made cakes & scones. Its outdoor patio gives great views over the North Tyne Valley. **£**

## FURTHER INFORMATION

ℹ **Bellingham Heritage Centre** Station Yard, Woodburn Rd, Bellingham NE48 2DG; ✆ 01434 220050; ⌂ bellingham-heritage.org. This multi-purpose visitor information centre & museum has friendly and knowledgeable staff, with masses of useful local information and tips. Its excellent local museum has an impressive collection of tableaux focusing on the region's diverse heritage of mining, farming and countryside crafts.

# 10 BELLINGHAM TO GREENHAUGH LOOP

| | |
|---|---|
| **START/FINISH** | Bellingham |
| **DISTANCE/TIME** | 21.4km/2–2½hrs |
| **DIFFICULTY/TERRAIN** | ① This is one of our shorter rides, all on quiet back roads and farm lanes with only a few hills, so is suitable for any reasonably fit cyclist, including families with older children |
| **SCENIC RATING** | ⑧ The moorland and fells of the Northumberland National Park, the North Tyne Valley, and historic Border Reiver bastles |
| **SUITABLE FOR** | Road bike, gravel bike or hybrid bike |
| **NCN ROUTE** | NCN10 and NCN68 |
| **MAPS** | OS Explorer 42 (1:25 000) |
| **KOMOOT REF** | 972477193 |

This slightly wonky-looking figure-of-eight loop is a shorter and less strenuous version of the Bellingham Bastle Loop (see page 90). Starting from Bellingham, on the banks of the North Tyne, we follow the North Tyne Valley upstream, then up through Lanehead and into the Northumberland National Park, with glorious views over the valley to Kielder Forest. From here, we wind across the fells to Greenhaugh ('-haugh' pronounced '-hoff'), before returning down the valley to Bellingham. En route, we also pass Hesleyside Hall, historic home of the Charlton family, one of the former Border Reiver clans; and Snabdough Farm, a 16th-century bastle farmhouse fortified against the Reivers (see box, page 95).

The first part of the ride is uphill, slowly but steadily. Also, as one of the main roads to and from Bellingham, sometimes it's relatively busy with traffic, by Northumberland's standards, that is. If you'd rather avoid the traffic, though, take the quieter road along the south bank of the North Tyne to Lanehead instead: the same way we take on our return to Bellingham, via Snabdough and Hesleyside (though, sorry, you'll still have to tackle the climb up to Lanehead!).

## THE ROUTE

Start from ❶ **Manchester Square**, in the centre of Bellingham, with a small car park. Turn left on to King's Street and out of Bellingham on the

B6320. As the road bends left towards the river, with the fire station on the corner, turn right, signposted Greenhaugh. Pass **Riverdale Hall Hotel** (see page 212) on your left and climb slowly out of town.

We're going up the North Tyne Valley here, with the river below us on our left. Pretty soon, we climb above the trees lining the riverbank, giving us wider views over the valley. Keep alert on this B-road as there can be some traffic, including the occasional timber truck. It's not that busy, though, compared with similar countryside roads in most other parts of the UK.

After about 1.5km we start to descend down to the valley floor, now with closer views of the North Tyne on our left, then start to climb again, entering the high moorland of Northumberland National Park. As we pass **The Boe Rigg** campsite (with café and shop; see below and page 212) on our right, the hill gets going in earnest; not steep, but all the way to Lanehead, about 2km further up the road.

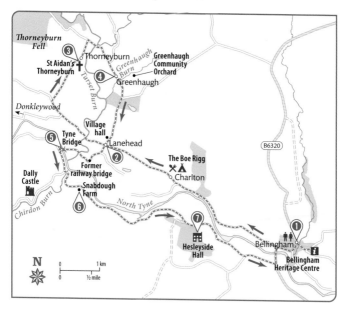

When we finally climb over the top of the hill, we come to a dogleg junction at ❷ **Lanehead**. Turn right here, then immediately left, signposted Donkleywood. The road descends here for around 500m, all the way down to a bridge over Tarset Burn. Make the most of this downhill spree, though, as the road then proceeds to climb, longer and steeper up the other side. Your efforts will be rewarded at the top, however, with breath-taking views westwards over moorland fells towards Kielder Forest on the horizon.

As the road begins to descend again, after around 500m we cross a cattle-grid and come to a fork. There's a signpost pointing left towards Donkleywood, but we turn right here. This roughly paved farm lane crosses the moorland through a field of sheep and cattle so, as always, cycle carefully, especially if there are cows with young calves, as they can be defensive if startled. We're heading northwards, across the slopes of Thorneyburn Fell and towards the hamlet of Thorneyburn. After a couple of hundred metres, at another fork, we take another right-hand turn (also unsignposted) on to a rougher track climbing up across the fell. Meanwhile, the main track continues straight on, running along the side of the valley towards Kielder (the alternative off-road trail on our Falstone–Bellingham Route 8; see page 88).

After about 500m, we come to a gate at the brow of the hill, with Thorneyburn tucked between the trees ahead of us below. Descending into this little hamlet, we go through another gate and wind right to pass the church of ❸ **St Aidan's Thorneyburn** on our right. Built in 1818, the solid stone church has some stained-glass windows and historic coats of arms inside. Looking somewhat outsized for this tiny settlement, the Grade II-listed church was funded by the Greenwich Hospital Commissioners to re-employ former Royal Navy chaplains in the aftermath of the Napoleonic wars. It also serve as a local information hub, with a selection of leaflets in its entrance-way, including nearby walk guides and wildlife displays.

Continue downhill from the church, and back on to a smoother paved road again now. After around 500m we come to a T-junction where we turn right, signposted Greenhaugh and Bellingham. The road winds gently uphill for around 1km to ❹ **Greenhaugh**, a pretty little village on the edge of the national park.

## NORTHUMBERLAND NATIONAL PARK

Stretching from north to south, from the Breamish Valley down to Hadrian's Wall, and bordering Scotland and Cumbria, the Northumberland National Park covers more than 1,060km$^2$ of England's northernmost and least populated region, providing a great opportunity to get away from it all and explore its wild, open spaces. Its varied landscapes comprise the rolling Cheviot Hills, fells and moorlands, rivers and valleys, peat bogs and ancient woodlands. With large areas protected as Sites of Special Scientific Interest (SSSIs), the park is rich in rare wildlife, such as ospreys, red squirrels, black grouse and otters.

Apart from Hadrian's Wall, stretching across the park's southern boundaries, it is also home to many other historic sites, including Roman temples, Iron Age hill forts, and bastles: fortified farmhouses built to repel the Border Reivers – Anglo-Scottish raider clans.

The park also lies within Northumberland's International Dark Sky Park (see box, page 69) with many Dark Sky Discovery Sites dotted around its remote corners (including some mentioned in our cycle routes, eg: at Tarset village hall on Route 9, page 93, and at Kielder Water and Forest Park, page 68).

Besides the park's myriad footpaths and bridleways, its miles of quiet countryside lanes and off-road trails are great cycling territory. Several tried-and-tested cycle routes, including Hadrian's Cycleway, the Pennine Cycleway

Just as we come into Greenhaugh, note the turning on the left, signposted **Black Middens Bastle**, which we visit on Route 9 (see page 94). If you're in need of a bite to eat, Greenhaugh has a bustling local pub, the **Hollybush Inn** (below), right in the middle of the village. Or on a sunny day, the **Greenhaugh Community Orchard** makes a lovely picnic spot, with great views over the moor from the top. It's a short walk of around 1.6km up Greenhaugh Burn, the stream that crosses the edge of the village on our way out. The path is on the left immediately after crossing the stream, with steps going up through the trees.

Leaving the village and crossing the bridge over Greenhaugh Burn, we climb up and over a couple of humpback hills, returning to Lanehead after

and the Reiver's Cycleway, wind across the park, as covered by many of the rides in this book. The park's intricate shape means that some places, such as Kielder Forest and Bellingham, lie outside its formal boundaries, although they are virtually surrounded by it. For more details, including up-to-date information on no-go areas, such as the Ministry of Defence's Otterburn Ranges, and ongoing clearance of forest storm damage, visit ⌘ northumberlandnationalpark.org.uk.

about 1.5km. As we come into Lanehead, note the red-painted **village hall** on your right, with picnic benches and Dark Sky display. We're in an International Dark Sky Park here, one of the best places in the UK for stargazing (see box, page 69).

And now, prepare for a lovely long downhill run for 1km or so, all the way to the bottom of the valley. Carry straight on through Lanehead, past the junctions we crossed over on the way up from Bellingham. Cross over the ➎ **Tyne Bridge** at the bottom of the hill and turn left, signposted Hesleyside, heading eastwards now back towards Bellingham. For the rest of the ride, the road is either gently undulating or level, running mostly parallel to the North Tyne on the left.

↑ Milecastle 39 on Hadrian's Wall in the Northumberland National Park (Michael Conrad/S)

Wind through the valley, the road turning left just after passing the road on the right that leads to Dally Castle (see page 87). And shortly after the bridge, as the road winds right we pass ❻ **Snabdough**. The farm, also a B&B (see page 213), is a fine example of the bastles: fortified farms built in Tudor times, during the troubled Anglo-Scottish wars, to fend off raids from Reiver clans (see box, page 95).

Climb gently uphill after Snabdough, with views left across the river valley, before dropping down again to come to ❼ **Hesleyside Hall** on your right. This landscaped estate has been home of the Charlton family for more than 700 years; the 18th-century hall is now a luxury hotel and glamping site (see page 209). Follow the road winding around the perimeter of the grounds, with Hesleyside Hall coming into view between an avenue of trees on the right after around 400m.

It's a final short climb again after Hesleyside, winding up through a small copse then dipping down again until we go through a straight avenue of plane trees. After a few hundred metres, we come to a T-junction with the B6320. Turn left here and across the one-way bridge back into Bellingham. Note that the road across the bridge is one-way, with priority for oncoming traffic, but there is a shared footpath/cycleway on the right. Follow the road winding right and into Bellingham. Manchester Square is on your right as you re-enter the town.

If you haven't slaked your thirst already in Greenhaugh, there's also the Rocky Road café on Manchester Square in Bellingham (below). Like all the best bike rides: start and end at a good caff!

## THE ESSENTIALS

**GETTING THERE** By road, Bellingham is 53km west of Newcastle upon Tyne, via the A69, A68 and B6320. The nearest train station is at Hexham, 27km south of Bellingham, with direct trains from Newcastle and connecting 680 bus service; average journey time around 1¾ hours.

**FACILITIES** There are public toilets in Bellingham, next to Fountain Cottage Café on the High Street, and customer toilets at the Hollybush Inn, Greenhaugh.

## WHERE TO EAT

✖ **Rocky Road Café** Manchester Sq, Bellingham NE48 2AH; ✆ 01434 220510; ⊘ rockyroadcafe.co.uk. This cheerful little take-away is right in the heart of Bellingham, and is open all day for b/fast, lunches & afternoon tea. There are daily specials & homemade cakes, including a locally famous Mars bar cheesecake: perfect for refuelling after a long bike ride. **£**

✖ **The Boe Rigg** Charlton NE48 1PE; ✆ 01434 220510; ⊘ theboerigg.co.uk. Based at the campsite overlooking the moorland between Bellingham and Lanehead, this bistro-style restaurant has perhaps a surprisingly good menu, with steaks, burgers, curries & fish dishes, not to forget some great sticky puddings; it also has a take-away, with sandwiches & light bites, all made on the premises. **££**

✖ **Hollybush Inn** Greenhaugh NE48 1PW; ✆ 01434 240391; ⊘ hollybushinn.net. Smack in the centre of this village on the edge of Northumberland National Park, this great little pub is open for b/fasts so, if you time it right, you can tuck into full English or other variations, including vegetarian options, on your way back to Bellingham (08.30–09.30 Mon–Fri & 09.00–10.00 Sat–Sun; evening meals & take-aways 17.30–20.30 Mon–Sat). **££**

## FURTHER INFORMATION

🛈 **Bellingham Heritage Centre** Station Yard, Woodburn Rd, Bellingham NE48 2DG; ✆ 01434 220050; ⊘ bellingham-heritage.org. This multi-purpose visitor information centre & museum has friendly and knowledgeable staff, with masses of useful local information and tips. Its excellent local museum has an impressive collection of tableaux focusing on the region's diverse heritage of mining, farming and countryside crafts.

# 11 BELLINGHAM TO WARK LOOP

| | |
|---|---|
| **START/FINISH** | Bellingham |
| **DISTANCE/TIME** | 24.9km loop/2½–3hrs |
| **DIFFICULTY/TERRAIN** | ② On the B6320 at the start, but mostly on quiet country roads; hilly throughout, including several steep climbs and descents; best suited for fit and experienced cyclists |
| **SCENIC RATING** | ⑧ Majestic moorland and undulating North Tyne Valley |
| **SUITABLE FOR** | Gravel bike or hybrid |
| **NCN ROUTE** | Partly on NCN10 and NCN68 |
| **MAPS** | OS Explorer 42 (1:25 000) |
| **KOMOOT REF** | 984495879 |

This moderately rigorous but rewarding ride explores the moorland and North Tyne Valley south of Bellingham, just outside the Northumberland National Park. Starting from Bellingham, we wind south down the east side of the valley, via Redesmouth and Birtley. We cross the North Tyne at Wark, a historic riverside town that was formerly part of Scotland, before heading back to Bellingham, up the west side of the valley.

## THE ROUTE

Start from ❶ **Manchester Square**, with a small car park, in the centre of **Bellingham**. Turn right on to the High Street, then first right again, by the post office. Just 100m later, at a fork, take another right-hand turn, signposted Redesmouth (and NCN10). Pass Bellingham primary and middle schools on your right, and within minutes we're out in the countryside, winding uphill with the North Tyne running close alongside us in the valley below.

After about 2.5km, we wind left and under a railway bridge, before descending again and crossing a modern bridge over the ❷ **River Rede** at Redesmouth.

Continue climbing upwards, over a couple of humpback hills (keep alert for oncoming traffic on blind spots). The climb, steep in parts, carries on through woods for about 700m from the bridge, before we come out

← St Giles' Church in Birtley, with its distinctive spire above the porch (Huw Hennessy)

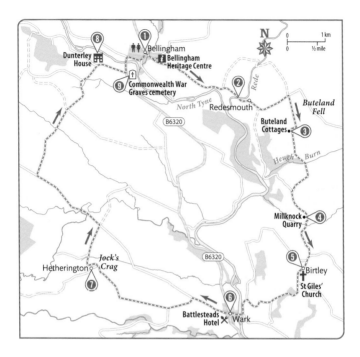

of the trees with sweeping moorland opening up in front of us, left and right. In about another 700m, just below the brow of the hill, we come to a crossroads, with a signpost to Matfen and Stamfordham. Turn right here, looking out for oncoming traffic as it's particularly steep just before the junction, with a blind summit warning sign on the left.

We're on a quieter, narrow country lane now, still climbing, gently at first then steeply, as we wind around to the right. If you pause for breath on the corner, notice an imaginative sculpture of a horse and foal, behind the fence on the right: a sort of eco-sculpture, with the horse's body made of horseshoes, a bicycle chain for its mane, and the foal made of chicken wire. We reach the hilltop of **Buteland Fell** soon after, turning left and passing ❸ **Buteland Cottages**, a row of holiday homes, on the right.

Continue straight ahead, coming down the fell, with stunning expansive views over the moor. This lovely long downhill run continues for 1km or so, winding left and right until we reach a small ford (Heugh Burn) at the bottom of the hill. Go through the ford and into a field, climbing for 100m or so: this farm lane is paved, but it's a rough and rubbly patchwork, with the central grassy strip sometimes smoother than the furrowed sides. Keep alert for livestock: on my recent ride, a pair of llamas were grazing the hillside, looking slightly quizzical but otherwise apparently as content here as in the Andes.

About 1km after the ford, we come to a left-angled T-junction, where we turn left, signposted Birtley (still on the NCN10). Climb up to a narrow brow of pine trees on the hill crest, then wind around to the right, past ❹ **Millknock Quarry**, behind the trees. Continue winding right and left down the hillside for a few hundred metres until we come to another T-junction, with Piper Gate. Turn right here, towards Birtley and Wark (leaving the NCN10, which continues eastwards to Tynemouth).

↑ Horseshoe and chicken wire sculptures, Buteland Fell (Huw Hennessy)

## DRY STONE WALLS

The rolling Northumbrian moors and meadows are interlaced with dry stone walls, which have become as integral to its landscape as the forests and rivers. Just as hedgerows are vital homes for flora and fauna, so too are dry stone walls important wildlife habitats, from the mosses and algae that carpet the stones, to the reptiles and insects that live inside their cavities, and the sheep that shelter from the elements behind the walls' solid line of defence.

Dry stone walls have been used throughout the UK for at least 3,500 years, with some of the earliest remains found in the Orkneys and in north and western Scotland. The walls are more common in parts of the country where stone is more common and where trees and hedgerows don't grow so easily, hence their prominence in northern and western regions. Different stones are used in different areas: slate and whinstone in Cumbria, basalt and granite in the west coast of Scotland, for instance, while Northumbrian walls are typically made of limestone and sandstone.

To the casual observer, the walls may look rough and uneven, but they are all carefully built according to a traditional structure and design. The average wall is at least 1.2m tall, with two layers of 'through' or 'thruff' stones spanning the whole width for extra strength, and topped by upright coping stones or 'caeps', almost making them look like a reptile's spine.

Today, professional dry stone wallers often have advanced qualifications, as certified by the Dry Stone Walling Association (DSWA) of Great Britain. The Northumbrian branch of the DSWA runs training courses and gives presentations at rural shows throughout the region. For more details, visit ⊘ northumbria-dswa.co.uk.

About 100m after the T-junction, we come to ❺ **Birtley**. It's a quiet, attractive little village, with honey-coloured stone cottages lining the main road and a village hall, playground and sports field on the left. There's no pub or shop here, but **St Giles' Church**, on a left-hand corner at the far end of the village, is worth a peek. It's a small but distinctive Norman church, with a spire above the porch rather than at the far end or centre.

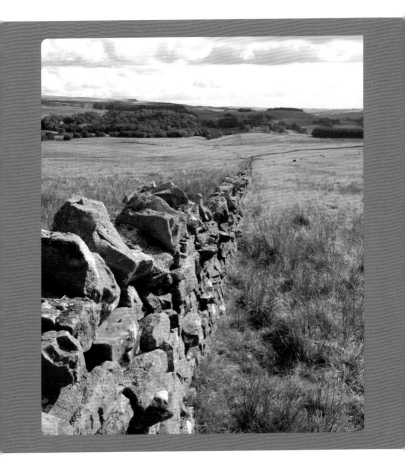

It's dark and sombre inside, with no windows in the north wall but with impressive stained glass on the south side, and three imposing, age-worn gravestones standing, as if on guard, in the porch.

Continuing past the church on your left, the road bends to the left, then hold on tight for a steep downhill stretch for about 2km to Wark, overlooking the North Tyne (and formally called Wark on Tyne). Take

↑ Dry stone walls span the high moorland around Bellingham (Huw Hennessy)

care as we approach the village, around several sharp hairpin bends and over a humpbacked bridge, before we finally come to a T-junction on the banks of the North Tyne. Turn left here and follow the riverbank, with a couple of picnic benches under the trees. After about 200m, turn right on to the bridge, an impressive iron construction with white-painted latticed railings. It's a great photo stop here too, looking across the wide and slow-moving Tyne with Wark town hall and clock tower peeking over the rooftops on the opposite bank. Cross the bridge and up Main Street, past the village green on your right with its spreading chestnut tree, planted in 1887 to mark Queen Victoria's Golden Jubilee.

With its riverside setting and weathered stone cottages lining the green, ❻ **Wark** (pronounced to rhyme with 'ark') is a handsome village with roots dating from Anglo-Saxon times. From 1150 to 1295, when the town was in Scotland, the Scottish kings held court in Wark Castle, as the capital town of Tynedale. Today, the castle is long gone and Wark is a peaceful place, with several comfortable inns and pubs, as well as a convenience store and a butcher's shop/deli opposite. The store, on the right at the top of Main Street, sells take-away snacks and hot drinks, with picnic benches

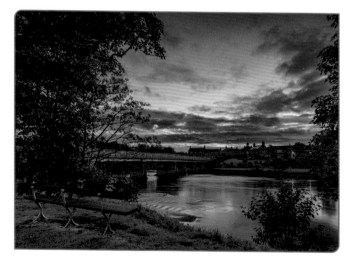

↑ Wark Bridge over the River North Tyne (Dave Head/S)

outside. With plenty to choose from here, it makes an ideal spot for a break, midway through our ride.

Leaving Wark, go straight ahead on the B6320, with the store on the right. Coming almost immediately to another junction, continue straight on to a smaller road, signposted Stonehaugh and Whygate, while the B6320 winds right, northwards towards Bellingham.

Soon leaving Wark behind, carry on uphill for 1km or so: steadily at first, then steeply. Just as a casual observation, you might notice that while dry stone walls dominate the open moors (see box, page 112), lower down in valleys and sheltered areas hedgerows are more the norm, with blackthorn, hawthorn, wild roses and honeysuckle among a profusion of trees and bushes; also, in wetter areas, the tall and fluffy purple loosestrife is abundant.

Eventually, the road levels out and winds down to the left, again signposted Stonehaugh and Whygate, with a green-painted bench on the corner, handy if you need a breather before enjoying a short freewheel spree. Make the most of it! For the next couple of kilometres there are lots more ups and downs, with more uphill climbs than descents. If it's any help as you puff uphill, though, we're treated to some lovely views here, particularly to the left, over moorland, meadows and tree-lined valley. It's very peaceful too, only the occasional cawing crow or twittering songbirds in the hedgerows (plus, possibly, the sound of grinding gears and panting cyclists).

We finally reach the brow of the hill, about 3km from Wark, just before the road bears right and starts descending towards Hetherington, about 1km from here. At this lonely bend in the road there are glorious views all round, over cattle pastures to the rolling moorland, stretching beyond to the horizon. Excuse the cliché, but it really does feel like the top of the world.

Continuing to the right, at the hamlet of ❼ **Hetherington** we wind around a little duck-pond on the left and the rocky overhang of **Jock's Crag** on the right. Turn right immediately after this, signposted Lineacres and Lowstead, and over a cattle-grid. The next couple of kilometres are another roller coaster of ups and downs – now thankfully more down than up – between the fields (now on the NCN68 Pennine Cycleway). And note that here we're back to the dry stone walls rather than hedgerows (but in some places both, just to contradict my previous assertion) until, after about 1km, we reach a T-junction where we turn left.

For the next 2km, following the straight road, there's more rolling up and down, with conifer plantations on our left including several massive trees lying uprooted by recent storms. Turn right, signposted Bellingham, crossing a cattle-grid and on to another straight road through open moorland, now undulating more gently. Pass a small grove of pine trees on your right, with colourful (and probably poisonous) fungi dotting the grass and moss at their feet.

Carry on straight ahead, sweeping down and up again (ignore the unsignposted farm track just before the brow of the hill). Coming over the summit at last, treat your weary legs to one final lovely long freewheel for 2km, leading to a T-junction in front of another small pine copse. Turn right here, signposted NCN68 and NCN10, now approaching the outskirts of Bellingham. At another T-junction a few hundred metres further on, opposite ❽ **Dunterley House**, turn right again and go through a shady tunnel of plane trees. This leads shortly to a final T-junction, where we turn right on to the B6320, in front of a ❾ **Commonwealth War Graves cemetery**. Turn left here and, after 300m, cross the bridge (one-way with priority for oncoming traffic, and with a cycle/pedestrian lane on the right). Coming into Bellingham, bear right along the High Street, with ❿ **Manchester Square** on your right.

## THE ESSENTIALS

**GETTING THERE** By road, Bellingham is 53km west of Newcastle upon Tyne, via the A69, A68 and B6320. The nearest train station is at Hexham, 27km south of Bellingham, with direct trains from Newcastle and connecting 680 bus service; average journey time around 1¾ hours.

**FACILITIES** There are public toilets in Bellingham, next to Fountain Cottage Café on the High Street, and customer toilets in Wark's pubs on Main Street.

## WHERE TO EAT

✕ **Battlesteads Hotel & Restaurant** Wark on Tyne NE48 3LS; ✆ 01434 230209; ⟁ battlesteads.com. On the south side of the village, by the B6320, Wark's smartest hotel also has a highly acclaimed restaurant. Its menu mostly features contemporary British cuisine, specialising in smoked meats and fish from its own smokery, as well as a selection of familiar international dishes, vegetarian options, & five- or eight-course tasting menus. **££**

✕ **The Gun at Ridsdale** Ridsdale NE48 2TF; ✆ 01434 270500; ⟁ thegunatridsdale.co.uk. This community-owned rural pub has a great countryside location, to the east of Wark, inside the Northumberland International Dark Sky Park. Its menu features good & nicely presented traditional pub fare, as well as pizzas & daily specials. There is also a coffee shop (open 09.30–16.00 Mon–Sat) for hot drinks, home-baked scones, cakes & pastries. **£**

✕ **The Cheviot Hotel** Bellingham NE48 2AU; ✆ 01434 220696; ⟁ thecheviothotel.co.uk. This recently refurbished hotel in the centre of Bellingham has a solid reputation for good, reliable pub grub based on locally sourced produce, but is best known for its carnivorous Sun lunch carvery; its live music nights also attract a loyal local following. **££**

## FURTHER INFORMATION

▮ **Bellingham Heritage Centre** Station Yard, Woodburn Rd, Bellingham NE48 2DG; ✆ 01434 220050; ⟁ bellingham-heritage.org. This multi-purpose visitor information centre & museum has friendly and knowledgeable staff, with masses of useful local information and tips. Its excellent local museum has an impressive collection of tableaux focusing on the region's diverse heritage of mining, farming and countryside crafts.

# 12 BELLINGHAM TO ROTHBURY

| | |
|---|---|
| **START/FINISH** | Bellingham/Rothbury |
| **DISTANCE/TIME** | 44.7km/5–6hrs |
| **DIFFICULTY/TERRAIN** | ② Mostly off-road, with some rough trails through boggy moorland and gravel roads through Harwood Forest; hilly throughout, including one or two steep stretches; best suited for fit and skilled MTB cyclists |
| **SCENIC RATING** | © Through wild and remote countryside in the Northumberland National Park: moor and fell, river valleys and conifer forest |
| **SUITABLE FOR** | Top-quality mountain bike |
| **NCN ROUTE** | NCN10, NCN68 and Sandstone Way |
| **MAPS** | OS Explorer OL42 (1:25 000) |
| **KOMOOT REF** | 984496628 |

↑ Heather covers the Simonside Hills outside Rothbury (Dave Head/S)

his adrenaline-charged ride winds northeast from Bellingham to Rothbury, cutting across the Northumberland National Park. We meander over moorland, up river valleys, through Harwood Forest, over the Simonside Hills and down into Rothbury. For the first 15km or so, starting from Bellingham, the going is mostly level, alongside the River Rede.

It's a long and challenging route in parts and mostly off-road, including some steep hills; over boggy, open moorland and rattling along rubbly forest roads; and with minimal signposting in the more isolated stretches. It's great fun, though, and spectacularly scenic – all in all, best suited for very fit and experienced cyclists on high-quality mountain bikes.

Part of the route follows the Sandstone Way and part on the Pennine Cycleway; on some of the off-road sections, for instance between points ❷ & ❹, ❾ & ❿ and crossing the moorland of the Simonside Hills, signage is minimal, so access to komoot navigation will be of considerable help.

Along with other forested areas of Northumberland, Harwood Forest is vulnerable to destructive winter storms and suffered considerable damage in the last couple of years, particularly from Storm Arwen in November 2021. At the time of writing, diversions were in place in the forest (see details in the route directions below), so for the latest information visit ⊘ visitnorthumberland.com/explore/destinations/forests.

Note also that I've estimated more time to complete this ride, allowing for the hills, diversions and winding off-road trails. Plan ahead and, if cycling alone, let someone know where you are going and when you expect to be back.

## THE ROUTE

Start from Bellingham, a historic village by the River North Tyne and one of the most popular gateways to the Northumberland National Park. Turn right out of ❶ **Manchester Square** (car park) on to King's Street, then right again, after the post office on the corner. After about 150m, at the fork in the road, take another right-hand turn, on to Russell Terrace/ Redesmouth Road (signposted NCN10), passing Bellingham primary and middle schools on the right, and soon leading out of the town.

As we climb gradually up the side of the valley, views open up all around, with the inky-dark North Tyne meandering slowly between the trees below on your left, and fields and woods stretching up the hillside beyond. After a couple of kilometres, we wind left away from the river and under a (disused) railway bridge.

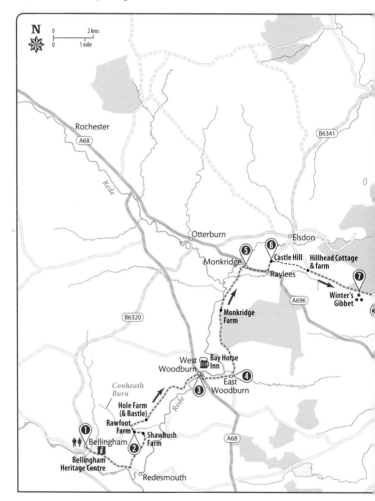

Shortly after going under the bridge, take a left-hand turning, on to a roughly paved track, signposted Sandstone Way. Follow this track uphill, then winding right along the side of the valley for around 700m, until you cross a small stream and come to a fork, where you turn left. Continue straight on for another 1km, to **Shawbush Farm**, where the path winds back to the left, running alongside another stream, Conheath Burn, and then turn right by ❷ **Rawfoot Farm**, leading up to a road. Turn right here at the T-junction, coming shortly to **Hole Farm**, with one of the historic former bastles: the tall and solidly built stone building overlooking the farm on the right (see box, page 95).

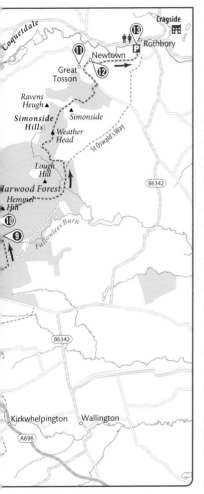

Follow this quiet back lane running along the valley, the way mostly level or downhill now, with the River Rede below you on the right. After about 4km, the road comes down to the River Rede and runs alongside it for another 1km, when we reach ❸ **West Woodburn**, a small village on the banks of the river.

Turn right at a T-junction in front of the **Bay Horse Inn**, on to the A68; keep alert on this road, though the traffic is not generally busy here, and there's a 30mph speed limit. Cross the bridge over the River Rede and after 200m take the first left, which continues eastwards with the river for just over 1km until we reach ❹ **East Woodburn**. Turn left at the crossroads at the end of the village and follow this country lane, still alongside the River Rede, through open moorland for around 3km, until the river winds left to the northwest and we continue straight on, climbing uphill to ❺ **Monkridge**, heading northeast towards Harwood Forest.

Passing **Monkridge Farm** on your left, turn right here on a cycle path on this side of the A696 – continuing behind a barrier for just over 1km – until you reach **Raylees**. Cross over the A696 here: again, it's not usually busy, but some vehicles speed up the hill from the left, so take care. Follow the lane uphill for about 1km, until you come to ❻ **Castle Hill**, with a bridleway on the right running alongside a dry stone wall, out now in wild, open moorland. Turn right here and follow this rough, roller-coaster trail up and down for just over 1km, until you come to **Hillhead Cottage** and farm on your left. Cross over a cattle-grid on to a fell road, which leads shortly to an angled junction with the B6342. Carry straight on here, climbing steadily uphill now. After a couple of kilometres, now approaching the edge of Harwood Forest on our left, we pass a forbidding-looking gallows on the right: ❼ **Winter's Gibbet**, a replica of the gallows where a certain William Winter was hanged in 1791 for the murder of Margaret Crozier, a local shop-owner. Or, to be more precise, it was near here that Winter murdered the unfortunate widow. He and his two accomplices were soon caught and subsequently hanged in Newcastle, but his dead body was brought back in chains to the site of his crime, where a gibbet was erected; the rotting corpse remained hanging here for many years.

With that gruesome story in mind, we're about to enter the deep and dark Harwood Forest! So, now would be a good time to test your gears and brakes, as some gnarly forest roads are coming up. This vast Forestry England conifer plantation covers more than 1,000ha within the Northumberland National Park. It was badly damaged by major storms during the winter of 2021, with more since in 2022. The main forestry roads remain open, with ongoing recovery work in progress, but at the time of writing there were some diversions. Access through to Rothbury is still possible, but your ride might take longer than expected, so plan ahead accordingly.

Continue downhill past Winter's Gibbet and, after about 1km, we come to the entrance to ❽ **Harwood Forest** on the left. Turn left here into the forest (signposted Sandstone Way – tucked on the back of a fingerpost on the left), through a gate and uphill on to the gravel forest road. If you have already cycled on forestry roads (eg: Route 7, page 74), you will probably be familiar with these rough gravel tracks with cambered edges and drainage ditches. If not, be wary of riding too close to the edges, in case of skidding into the side ditches; on the other hand, also keep alert for forestry trucks and other vehicles, which will probably take the flattest and easiest route along the centre of the road.

Continue climbing uphill, coming shortly to the car park at the entrance to the forest. Turn right from the car park on to the forest road: a wide and rough gravel trail between densely packed rows of tall conifers (predominantly Sitka spruce trees). Apart from the trees, which seem to go on forever into the darkness, the main impression here is of a peaceful but slightly eerie silence.

Follow this dead straight road downhill for just over 2km until we come to a junction, where we take the left fork – a continuation of the main road – carrying on downhill until we cross a little bridge over a stream, ❾ **Fallowlees Burn**. Climb uphill to the left here for around 700m, until we reach a right-angled junction. Turn right here – diversion, due to storm damage – on to ❿ **St Oswald's Way**. This long-distance trail runs across Northumberland for 156km, from Lindisfarne south to Hadrian's Wall, following sites associated with St Oswald, an early Christian pilgrim and ruler of Northumbria when it was a kingdom in the early 7th century.

Still on a wide and clear gravel road, and still climbing uphill, this detour winds, mostly eastwards, around the feet of **Hemmel Hill** and **Lough Hill**. After around 4km, the road goes around to the left/northwards, dipping down over another stream, then climbing steeply up again. As the road eventually levels out we come into a clearing, giving longer views northwards over the wall of trees and beyond to the fells of **Simonside Hills**. From here, the road winds to the left and after around another 2km

## CRAGSIDE

Former home of Lord William and Lady Margaret Armstrong, this house on a rocky crag overlooking Rothbury and the Coquet Valley was the site of the world's first hydro-electric power system, dubbed 'the Magician's Palace' after Armstrong, who was known to some as the 'Magician of the North'. The Armstrongs built their magnificent Arts and Crafts house on the bare

uphill climb, we come to the crest of the hill at the edge of the forest. On our left is the forest road that we turned off earlier, on to the St Oswald's Way diversion.

Take the trail forking right ahead, which winds down and then up again for a few kilometres across scrubby gorse and moorland. Be warned: this section of the route is unclear and unsignposted, with lots of side-paths made by walkers and cyclists, dodging boggy puddles and flooded streams at the bottom of hills. Use the komoot map to help your navigation:

↑ Cragside (yahiyat/S)

heathland, completed in 1885 after 15 years in the works, creating what is considered to be the world's first 'smart house'. Much of the house was designed by Richard Norman Shaw, one of the greatest architects of the Victorian era, incorporating an eccentric mix of Tudor, Renaissance and Gothic styles into the Armstrongs' whimsical castle.

William Armstrong, one of the Victorian era's great industrialists, also designed and installed electrical systems around his house, using hydraulics driven by the nearby River Coquet. With his scientist's passion for invention and technology, Armstrong filled his house with what at the time was advanced domestic innovation, including central heating, electric lights and even a hydraulic luggage lift. It is also brimming with the finest examples of Victorian domestic décor and taste, from William Morris stained-glass windows to collections of taxidermy and seashells. A massive and intricately carved Italian marble fireplace dominates the drawing room: standing around 6m tall and thought to weigh around 10 tonnes, it is supported by the solid rocky crag on which the house stands.

The 405ha grounds also offer a range of attractions including the powerhouse, a rock garden, a pinetum and formal gardens. There's also Carriage Drive (accessible to visitors to the house), a 9km circular route past lakes, waterfalls and moorland. It's all paved and mostly level, with picnic benches by the roadside, and so makes a perfect cycle ride for the family. For details, including Cragside's opening times and special events, visit ⚲ nationaltrust. org.uk/cragside.

we're heading generally northeastwards, skirting around several bare, craggy fells – first, to the left of **Weather Head** and, beyond that, between **Simonside** on our right and **Ravens Heugh** on the left.

As we approach the foot of Simonside, the path becomes clearer, with a T-junction where we turn right on to a wide gravel trail. This continues right, winding around Simonside, past a footpath to the peak on your right (no cycling allowed, but there are amazing views over the forest and rocky moorland of Coquetdale from the top). After about another 1.4km, the path comes to a junction, where you turn left. This path winds left and right downhill for about another 1.5km, with the Coe Burn stream on your right, and coming to another T-junction with a paved road. Turn left again here, leading to ❶ **Great Tosson** – we're off the wild moors now and back to 'civilisation', the terrain levelling out and into the gentle pastures of the Coquet Valley.

Turn first right on a hairpin bend before the hamlet and then, after another 600m, turn right again at a T-junction with Carterside Road, which goes past the edge of another hamlet, ❷ **Newtown**. Follow the road running parallel to the River Coquet on your left for a couple of kilometres, turning left on to Whitton Bank Road, passing Rothbury Golf Club on your left. Coming into the outskirts of **Rothbury** now, as the road runs downhill towards the river, note the elegant spires of Cragside – the magnificent country home of pioneering Victorian engineer, William Armstrong – in the trees across the valley (see box, page 124).

As you approach the bridge over the Coquet River into Rothbury, turn left instead to ❸ **Haugh car park** (free). There's a footbridge from here over the river and into the attractive old market town, often called the 'capital of Coquetdale'. Sheltered to the north by wooded hills and on the edge of the Northumberland National Park, it's a popular base for walkers and, of course, cyclists; it also provides convenient access to **Cragside**.

Here endeth the wildest and, for this writer at least, the most exciting ride in the book!

## THE ESSENTIALS
------------------------------------------------------------------

**GETTING THERE** By road, Bellingham is 53km west of Newcastle upon Tyne, via the A69, A68 and B6320. The nearest train station is at Hexham, 27km south of Bellingham, with direct trains from Newcastle and connecting 680 bus service; average journey time around 1¾ hours.

Rothbury is just under 50km northwest of Newcastle upon Tyne, via the A1, A697 and B6344. There's no train station in the town, but Arriva North East (⊘ arrivabus.co.uk/north-east) runs the X14 bus service direct from Newcastle, which takes about 1¼ hours.

If you're planning to return to Bellingham, the only option is by car, as there is no train service in either town.

**FACILITIES** There are public toilets in Bellingham, next to Fountain Cottage Café on the High Street, and in Rothbury, on Bridge Street.

## WHERE TO EAT

✘ **Bewicks Kitchen & Coffee House** Church St, Rothbury NE65 7UP; ✆ 01669 621717; ⬙ bewicksrothbury.com. Serving what is probably the best gourmet food in town, Bewicks is based in a tastefully decorated old townhouse in the heart of Rothbury. Under the guidance of head chef Kevin Mulraney, the menu comprises excellent contemporary British cuisine, including game meats, fish pie, home-smoked salmon & local shellfish. Afternoon teas, with or without prosecco or champagne, also look tempting; not cheap but top quality. **£££**

✘ **La Mensa** High St, Rothbury NE65 7TE; ✆ 01669 620461; ⬙ La Mensa. This highly rated Italian restaurant at the end of Rothbury's High St has all the favourites on its menu, including pasta, pizza, focaccia & risotto, as well as chicken & seafood dishes, all nicely cooked & good value for money. The ambience is laid-back & friendly & it's extremely popular too, so booking is advisable, especially at w/ends (take-away also available). **££**

✘ **Newcastle House** Front St, Rothbury NE65 7UT; ✆ 01669 620334; ⬙ rothburynewcastlehouse.co.uk. This traditional hotel in the centre of Rothbury has a popular restaurant, open all day for b/fast, brunch, light lunch (& Sun lunch carvery) & dinner. Its menu has a good mix of family favourites, including burgers, fish'n'chips, roast meats & lasagne. Apart from the tasty, good-value food, half the fun here is in reading the whimsical menu, with wacky dishes including baby shark whitebait, Rock the Kasbah nut roast and Whoa oh oh Sweet Stack of Mine pancakes. It also has an outside eating area in front, so you can prop your bike up against the railings while you eat. **££**

## FURTHER INFORMATION

🏛 **Rothbury Library** Front St, Rothbury NE65 7TZ; ✆ 01669 620428. In the absence of an official visitor information centre in Rothbury, your best bet is the public library, towards the western end of Front St (which runs parallel to the High St). Staff here will be able to help with local information & advice, with a selection of useful tourist leaflets available too. There is also a visitor centre at nearby Cragside (see box, page 124), with local tips and information.

# 13 WALLINGTON TO BELSAY LOOP

| | |
|---|---|
| **START/FINISH** | Wallington Hall |
| **DISTANCE/TIME** | 33.1km/3–3½hrs |
| **DIFFICULTY/TERRAIN** | ① Undulating terrain from start to finish, but no hills that are very steep or long; all on road, mostly quiet back roads, with a few short A-road crossings (one on a cycle path); suitable for reasonably fit and experienced cyclists |
| **SCENIC RATING** | ⑧ Meandering through the rural landscape of the Wansbeck and Blyth valleys via a clutch of country estates: Wallington Hall, Capheaton Hall, Belsay Hall and Castle and Whalton Manor and Gardens |
| **SUITABLE FOR** | Road bike, hybrid or gravel bike |
| **NCN ROUTE** | Between the Sandstone Way to the north and NCN10 to the south |
| **MAPS** | OS Explorer OL325 and OL42 (1:25 000) |
| **KOMOOT REF** | 984496227 |

↑ Bolam Lake (Dave Head/S)

This loop route meanders across the Wansbeck and Blyth valleys, via leafy historic estates and a lakeside park. Starting at Wallington Hall, one of Northumberland's greatest country homes, we head south across the valley through Capheaton, a farming village on Capheaton Hall's estate. Winding east, we pass Belsay, home to another handsome historic pile, Belsay Hall and Castle (a short detour off route). Continuing eastwards, we cross the River Blyth and head north to Whalton, whose Whalton Manor boasts Lutyens-designed gardens. From Whalton, we loop further north and then west past Bolam Lake and Country Park, before crossing back over the Wansbeck River and returning to Wallington.

Maybe it was something to do with the cyclist-friendly café at Capheaton (see below), or just because this is such a pleasant route, but I saw more cyclists on my recent ride – around 35 – than I'd seen in all the previous 11 put together. We're not talking shoulder-to-shoulder pelotons, but it was nice to have a little company and to see that other cyclists like these peaceful back roads too.

## THE ROUTE

❶ **Wallington Hall**, where we start our ride, is one of Northumberland's most impressive stately homes (see box, page 132). Covering more

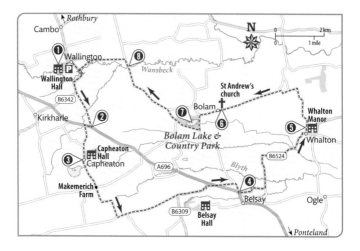

than 5,400ha of woodlands, grazing pastures and gardens, Wallington is the largest estate managed by the National Trust, with its 17th-century mansion built by Sir William Blackett, a shipping and mining magnate from Newcastle. Wallington's stunning landscaped grounds were designed by Lancelot 'Capability' Brown, who was born nearby in Kirkharle.

Coming out of the car park, turn right on to the B6342, through the woods and past the distinguished Palladian façade of Wallington Hall on your right. There are four dragons' head gargoyles on the lawn in front, grinning – or perhaps grimacing – as we cycle past.

Follow the road downhill and across the old stone Wallington Bridge (look out for oncoming traffic, it's single file only) over the Wansbeck River. As the road winds uphill to the right, note the large bed of massive, leafy gunnera plants by the verge, alongside the perimeter wall of the Wallington Estate. Continue climbing, away from the river and out into the open countryside.

If you've already cycled in and around the nearby Northumberland National Park (see Routes 8–11, pages 82–117), you'll have experienced its wild moors, fringed with rugged dry stone walling. Here, though, in mid-Northumberland, the undulating landscape feels tamer, with cattle and sheep grazing lush meadows, and roadside hedgerows thick with shrubs and wild flowers, including bramble, wild rose and elderflower.

As we approach the top of the hill, after around 400m, the B6342 winds around to the right. Carry straight on here, on to a smaller, unsignposted side road, and continue straight ahead, southwards and gently downhill. After winding downhill for a few hundred metres, we go over a stone bridge across the little Swilder Burn, and uphill shortly to a T-junction with the ❷ **A696**. It's only a two-lane A-road, but traffic can be quite busy here so keep alert. Thankfully, there's a cycle path running alongside the road on the right for around 50m, from where it crosses over to another cycle path opposite. This path continues to the right for another 50m or so, until we reach a side road, where we turn left, signposted towards Capheaton.

Continue along this quiet country lane for around 1.5km, downhill then up again, before coming to the hamlet of ❸ **Capheaton** with a row of solid stone farm cottages lining the road. Hidden behind trees to the left is the grand country pile, the 17th-century **Capheaton Hall**, home to the Swinburne family since 1260 and now a luxury hotel (see page 210). And just as the road bears right, there's a little green, corrugated-tin hut on the right, which houses the **Capheaton Tearoom** (see below), a likely tempting stop after that modest uphill climb if you're here at the weekend, as it's only open on Saturday and Sunday. Otherwise, there are no refreshment options for around another 10km, at the detour to Belsay.

From Capheaton, follow the road bearing right and straight ahead at the crossroads by **Makemerich (!) Farm** on your right. We're heading downhill now, until after around 3km we reach a T-junction where we turn left. Continue along this nice, level and straight road through the fields for another 4km, joining the B6309 and coming to the A696 again. Here there's a dogleg junction with the B6309 continuing across the other side, so turn right briefly and then immediately left (or if you're not so confident, you can simply go on to the triangle between the roads and wait until it's clear to cross).

Continue along the B6309, still heading eastwards along the level valley. After about another 1km we come to a T-junction, signposted left to

Rothbury, but we turn right here, heading south towards Belsay. And in another 400m we come back to the A696 – for the last time! Again, it's an easy junction, and our main route turns left here on to the ❹ **B6254**, avoiding the A-road. If you're interested in a short detour, though, **Belsay Hall** is about 500m to the right, down the A696.

Managed by English Heritage, Belsay is an impressive estate, with a castle, hall and gardens. The castle was originally medieval but enlarged in the 17th century; the hall is a Greek Revival mansion dating from the 19th century, and between the two are beautiful gardens, created in and around the quarries that provided the stone for the buildings. Belsay has

## WALLINGTON'S WHITE-CLAWED CRAYFISH

The magnificent 17th-century Wallington Hall in the heart of mid-Northumberland is one of the most important historic houses in the county, with a 5,463ha estate, including landscaped gardens designed by Lancelot 'Capability' Brown. Besides an opportunity to explore the house, with its Italianate central hall, there are walks around the grounds. And, for cyclists, the Dragon Cycle Trail is a special highlight: 6km of off-road paths (a 1.5km easy Green woodland route and a longer Blue route of just under 5km around the estate fields), ideal for families and as a warm-up for our ride to Belsay.

In addition to its range of visitor activities, however, Wallington also runs various conservation projects aimed at protecting its natural habitats and their resident wildlife. One such project is for the white-clawed crayfish, the only native freshwater crayfish found in the UK. Sadly, this protected species, which grows up to 12cm long, is in decline across the rest of the country, threatened by a fungal disease carried by the larger, invasive American signal crayfish. Here in Wallington, though, the water is particularly clean, and special 'ark' sites have been set up where the crayfish can be cared for in isolation from outside water sources. The long-term aim is to build up their population to around 300 crayfish, which could then be safely reintroduced to river systems should the species be wiped out. The crayfish ark site is in the Fountains plantation area, which can be visited from the green Dragon Cycle Trail. Alternatively, they

been going through major conservation work since 2021 and is due to reopen in July 2023, so check in advance at ⌀ english-heritage.org.uk.

The entrance to the hall is on the right, as the A696 bears left. Or, if you're in need of refreshment, Belsay Shop is opposite the side-turning to Belsay Hall on the left, with take-away snacks, hot and cold drinks, and a picnic bench outside in front.

Continuing from the junction with the B6254, above, carry on eastwards and mostly level along the side of the valley. After just over 1km, the road winds left, crossing the River Blyth (just a trickle here), and heads northwards now.

also keep some white-clawed crayfish in an aquarium at the Visitor Reception Centre, as part of a display about the project.

For more information, including a map of the Dragon Cycle Trail, visit ⌀ nationaltrust.org.uk/wallington.

↑ A white-clawed crayfish shows the pale underside of its claws, which gives the species its name (naturepl.com/Linda Pitkin/2020VISION)

After about 4km from Belsay, we reach Whalton, quite a prosperous-looking village and home to another country house and garden: ❺ **Whalton Manor**. The main road through the village winds right, then take the first turning on the left, signposted Bolam Lake and Country Park, just before the Beresford Arms pub. If you're keen on visiting Whalton Manor, though – and tick off the complete set of historic houses on this ride – carry straight on past the pub, and it is another 300m beyond on the left. The house itself dates from the 17th century, but only its gardens and summer house are open to the public (from April to October, by prior appointment; for details, visit ⬦ whaltonmanor.co.uk). Whalton's magnificent 1.2ha gardens were designed by Sir Edwin Lutyens, advised by his mentor Gertrude Jekyll, who also designed Lindisfarne Castle's walled garden.

To return to the left-hand turning from Whalton, follow the road winding uphill for about 2km, before making a 90-degree bend to the left and levelling off, as we head westwards back towards Wallington. In about 3km, as the road bends to the left before we come to Bolam, there's the little church of ❻ **St Andrew's, Bolam**, just off the road, down a short

↑ Belsay Castle (verityjohnson/S)

narrow lane on the right. It's well worth a peep, if you're as into churches as this writer is. It's a handsome and solid church, with a stone tower dating from the Saxon era. Its interior is largely Norman, with some fine stained glass and, in a side-chapel, the carved gravestone of Robert de Reyne, a knight who fought in the Anglo-Scottish wars in the late 12th and early 13th centuries. Its main historical claim to fame, though, is that four German bombs landed in the churchyard during World War II. Three bombs went off, but one somehow 'bounced' in through the south wall of the church, where it wedged itself in, unexploded. Some 60 years later, the German bomber pilot, Willy Schludecker, learned of this and so visited the church to apologise. The event has been commemorated in one of the stained-glass windows in the south wall. This is one of the many reasons I love churches: to misquote Forrest Gump, you never know what you might find.

Back on the road from the church, carry on to the right and, in 1km, turn left at a T-junction. About 50m after the T-junction, we come to the entrance to ❼ **Bolam Lake and Country Park** on your right, with a visitor centre and café next to the car park. This popular public park and gardens (free entry) has lakeside trails, with swans, ducks and other waterfowl to be

↑ St Andrew's Church, Bolam (Huw Hennessy)

seen on the water. The mature woodlands around the lake are also home to a variety of animals, including roe deer, stoats, weasels and red squirrels.

Continue along the road running south down the side of the park. At the angled T-junction shortly after the lake, turn right, signposted Cambo and Rothbury, and enjoy a nice long, straight downhill run through the trees. There are forestry plantations here, though, on both sides of the road, so keep alert for warning signs of forestry trucks coming out of side roads.

At the bottom of the valley, about 4km from Bolam Lake, we cross back over the ❽ **River Wansbeck**. And in about 400m, before the road starts winding uphill, turn left, signposted Wallington.

Continue alongside the river on your left, happily downhill again; note on your left more of the leafy gunnera plants that we saw at the start of the ride. Finally, the road comes to another T-junction, just above the bridge over the Wansbeck, where we started. Turn right here on to the B6342, climbing uphill past ❾ **Wallington Hall** on your left – gargoyles definitely grinning now. Follow the road bearing left around the bend and turn left again into the car park.

## THE ESSENTIALS

**GETTING THERE** By car, Wallington is just over 32km northwest of Newcastle upon Tyne, via the A696 and B6342. The nearest station is at Morpeth, 21km to the east, with CrossCountry trains from Newcastle taking around 15 minutes.

**FACILITIES** There are customer toilets at Wallington Hall and Belsay Hall, and public toilets at Bolam Lake and Country Park

### WHERE TO EAT

✕ **Capheaton Tearoom** Silver Hill, Capheaton NE19 2AA; ⊘ capheatontearoom. co.uk. Right on our route in the rural hamlet of Capheaton, this little community-led tearoom is a surprise find, housed inside the village hall: a corrugated-tin shack by the side of the road.

Open at w/ends (10.00–15.00), it does hot & cold snacks, soups, sandwiches, tea & coffee, & freshly made cakes, with vegan & gluten-free options. It's a favourite stop-off for local cycling clubs (with even a Capheaton Cycling jersey on sale here). £

✕ **The Belsay Shop Post Office** 12 The Arcade, Belsay NE20 0DY; ℘ 01661 881207. This village shop across the road from Belsay Hall has a take-away counter with snacks, freshly made cakes & pastries, tea & coffee. There are picnic tables outside – handy for a bite on the go. £ (Note too, that if you plan to visit **Belsay Hall**, opposite, it will also have a café after its refurb, though details were not available at the time of writing.)

✕ **Clocktower Café** Wallington Hall, Cambo NE61 4AR; ℘ 01670 773606; ⌂ nationaltrust. org.uk/wallington. This spacious café, overlooking Wallington Hall's courtyard and gardens, is open all day, serving b/fasts, brunches & light lunches, including jacket potatoes, soups & savoury snacks; eat indoors or outside in the courtyard. £

## FURTHER INFORMATION

ℹ **Wallington Hall** Cambo, nr Morpeth NE61 4AR; ℘ 01670 773606; ⌂ nationaltrust. uk/wallington. Staff at Wallington Hall's Visitor Reception and Information Centre are available for advice on local attractions and amenities, with a wide selection of maps & books for sale.

# 14 ALNWICK TO WARKWORTH LOOP

| | |
|---|---|
| **START/FINISH** | Aln Valley Railway |
| **DISTANCE/TIME** | 22km/2½hrs |
| **DIFFICULTY/TERRAIN** | ① All on road or cycle path; mostly level with only a few moderate hills; only one A-road crossing so, all in all, suitable for beginners and leisure cyclists |
| **SCENIC RATING** | ⑧ Mix of rural back lanes, river valley and coast |
| **SUITABLE FOR** | Road bike, hybrid or gravel bike |
| **NCN ROUTE** | NCN1 |
| **MAPS** | OS Explorer 332 (1:25 000) |
| **KOMOOT REF** | 984497657 |

This scenic and easy ride loops around the rural Aln Valley and the coast, between Alnmouth and Warkworth.

We start from the Aln Valley Railway, a heritage line on the outskirts of Alnwick, along a permissive path by the railway line, heading east down to the Aln Estuary at Alnmouth. From here, we follow the Coast & Castles Cycle Route (NCN1, the long-distance, 315km route from Tynemouth to Edinburgh) southwards to Warkworth, with glorious views over fields to the sand dunes lining the coast, and glimpses of the lighthouse on Coquet Island offshore. On the outskirts of Warkworth, with its magnificent medieval castle, we wind inland again and meander northwards through country lanes between the fields, back to Alnwick.

As it's a loop route, you can choose to go in whichever direction you prefer, but I'd recommend going clockwise down the coast and inland back up to Alnwick as described here: it's an easier downhill gradient overall and you're more likely to have the prevailing winds behind you going southwards down the coast.

## THE ROUTE

Start from the ❶ **Aln Valley Railway** on the southern outskirts of Alnwick, across the A1 and next to the Lionheart industrial estate. The Aln Valley Railway Trust (⊘ alnvalleyrailway.co.uk) is a charitable heritage project on this disused former branch line, with trains currently running to Greenrigg Halt, 1.5km down the line. With ongoing volunteer work, they are hoping

← The lighthouse on Coquet Island (Dave Head/S)

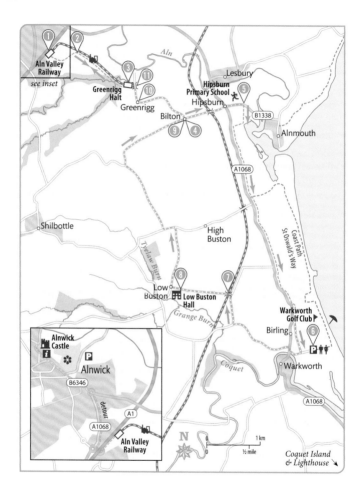

eventually to extend the line to link up with the East Coast Main Line at Alnmouth, providing onward connections to Edinburgh and London. There's a collection of vintage steam locomotives, wagons and carriages in the old station yard, as well as a museum of railway memorabilia, café and car park.

Turn left out of the station and follow the cycle and footpath to the left, signposted Alnmouth. After about 500m, winding uphill to the left on a gravel track, we come down again to a T-junction by the ❷ **railway line**. Turn right here, with the path running alongside the line, heading eastwards towards the coast. A few hundred metres later we cross over a high bridge, with views left and right over the treetops; in the distance is a faint hiss from traffic on the A1, but otherwise it's very leafy and peaceful here with just a few dog walkers for company (in fact, I only saw two other cyclists on the whole trip when I was here in autumn 2022).

Around 300m after the bridge we come to ❸ **Greenrigg Halt** station, where we leave the railside path and take the fork up to the road on the right. Here we come to a T-junction where we turn right, signposted Alnmouth, then climb uphill and continue straight ahead past the hamlet of Greenrigg, a row of cottages and farm on the right.

Follow the road winding right and left, with wide views westwards over the Aln Valley and towards the Cheviot Hills in the Northumberland National Park. After about 1km we descend to ❹ **Bilton**, with Bilton Farm on your right. Coming to a T-junction, signposted Alnmouth, turn left downhill through the village. Carry on downhill, over the railway bridge (near Alnmouth station) and through Hipsburn. After about 300m, we come to a roundabout with the A1068; take the second exit, straight ahead, on to the B1338. Pass **Hipsburn Primary School** on your left, followed by Alnmouth Croquet Club and Alnmouth and Lesbury Cricket Club. Opposite the entrance to the playing fields, turn right on to a compact gravel/cinder path, signposted ❺ **Coast Path**.

The path winds right around the broad Aln Estuary, with views southwards over the dunes to the sea. If the tide is out this is a good spot for birdwatching, particularly on the mudflats. Geese, mallards, lapwing and wading birds are common here. And if you're lucky, you might spot rarer species, including marbled ducks and several different warblers.

Heading inland, the path then makes a right-hand bend leading to the A1068, where we turn left, but protected from the road by trees and hedgerows. Soak up the glorious views over the sea to our left now, over the fields and dunes, with Alnmouth across the estuary and, silhouetted against the sea, to the south, is **Coquet Island and Lighthouse**. The island is a superb RSPB nature reserve, with some 40,000 seabirds nesting here every year, including the UK's only breeding colony of roseate terns (see box, opposite).

As we continue southwards, ignore side roads and paths leading down to the sea, although part of our Warkworth West route does follow the Coast Path for a short distance (see page 148). This shared footpath and cycleway makes for some very pleasant cycling down the coast; it's mostly very flat with one or two short climbs, which have the advantage of giving wider views to the north and south, over the sea.

Carry on along this path for around 4km, until we reach a fork at Birling, where we turn left on to a rough, rubbly road, leading to the outskirts of **Warkworth**. After about 700m, passing Warkworth Golf Club on your left and a caravan site on your right, we come to a T-junction with ❻ **Warkworth Beach car park** on the right. Turn right here, signposted NCN1, and after a couple of hundred metres we come to another T-junction with the **A1068**, with the two bridges across the River Coquet on your left, leading into Warkworth's town centre.

Turn right here, across the A1068 and on to a cycle lane – take care crossing the road, with a blind spot from oncoming traffic from the right in particular – and then turn left almost immediately on to Station Road.

Follow this road for around 1.5km, climbing uphill through Warkworth's suburbs, and then downhill to a turning on the right just as the road bears left, signposted Shortridge Hall and Buston Barns. Turn right here and follow this road, levelling out now and winding left through the arable fields, shortly to cross the main-line railway line. After around 600m we come to a left-hand turn, signposted High Buston and Low Buston. Turn left here, over the ❼ **railway bridge**, and continue straight for about 1km to **Low Buston**, a little farming hamlet.

At the next junction, just after passing ❽ **Low Buston Hall** on your left and as the main road bears left, turn right, signposted High Buston and Alnwick. We're heading northwards now, the road mostly level or undulating. This is pleasant and peaceful rural countryside, with little traffic on these back roads apart from the occasional tractor or potato

## COQUET ISLAND

Lying only 1.5km offshore from Amble, just to the south of Warkworth, Coquet is a low-lying grassy island spanning some 7ha and topped by a sturdy lighthouse. Coquet is best known today as an RSPB nature reserve, but it has quite an interesting back story too. It was first inhabited by the Culdees, early Christian pilgrims who sought sanctuary here during the warring times of the Northumbrian kingdom in the 7th century. Subsequently, Benedictine monks built a monastery here as a place for secluded meditation, perhaps inspired by the North Sea's wrathful storms, keeping them in awe of God's omnipotence.

Together with the rest of Northumbria, Coquet was occupied by the Scots during the reign of Charles I, not returning to English rule until 1641. While civil war raged across mainland England, Coquet Island was left in peace, until the construction in 1841 of the Coquet Lighthouse. Standing over 24m tall, the lighthouse's first keeper was William Darling, elder brother of Grace Darling, whose heroics in 1838 saved passengers and crew from the paddle steamer *Forfarshire*, wrecked off the Farne Islands, nearby to the north.

Today, though, Coquet is all about the birds. Since the 1970s, Coquet has been managed by the RSPB as a nature sanctuary. It is home to around 40,000 breeding seabirds, some migrating here from as far as Africa. Its star attraction are the roseate (or rosy) terns, for whom the island constitutes the only breeding site in the UK. Tragically, avian flu has hit the tern population very hard; in summer 2022, 55% of the adult birds died out of its colony of 154 pairs.

With or without avian flu, landing on Coquet Island is prohibited as a protected reserve. Several local boat companies do run cruises around Coquet and other offshore islands, with the opportunity of seeing many other birds besides the terns. These include puffins, kittiwakes and fulmars, with the bonus of around 600 grey seals.

For more information about cruises around Coquet and other sites along the Northumberland coast, a couple of recommended operators are Puffin Cruises (𝒷 puffincruises.co.uk) and Billy Shiel's (𝒷 farne-islands.com).

truck (lots of potatoes are grown here). And we're never more than a few kilometres from the coast, so you can still catch glimpses of the sea over the hedgerows on our right. Follow the road around to the left after about another 1km, signposted Shilbottle and Alnwick. Shortly after that, in about 300m, take the next right-hand turn: it's not signposted, but it's in front of a steel gate at the corner of the field.

After just over 1km, climbing gently uphill, we pass on our left a slightly sinister-looking RAF radio transmitter base, bristling with razor-wire fencing, and then come to a T-junction. Turn right here (though note that it's signposted Alnwick left and Alnmouth right), and enjoy a wonderful downhill run towards the coast now for a couple of kilometres until you come to ❾ **Bilton**, with a left-hand turning signposted **Greenrigg**. Turn left here, on to the same road as we came down at the start of the ride. This winds uphill through the fields for around 1km, until it bears left at

↑ A carved lion stands guard on the road to Alnwick Castle (D K Grove/S)

a ⑩ **little triangle**, in Greenrigg, with a farm and a row of cottages at the top of the hill. Carry straight on here, on the narrow track signposted cycle/footpath to Alnwick.

After a short downhill stretch from the Greenrigg junction, we come to a ⑪ **railway bridge**. Turn left in front of the bridge, through a gate, leading downhill to the path back to Alnwick. After around 1.5km, coming into Alnwick, take the left fork, winding up and down, back to the ① **Aln Valley Railway**.

**OPTIONAL ADD-ON** Alnwick (pronounced 'Annick') is an attractive, historic town, about 10 minutes by bike from here: turn right out of the car park, through the Lionheart industrial estate. Turn left on to the A68 (with cycle path alongside the road) and under the A1. At the roundabout, take the third exit, following the A68 up to another roundabout with the B6346. Take the second exit and continue up the road for around 1.4km, past **Barter Books** on the left, and into the town centre. At the top end of the town is the magnificent medieval **Alnwick Castle**, the second-largest inhabited castle in the UK. Best known today for its appearances on film and TV, from *Harry Potter*'s Hogwarts School of Witchcraft and Wizardry to TV's *Downton Abbey*, the castle has a regular schedule of guided tours, including a highly entertaining 'Film Tour' (and even broomstick training lessons). For bookworms, the town also has one of the largest secondhand bookshops in the UK: Barter Books is housed in the former train station, with a model railway line running around the labyrinthine building above the bookshelves, along with the excellent **Station Buffet** café (see below).

## THE ESSENTIALS

**GETTING THERE** By road, Alnwick is just under 60km north of Newcastle upon Tyne via the A1 and B1340 (or just under 72km by the more scenic coastal route via Tynemouth, Whitley Bay, Blyth, Amble and Warkworth, on the A189 and A1068). The nearest train station is at Alnmouth, which has direct trains from Newcastle on LNER (⊘ lner.co.uk) taking 25–45 minutes, with the connecting X20 MAX Arriva North East bus service (⊘ arrivabus.co.uk/north-east) taking around 15 minutes.

**FACILITIES** There are toilets at Aln Valley Railway and public toilets next to Warkworth Beach car park.

## WHERE TO EAT

✗ **Buffet Stop Café, Aln Valley Railway** Lionheart Enterprise Park, Alnwick NE66 2EZ; ⌀ alnvalleyrailway.co.uk/cafe/. Handy for the start and end of the ride, this little café based in the old station yard serves a range of hot & cold light meals & snacks, including b/fast bacon rolls, jacket potatoes, sandwiches & cakes (open w/ends Easter–Sep, Wed during summer holidays & on other special railway opening days during the year – check online for details). £

✗ **The Station Buffet & Paradise Ice Cream Parlour** Alnwick Station, Alnwick NE66 2NP; ✆ 01665 604888; ⌀ barterbooks.co.uk. This brilliant little café is based in the old waiting room of Alnwick's former station, now housing the wonderfully eccentric Barter Books. The menu features classic comfort-food favourites, such as chip butties, fish-finger butties, burgers, homemade soups, brownies and Earl Grey tea fruit cake. The adjacent Paradise ice-cream parlour has 12 different flavours (made with

↑ The high-level model train in Barter Books chugs past Peter Dodd's *Famous Writers* mural (Huw Hennessy)

Jersey cows' milk from Wheelbirks Farm, between Hexham and Hamsterley), as well as homemade cakes, milkshakes, ice-cream sodas, teas & barista coffees. £

✂ **Caffe Tirreno** 45 Bondgate, Alnwick NE66 1PR; ✆ 01665 605455. This bustling & very popular Italian restaurant opposite the Playhouse in the centre of Alnwick serves delicious and authentic Italian classics, including calamari, spaghetti carbonara, risottos & pizzas. It's very reasonably priced too; they don't take bookings, so get here early to be sure of a table – if none is available, you can wait in the Fleece Inn next door, and they'll come and get you when one is ready. ££

## FURTHER INFORMATION

▪ **Alnwick Tourist Information Centre** Bondgate Without, Alnwick NE66 1PQ; ✆ 016670 622152. Based in Alnwick library, within the Playhouse, this information centre in the centre of Alnwick has helpful staff on hand for advice, with plenty of local leaflets, maps and guidebooks available too.

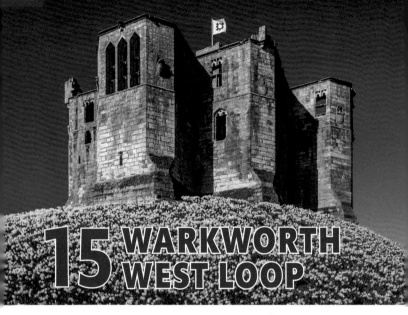

# 15 WARKWORTH WEST LOOP

| | |
|---|---|
| **START/FINISH** | Warkworth |
| **DISTANCE/TIME** | 18.8km/1½–2hrs |
| **DIFFICULTY/TERRAIN** | ② Mostly on level or undulating terrain, with a few steep climbs over the sand dunes; mainly on quiet country lanes, with some off-road tracks (but not hair-raising or needing MTB skills) |
| **SCENIC RATING** | ⑧ A tranquil mix of rural countryside and unspoilt coastline, with stunning views of the sea, sand and dunes, and Coquet Island on the horizon |
| **SUITABLE FOR** | Gravel bike, robust hybrid or MTB (all with knobbly tyres) |
| **NCN ROUTE** | Partly on NCN1 |
| **MAPS** | OS Explorer 332 (1:25 000) |
| **KOMOOT REF** | 937728780 |

↑ Warkworth Castle (Michael Conrad/S)

This short but diverse loop meanders through the undulating Coquet Valley, flanked by the coastal dunes and sandy beaches between Warkworth and Alnmouth. If this is your first visit to the area, it should make the perfect introduction to the Northumberland coast's breath-taking natural beauty.

Starting from Warkworth, on a bend in the River Coquet just inland from Amble, we head west into the valley, along country lanes between sleepy hamlets, before looping northwards and zigzagging on bridleways and farm tracks across arable farmland. As we approach the Aln Estuary, we head eastwards and down to the coast. Here, we join the Coast Path and the Coast & Castles Cycle Route (NCN1) to return southwards down the coast to Warkworth. There are a few moderate hills including some fun ups and downs through the dunes, with one or two short but steep climbs where you might need to dismount and push your bike up the hill.

Overall, the route should be easily accessible for most cyclists, including families with older children.

## THE ROUTE

Start from ❶ **Dial Place**, at the bottom end of Warkworth's main street, with its massive medieval castle towering over the town. Turn left on to Bridge Street (A1068), and left again after around 100m to cross the old medieval bridge over the River Coquet, now a shared footbridge (it's cobblestoned, so it's probably easier to dismount and walk across the bridge).

Turn left to join the A1068, briefly, then first left again up Station Road. The suburban road is lined by some of Warkworth's grander houses, and it winds uphill out of the town and soon we're into the countryside. After about 1km, pass the ivy-clad Hermitage Farm on your right; the road then starts to level off and bear left, heading southwards towards the railway line, about another 1km beyond the farm.

Go over the ❷ **level crossing** (the East Coast Main Line) and, after another 300m, take the first left, signposted Brotherwick and Guyzance, continuing southwards for just under 2km. This is quiet rural countryside, the road gently undulating through broad arable fields, fringed by hedgerows; the few houses mostly either farms or farm cottages. At the next junction, follow the main road as it bears right, still signposted Guyzance, a hamlet nearby to the south.

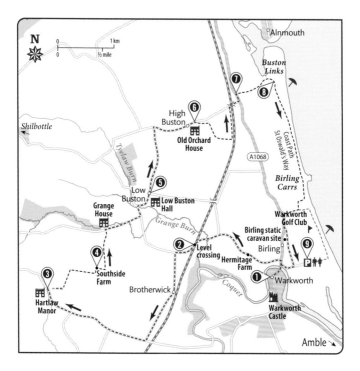

After about 2km, climbing gently, turn right on to a ❸ **public bridleway**, just as the road bears left and climbs more steeply uphill, towards **Hartlaw Manor**. Go through a gate on to a grassy and gravelly farm track. This winds gradually uphill for around 500m, before starting to descend again as it heads east towards the coast. If it's a clear day, you should be able to glimpse the sea from here, and perhaps **Coquet Island and Lighthouse**, further south, offshore from Amble.

After around another 700m, still descending down the rough track, pass ❹ **Southside Farm** on the right to come to a T-junction. Turn left here, back on to a paved road and now heading north again, towards **Low Buston**. After about 200m, we come to another T-junction; no signpost here but there's a cluster of cottages across the road, including **Grange**

**House**, tucked behind the hedgerow and trees. Turn right here, towards the sea again, and going under a line of tall electricity pylons straddling the fields.

This straight road dips down over Grange Burn and then climbs for about 700m to another T-junction where we turn left, signposted Alnwick, Shilbottle and Low Buston. Just after crossing another stream, Tyelaw Burn, turn right on to a smaller lane at the bottom of the hill, looking out for oncoming traffic around the blind turn to the left. After about 400m, passing ❺ **Low Buston Farm** on your left, you come to a junction with a smaller road, signposted High Buston and Alnwick, while the main road bears right. Go straight on here on the smaller road.

Carry straight on along this level road through the fields for around 1km, coming to a T-junction, signposted High Buston and Alnmouth, where we turn right. Coming to **High Buston**, another farm hamlet, after about 700m, pass High Buston Farm on your right, then in front of ❻ **Old**

↑ The River Coquet estuary, Amble (Caitlin Hennessy)

**Orchard House** turn right (through a gate) on to an unpaved track. After around 400m, this leads through another gate, and left on to a narrow grassy path across fields and between hedgerows of gorse and brambles. This is a permissive path, so give way to walkers and other users (and be prepared for possible diversions around sown arable fields).

After around 800m we come to the railway line again. Turn left here and follow the path next to the line, protected by a stone wall, and then alongside a grove of silver birch trees (look out for colourful toadstools speckling the shady moss below).

After about 200m the path comes to a small car park, where we turn right on to a paved road going immediately under a railway bridge. Coming shortly to a T-junction, turn left briefly on to the A1068 before taking the next right after about 100m – look out for oncoming traffic – on to a public bridleway signposted ❼ **St Oswald's Way** and **Buston Links**, a popular stretch of secluded beach and dunes at the end of the road ahead. This is a rough and rubbly path but, if you can ignore your teeth jangling in your head, there are gorgeous views from here to the sea sparkling not far away now, beyond the bank of sand dunes ahead. Follow the path downhill towards the sea until, after a few hundred metres, we reach the dunes and turn right on to a ❽ **bridleway** signposted **Birling Carrs**, a rocky headland just to the south. We're on a rough gravel track here, but starting to open up stunning views over the dunes to the wide sandy beach and south down the coast towards Warkworth.

Follow the path southwards through the dunes. The way is rolling up and down now and narrower in places so go carefully, especially on downhill stretches where it's easy to skid on loose sand. After around 1.6km, at Birling Carrs, the path diverts inland through a static caravan site; as you enter the site, follow the bridleway signpost at the fork where you turn right. Go carefully between the caravans, looking out for children and dogs in particular.

Continuing beyond the caravan site, the bridleway winds across the fairway of **Warkworth Golf Club** (look out for low-flying balls!). After about 200m turn left on to the NCN1, which heads south alongside the A1068, running parallel behind a hedgerow.

# WARKWORTH CASTLE

At the peak of its importance, Warkworth Castle was home to the Percy family, one of the most powerful dynasties in medieval England. With its natural defensive site on a mound overlooking a loop in the River Coquet, around 1.5km inland from its mouth at Amble, the castle was a vital stronghold during the long Anglo-Scottish wars and subsequent Wars of the Roses, when its control flipped sides from the Lancastrians to the Yorkists.

The castle's beginnings are uncertain: it is thought that the Anglo-Saxon earls of Northumberland had a residence on the site before the 1066 Norman Conquest, but the castle itself may have been built by Henry II in the 1150s, to strengthen his control of Northumberland. It was further fortified during the late 13th century during the Anglo-Scottish wars, and extended in 1377 by the 1st Earl of Northumberland, whose family, the Percys, owned Warkworth from the 14th to the 17th century. The present-day Percy family are still in residence up the coast at Alnwick Castle (see page 145).

The last major restoration work took place in the mid-19th century, but most of the castle's appearance today is much as it was in the 14th century. The Great Tower dominates the site: a cross-shaped fortified keep, standing on top of the mound, or motte. This central part of the castle housed some of its most important rooms, including the chapel, great hall and the Percy family's chambers.

Exploring the castle's labyrinthine corridors, with the aid of audio guides, visitors can enjoy a virtual historical experience. Climbing its gatehouse and turrets also provides stunning views along the coast, imagining the invading armies that bombarded the massive ramparts. Also connected to the grounds is the Hermitage (additional entry fee), a chapel built into the rocky cliff by the riverbank and used by the 1st Earl of Northumberland for private family services. It's a 1km walk up the river, followed by a boat ride across to the secluded site.

For more details about visiting Warkworth Castle, visit ⊘ english-heritage. org.uk.

After around 200m, the cycle path comes to a junction, where we take the left fork on to a rubbly road leading through Birling, with another static caravan site on the right. The road comes to a T-junction after another 700m, by ❾ **Warkworth Beach car park** on your right. Turn right here, signposted NCN1. After 300m we come a T-junction with the A1068, as we reach Warkworth. Cross over the A-road (look out for traffic) and turn left, back across the medieval bridge over the River Coquet. Continue up Bridge Street through the town and first right back into ❶ **Dial Place**. There are railings by the lamp posts here in the little square where you can lock up your bike, as well as a couple of pubs and a convenience store.

And it's definitely worth visiting **Warkworth Castle**, just up the hill (see box, page 153) – perhaps after some refreshment and giving your legs a rest before one last climb!

## THE ESSENTIALS

**GETTING THERE** By road, Warkworth is just over 50km north of Newcastle upon Tyne via the A1 and Morwick Road. By train, the nearest main-line station is at Alnmouth, with direct services on LNER (🖰lner. co.uk) from Newcastle taking 25–45 minutes, with the X18 MAX bus from Alnmouth to Warkworth, on Arriva North East (🖰arrivabus.co.uk/ north-east), taking approximately 15 minutes.

**FACILITIES** There are public toilets in Warkworth on Brewery Lane, off Dial Place, and opposite the Warkworth Beach car park near the end of this ride.

### WHERE TO EAT

✕ **Bertram's Café** Bridge St, Warkworth NE65 0XB; 🖰 01665 780700; 🖰 bertrams.co.uk. This popular little family-run café is a great pick for a tasty snack or homemade cake. The all-day b/fasts are a special highlight, including locally smoked Seahouses kippers & bacon butties, as well as several veggie options including avocado smash. Its two wood-burning stoves are a big draw in raw wintry weather; there's also a sheltered courtyard if alfresco dining appeals. **£**

✘ **Topsey Turvey** Dial Pl, Warkworth NE65
0UG; ☏ 01665 711338; ⌖ topseyturvey.
co.uk. This nostalgic restaurant in the centre
of Warkworth has a traditional English menu
to match, with classic favourites such as steak-
and-kidney pudding, & pie'n'chips; trifle,
lemon meringue pie & fruit crumbles feature
among its tempting desserts. It also does light
lunches, including jacket potatoes & sandwich
baguettes. Not sure why they chose the name –
perhaps because of the assorted knick-knacks,
paintings & gifts displayed for sale here too. **££**

✘ **Spurreli** The Old Chandlery, Coquet St,
Amble NE65 0DJ; ☏ 01665 710890; ⌖ spurreli.
com. A short ride down the riverside path to
Amble, this ice-cream parlour by the harbour
has avid fans across northeast England, winning
awards for its delicious, Italian-style artisan
ice cream (including non-dairy, gluten-free &
vegan flavours), as well as homemade scones,
cakes & warming soups in winter. Eat indoors or
at outdoor tables, or take-away. It's not cheap
but very highly recommended. **£**

## FURTHER INFORMATION

ℹ **Alnwick Tourist Information Centre**
Bondgate Without, Alnwick NE66 1PQ;
☏ 016670 622152. The nearest tourist
information centre is in Alnwick, based inside
the town centre's Playhouse. It has helpful staff
on hand for advice, with plenty of local leaflets,
maps and guidebooks available too.

# 16 CRASTER TO HOWICK LOOP

| | |
|---|---|
| **START/FINISH** | Craster |
| **DISTANCE/TIME** | 18.7km/2hrs |
| **DIFFICULTY/TERRAIN** | ① Mostly on paths and bridleways or quiet country roads, with some long but gradual hills |
| **SCENIC RATING** | © Beautiful coastline, with sandy beaches and sheltered coves; stunning views up the coast to Dunstanburgh Castle |
| **SUITABLE FOR** | Hybrid bike, gravel bike or MTB |
| **NCN ROUTE** | NCN1 |
| **MAPS** | OS Explorer 332 (1:25 000) |
| **KOMOOT REF** | 941999000 |

↑ The harbour at Craster (Gordon Bell/S)

This stunning coastal ride follows a figure-of-eight loop, sweeping southwards from Craster to Boulmer, then winding back inland via Longhoughton. En route, you could break the journey at Sugar Sands Beach, where oystercatchers, redshanks and curlews browse the shoreline. Or have a mosey around Howick Hall, where Earl Grey tea was invented. If you've got the time and energy to spare after all that, about an hour's walk up the coast are the majestic ruins of Dunstanburgh Castle. Lastly, you might be tempted to treat yourself to Craster's famous smoked fish and seafood, at its harbourside Jolly Fisherman Inn (see below).

The route is mostly off-road, including some rough and bumpy gravel tracks, narrow bridleways and paths, plus there are one or two long, but not steep, hills on B-roads and quiet back lanes. The first off-road section, across fields and through woods for a couple of kilometres to Howick Hall, is a little fiddly, so you'll probably have to go slowly and follow the directions carefully. But from then onwards the way is clear and well signposted. Overall, it's suitable for more confident and reasonably fit cyclists, including families with older children.

## THE ROUTE

Start from ❶ **Quarry car park** (pay-and-display), tucked inside a quarry behind Craster village. Turn left out of the car park, past the **Tourist Information Centre** (see below) on your left. Take the next left-hand turn soon after, on to **Windside Hill**, signposted Alnmouth.

Wind gradually uphill, coming shortly to **Craster Tower Gateway**. At the time of writing, this impressive 18th-century stone entrance to Craster is under repair and closed to motor vehicles, but accessible for cyclists and pedestrians. The gateway is made of whinstone rubble, the same stone as used for the core of nearby Dunstanburgh Castle. It originally formed part of Craster Tower, one of nearly 100 historic pele towers, which were built along the Anglo-Scottish border areas as a defence against Reiver raiders (see page 95).

Carry straight on, passing the Stable Yard Café (see below) on your left. After about 250m, go straight on over the crossroads (note that we come back here, from the left, at the end of the ride). Continue along the undulating road for around 1km, until just before **Craster West Farm** on the left you come to a ❷ **public bridleway** also

on your left, signposted Howick Hall Gates.

Turn left here and follow this muddy, grassy path through the trees. After about 100m, when you come out into a field, carry straight on. There's hardly any discernible path to follow here, but keep to the edge of the field. At the corner of the field, after another 200m, follow it around to the left, then after around 100m turn right through a gate, just before a line of electricity posts.

Carry straight on along the left-hand edge of another field, with ❸ **Northmoor Wood** on the left until, midway across the next field, you come to a gravel road, where you turn left. Follow this road, going gently downhill, for about 200m until it comes to a line of trees, where it winds left. Turn right off the road here and on to a grassy path through the trees. It's a narrow path under low-hanging branches, so go carefully.

Carry on downhill, keeping the stream on your left until, after around 300m, you come to a sign ahead, marked 'Private'. Turn left just before the sign, across the stream and on to another narrow path, soon coming out of the trees and into another field. At the T-junction, at the corner of the field, turn right. Now that we're emerging out of this fiddly stretch at last, glimpses of the sea sparkle between the trees ahead of us, luring us on…

Meanwhile, carry on downhill along the edge of the field, and after around 200m join a gravel road leading straight ahead. In another 500m, we come to a triangle with the entrance on the right to ❹ **Howick Hall**, the ancestral residence of the Grey family. It was here, in the 1820s, that oil of bergamot was added to counteract the taste of lime in the water, producing what became Earl Grey tea. Howick Hall, with informal gardens and arboretum, is open to visitors ( howickhallgardens.com).

At the triangle, turn left on to the road, heading quite steeply down towards the coast. Continue for around 800m until we come to a junction, with the main road winding left. Turn right here, through a small car park and on to a wide but rough and rubbly farm track. Pass **Sea Houses Farm** on your left, with the rocky shoreline and sparkling sea just beyond.

Carry straight on, coming to a sign on the left after about 800m, marking the nearby site of an **Iron Age fort**. There's no sign of the fort here today, but the English Heritage sign tells of the Iron Age defensive settlements that were dotted all along the coastline, in readiness for potential invasions, such as the coming Viking raiders.

↑ Howick Hall (Gail Johnson/S)

A little further on we cross a bridge (too narrow to cycle) over Howick Burn and come right down to the shoreline, with sandy beaches sheltered between rocky headlands. The first is **Sugar Sands**, an idyllic soft-sand beach backed by grassy dunes, with terns, oystercatchers and skittering redshanks picking through the weeds and rock pools.

Continue past Sugar Sands and around the next headland is the similarly delightful ❺ **Howdiemont Sands** (with a car park). Ignore the side road here leading to Longhoughton, and carry on south along the shoreside path. The fields on our right are edged with low stone walls, decorated here and there with quirky bird sculptures which look as if they've been repurposed from old bits of farm machinery (see the komoot map for a wide-eyed owl and what might be a gull and a crow).

Around 1.8km later the track runs back on to a paved road as we come into ❻ **Boulmer**. Turn right at the junction just in front of **St Andrew's Church** on the corner, signposted Craster. Follow the road, a gentle climb inland, passing **RAF Boulmer** airbase on your left. After 2.5km, we come to a T junction on the outskirts of ❼ **Longhoughton**, a simple, working village with a supermarket and a couple of cafés, including the Running Fox (see below). Turn right here, signposted Craster: we're now, thankfully, heading downhill for a while. Pass the **Parish Church of Saints Peter and Paul** on your left and note the stone sculpture opposite, looking somewhat like a knotted cable. Made by Gilbert Ward, a local sculptor, it was erected in 2004 on the site of an ancient cross, which marked this point on the pilgrimage route from Holy Island to Durham.

Carry on through and out of Longhoughton, still pleasantly downhill. After 1km, after a right-hand bend in the road, we come to a junction where the B1339 bears left, signposted Craster. Turn right here (look out for traffic coming round the corner) on to a smaller road, signposted Howick Hall. The road winds between the trees along the banks of Howick Burn. After about 1km, it crosses the stream, dips under a footbridge and climbs back up to the entrance-way on the left to Howick Hall – where we came down the gravel trail earlier on.

Stay on the road now, though, as before, as it winds right and descends towards the coast. After around 500m, turn left (off the NCN1) into the

## KIPPERS!

Despite having a string of majestic, historic castles for neighbours, up and down the coast from Bamburgh to Warkworth, the little fishing harbour of Craster is still best known as the home of the humble kipper.

The salty fish, which is a smoked herring, has long been a traditional breakfast dish across the UK. The former estate of Craster Manor was held in 1785 by Shafto Craster, who is credited with starting the local fish-smoking industry which is still producing kippers today. The historical truth is perhaps disputed, though, as the origin of the kipper itself is attributed to a Mr John Woodger from Seahouses, some 20km up the coast from Craster. He apparently accidentally 'invented' the kipper sometime in the 1840s, when he discovered the smoked fish one morning, having accidentally left it over a smoking stove overnight.

I'm not able to dig any deeper into the history than that, and certainly wouldn't want to trigger a feud between the two towns. Nevertheless, Craster kippers are rated by many as the best in the country, with the Robson Smokehouse now the only remaining producer in the village. You can buy kippers here as well as smoked salmon, haddock and cod, but The Jolly Fisherman (see page 163) is also highly rated as one of the best places on the Northumberland coast for its fish dishes. And of course, all the best B&Bs around here include kipper on the menu, whether from Craster or Seahouses.

hamlet of ❽ **Howick**, a sleepy little huddle of bungalows and holiday cottages overlooking the coast. The road winds through the village and, at the T-junction on the coast, turn left to rejoin the NCN1 and head northwards back up the coast towards Craster.

As we climb up the hill from the T-junction, we come to a **lay-by** on the left and a small sign in the hedgerow on our right, pointing left along the cliff edge to **Howick Scar**, the tip of a prominent limestone escarpment that stretches across the fields and up to a headland, ❾ **Cullernose Point**. It's only a 5-minute walk to the clifftop, dramatically jutting out into the sea, which is a great place to see hundreds of fulmars, terns and other

seabirds swirling around to perch precariously on the narrow ledges of the guano-splattered rock face.

From Howick Scar, continue up the road, bearing inland now and mostly level. After about 1.5km we come to a junction near **Dunstan**, where we turn right, signposted Craster and Dunstanburgh, on to **Windyside Hill**. Carry on along the straight road and through the **Craster Tower Gateway**, under which we passed at the start of our ride. The road then sweeps on a downhill run to a T-junction, where we turn right and back into Craster, with ❶ **Quarry car park** a few hundred metres ahead on the right.

This is the end of the ride, but Craster is a very picturesque fishing harbour worth spending some time in (famous for its smoked fish; see box, page 161). It's also the gateway to the magnificent clifftop ruins of **Dunstanburgh Castle**, about an hour's walk from here. These date from 1313, when the castle was first built by Thomas, Earl of Lancaster. It was built up over successive centuries and wars, with the Lancastrians holding off their Yorkist rivals until it finally fell in 1464.

## THE ESSENTIALS

**GETTING THERE** By road, the quickest way to Craster from Newcastle upon Tyne is via the A1, just under 66km; or for a scenic coastal route

↑ Cullernose Point (Dave Head/S)

via Tynemouth, Whitley Bay, Blyth, Amble and Warkworth on the A1058, A189 and A1068, it's just over 78km. The nearest train station is at Alnmouth, 14km to the south, which has regular trains from Newcastle on the East Coast Main Line (⌀ crosscountrytrains.co.uk; ⌀ lner.co.uk), taking 25–45 minutes.

**FACILITIES** There are public toilets next to the Tourist Information Centre in Craster (see below), as well as toilets for customers in cafés mentioned below, en route

## WHERE TO EAT

✖ **The Jolly Fisherman** Craster NE66 3TR; ✆ 01665 576461; ⌀ thejollyfishermancraster.co.uk. Overlooking Craster's tiny fishing harbour, this gem of a pub restaurant is famed for some of the tastiest fish & seafood on the Northumbrian coast, with local specialities including Lindisfarne oysters, Craster lobster & crab soup made from Craster crab. Tables in the fireside bar are cosy, or the seafront terrace is very scenic; the bar stocks local real ales & there's a take-away fish'n'chip van out front if you can't get a table. It's very popular so booking is highly advisable. **££**

✖ **The Running Fox** Longhoughton NE66 3AG; ✆ 01665 660721; ⌀ runningfoxbakery.co.uk. This cracking little café & artisan bakery in the middle of the village has tables indoors or outdoors on the front lawn. It does a huge range of b/fasts, from full English to porridge, including vegan & gluten-free, as well as lunches & afternoon teas. **£**

✖ **The Stable Yard Café** Craster Tower, Craster NE66 3SS; ✆ 01665 571240; ⓕ The Stable Yard. Next to the historic Craster Tower Gateway at the entrance to Craster, this cute little café has tables indoors or outside in the stable courtyard (handy for propping up your bike while you eat). It serves homemade cakes, scones & other hot & cold snacks – its sausage rolls & coleslaw are particular favourites. **£**

## FURTHER INFORMATION

ⓘ **Craster Tourist Information Centre** Craster NE66 3TW; ✆ 01665 576007; ⌀ visitnorthumberland.com. This handy little information centre is on the outskirts of town, opposite Quarry car park. Lots of useful leaflets & maps are available, as well as advice & booking of local attractions.

# 17 AMBLE TO BAMBURGH

| | |
|---|---|
| **START/FINISH** | Amble/Bamburgh |
| **DISTANCE/TIME** | 47.6km/5–5½hrs |
| **DIFFICULTY/TERRAIN** | ② Mostly on quiet country lanes or off-road coastal paths; there are not many hills but, as the longest ride in the book, it's best suited for fit, experienced cyclists |
| **SCENIC RATING** | © Along one of the UK's most spectacular stretches of coastline, guarded by a chain of historic castles |
| **SUITABLE FOR** | Gravel bike, hybrid or MTB |
| **NCN ROUTE** | NCN1 |
| **MAPS** | OS Explorer 332 and 340 (1:25 000) |
| **KOMOOT REF** | 983461789 |

↑ Dunstanburgh Castle (Dave Head/S)

This stunning ride wends its way northwards along the beautiful Northumbrian coastline. We hop from one ancient castle to another, from Warkworth up to Bamburgh, looping inland around the majestic Dunstanburgh Castle, its jagged ruins still defying the elements today. This virtual historical tour illustrates the major role these citadels played in British history, from the Celts and the Romans to the Wars of the Roses and the Anglo-Scottish wars.

Starting from Amble, we follow the River Coquet up past Warkworth Castle, then on to Alnmouth, soaking up ever more breath-taking views up the coast with its sand dunes and long, sandy beaches. After Howick we wind inland, but return to the coast at Beadnell before finally coming to Bamburgh, the ancient home of the Anglo-Saxon kings of Northumbria.

The ride largely follows NCN1 (Coast & Castles Cycle Route), including one or two detours as indicated below.

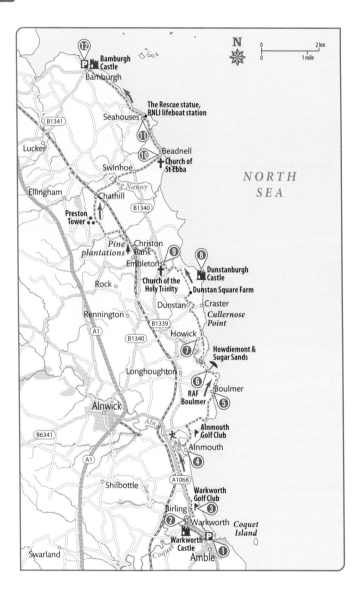

# THE ROUTE

Start at ❶ **Amble Braid car park** on the outskirts of Amble, a fishing port on the mouth of the River Coquet. Turn right out of the car park on to the cycle path, running along the right-hand side of the road with the river on your right. The riverbank and mudflats are favourite sites for wading birds including curlews, oystercatchers and avocets. And if you're as lucky as I was here, you might even see a shimmering cloud of starlings perform a murmuration over the water.

Follow the cycle path up to ❷ **Warkworth**, about 1km from here, with **Warkworth Castle** towering high over the Coquet. The castle dates from around the early 12th century, built on a strategic mound over a loop in the river. English Heritage has preserved the castle in its gracious state of ruin, like a battle-scarred boxer, marking its busy centuries of warfare. As we approach the town, the path winds left away from the river and up to a T-junction. Turn right here and then it's downhill through the town centre (it's safer to join the road now as the path crosses driveways and there may be more people walking here too).

Carry on down through the town, past the foot of the castle on your left. At the bottom of the hill, pass St Lawrence's Church behind Dial Place on your left, before coming to two adjacent bridges over the river. Take the cobblestoned medieval footbridge on the left, then cross over the **A1068** – look out for oncoming traffic – on to the side road opposite.

Follow this road uphill for 300m, then turn left on to a rough gravelly side road, passing ❸ **Warkworth Golf Club** on your right. It's one of many golf courses along this stretch of coast, perhaps inspired by the proximity to Scotland, birthplace of the noble sport. The gravel road soon winds left to a T-junction with the A1068; turn right here on to the cycle path, which runs alongside the A-road but is sheltered from the traffic by hedgerows. It undulates up and down between the road and the fields, giving sweeping views of the coastline, fringed with a bank of dunes and Alnmouth not far ahead, on the Aln Estuary. And if you look back southwards, you'll also see **Coquet Island**, its tall lighthouse silhouetted against the sea, just off Amble. This was one of various remote sites along the Northumbrian coast where St Cuthbert and other early pilgrims hunkered down against the raging North Sea. Today, though, Coquet is an RSPB protected nature reserve (see box, page 143).

Continue along the cycle path for around 3km, until we come to the mouth of the River Aln, with ❹ **Alnmouth** behind a fringe of pine trees on its north bank. The path winds downhill to the right, around the estuary mudbanks, then left to a T-junction with the B1338, which leads into Alnmouth.

Turn right here, opposite Alnmouth Cricket and Croquet Club, and on to the road. Cross the bridge over the river and straight on, uphill to a mini-roundabout on the edge of the town. Turn left, the first exit, signposted Boulmer and Foxton, still climbing up and over the headland. After 100m or so, pass the **Old School Gallery and Café** on the left (see below), with the road continuing uphill. It's getting quite steep now, but giving us expansive views inland. If you pause for breath at one of the gaps between the trees, you can see over a graceful U-bend in the River Aln and beyond to the rolling Cheviot Hills, inside the Northumberland National Park.

Eventually, after a steady climb for around 1km, we come out of the trees at the top and wind downhill for a few hundred metres until we come to an angled T-junction. Turn right here, signposted Craster, heading

↑ The 'Fence to Nowhere' at Sugar Sands, built to prevent grazing cattle from wandering across the rocky coastline (coxy58/S)

back towards the coast. Carry on downhill now for about 1.5km, past **Alnmouth Golf Club** on your right, then levelling out as we return almost to sea level and into ❺ **Boulmer**. This quiet hamlet comprises a scattering of seafront cottages, a cosy inn (see the **Fishing Boat Inn**, page 214), and a few fishing boats on the beach, though the peace may be shattered occasionally with overflying aircraft from the nearby RAF Boulmer.

Carry on straight ahead and out of Boulmer, with views of the wide sandy beach almost within reach now, close enough to hear the waves breaking on the shore. We're only 100m or less from the seashore here, the wide sands giving way to eroded boulders and rock pools – a haven for seabirds. At one point I was startled by the plaintive peep of oystercatchers picking through the seaweed along the high-tide line.

After continuing northwards for another 1km or so, you might make out the hazy outline of Dunstanburgh Castle on the horizon: beckoning us onwards or warning us off? A couple of kilometres beyond Boulmer, at the lovely soft-sanded beach of ❻ **Howdiemont Sands**, we come to an optional on-road detour inland, where the NCN1 splits in two. If you're not on a hybrid or gravel bike, or don't fancy the off-road rough and tumble coming up shortly, turn left here and right through **Longhoughton**, to rejoin the coast route again after around 7km at **Howick** (see Route 16, page 156). Otherwise, carry straight on, with increasingly gorgeous views of the coastline as we head north. After passing another stunning beach, **Sugar Sands**, cross a narrow bridge over a stream, Howick Burn. Hold on tight here, the forewarned bumpy stretch is coming up – with some sandy and grassy patches in the hollow dips, which could be slippery in wet weather.

Around 4km from Boulmer, by Sea Houses Farm on the right, we're finally off the rough track and on to a paved road – enjoy that while it lasts! And a few hundred metres further on, at ❼ **Howick**, the detour from Longhoughton rejoins our main route. The road begins to wind slowly away from the sea now and we start to climb uphill, heading towards a long, low stony ridge on the horizon to the north. After about 500m, as we come to the top of the hill and reach this rock fault, there's a sign on the right by a footpath to Howick Scar: a popular birdwatching site. A few minutes' walk from here, tall cliffs jut out into the sea at **Cullernose**

**Point**, offering a prime breeding site for seabirds including terns, fulmars and kittiwakes (the noisiest of the bunch, named after their screech).

Winding inland now, about 1.5km beyond Howick Scar we come to a crossroads near **Dunstan**. Turn right here towards **Craster**, then 500m later take the next left. Carry on for another 500m until the road climbs up through a small grove of trees, where we turn right through Dunstan. Go through the village and, after around 400m, turn right on to a farm road (signposted NCN1). Follow this towards the sea, then bear left at **Dunstan Square Farm** to skirt northwards across country, with ➑ **Dunstanburgh Castle** beyond the fields to the right. Its lonely tower stands proud on its coastal perch, as if still lording it over us mortals on two wheels below. Similar to Warkworth Castle, Dunstanburgh has been carefully preserved as magnificent ruins, much as it has been since the Middle Ages. (Unfortunately for cyclists, access to the castle is by foot only via the Coast Path, either from Craster or Dunstan Steads. If you have the time for a return visit, though, this is one of the most awesome historic monuments in Northumberland.)

The farm road joins the main road after around 1.7km at Dunstan Steads, winding to the left just before the village and coming out at a right-angled bend in the road. Carry straight on here, then wind downhill to the left and right steeply uphill again, into ➒ **Embleton**. Turn right at the T-junction after 1km and into this pretty village. Pass the Blue Bell Inn on your right then, around 100m later, turn right at the T-junction on to the B1339, in front of the **Church of the Holy Trinity** (note the book-swap stall in front, for the interest of bookworms like this writer).

Take the next left-hand turning shortly after the church to meander roughly northwest now, through flat arable fields and forestry conifer **plantations**. Turn left at a T-junction 2km after Embleton, then right after 500m in front of a modern housing development on the outskirts of **Christon Bank**. Go straight on over a level crossing (the East Coast Main Line) and through pine plantations either side of the road. Climbing uphill now, turn left at a T-junction signposted Seahouses. The road winds around to the north again now, past a turning to **Preston Tower** on your left. This 14th-century pele tower was one of the dozens of fortifications

## ST AIDAN'S CHURCH, BAMBURGH

Bamburgh Castle, unsurprisingly, is the major draw for most visitors to the little village midway up the Northumbrian coast. But the Norman Church of St Aidan is a historic gem that is full of its own ancient wonders. It is named after St Aidan, the early Christian saint who travelled to Lindisfarne in AD635 to spread the gospel. Aidan died here in this church in AD651, as was recorded by the Venerable Bede, author of the *Ecclesiastical History of the English People*, widely considered one of the most important English historical texts. In Aidan's lifetime, one of his best-known feats was when Bamburgh Castle was being threatened with fire by Penda, king of Mercia, in AD651. Aidan saw the fire from his retreat on the Farne Islands and, as a result of his prayers, the wind changed direction and the castle was saved. There is a beam inside St Aidan's Church tower which is thought to be the same 'incombustible' beam that Bede mentions as one of those from Bamburgh Castle, which survived the fire and which also supported the awning in the church under which Aidan died.

There is a memorial chapel to St Aidan inside the church today, which attracts pilgrims from around the world, particularly to mark the hour of the saint's death at 15.00 on 31 August each year.

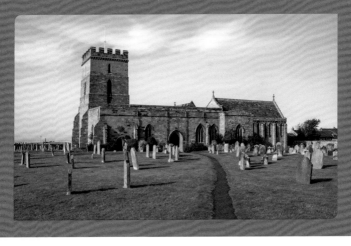

↑ The Norman Church of St Aidan in Bamburgh (chrisdorney/S)

built in Northumberland during the Anglo-Scottish wars (see box, page 95). The tower is open to the public and is around 250m down the road on the left (⚲ prestontower.co.uk).

Continuing northwards for around 1.5km, we go over another level crossing at **Chathill**, then eastwards, happily, back to the coast at Beadnell. (We're detouring here off the NCN1, which cuts across to Seahouses, in order to make the most of this glorious coastline.) So, carry straight on here, downhill at first over the Long Nanny stream, then uphill to **Swinhoe**. It's nice to see fields of sheep and cattle again, here at this farm hamlet, after the rather bland arable fields we've just been through. Continue straight ahead, joining the B1340 at Swinhoe until, after a couple more kilometres, we reach the coast again at ❿ **Beadnell**. This popular little seaside resort has a handful of holiday cottages, a campsite and a good café (see Saltwater Café, below) opposite the parish **Church of St Ebba**. We're more than three-quarters of the way to Bamburgh by now, so you might be feeling peckish.

Follow the road to the left around Beadnell, then join the compacted gravel path running along the right-hand side of the road. Note that the Coast Path also runs parallel here, so there are unlikely to be many walkers on the roadside path with you, but still give way if you do come across any pedestrians. The roadside path continues all the way up to Seahouses, around 3km north of Beadnell. You can't always see the sea from here – it's mostly hidden behind a grassy bank of dunes – but it's a lovely flat road and you can at least smell the salty sea air!

Coming into ⓫ **Seahouses** the path comes to an end, so join the main road and turn right at a mini-roundabout into the town centre. Similar to Beadnell, Seahouses is a slightly bigger and more bustling seaside resort, with the addition of a few souvenir shops, fast-food take-aways and an **RNLI lifeboat station**. There are also several harbourside companies here, offering boat trips to Coquet Island and the Farne islands (see box, page 143). At the next roundabout, take the second exit, then join another roadside path on the right next to the *Rescue* statue (above the RNLI).

Similar to the Beadnell roadside path – also with a parallel Coast Path – continue northwards up the coast. Now, though, we have the added

spectacle of Bamburgh Castle, looming larger on the horizon, and the crashing waves beyond the sand dunes on our right. About 1km out of Seahouses the path on the right comes to an abrupt end at a small car park, so cross over the road here as it continues on the left instead.

As we approach ⑫ **Bamburgh**, just over 4km from Seahouses, it's safer to join the road since we're passing suburban houses with driveways crossing the path. Looming ahead on a steep rocky outcrop are the massive ramparts of **Bamburgh Castle** (⊘bamburghcastle.com), another majestic sentinel of the Northumbrian coast. Unlike the ruins at Warkworth and

↑ Bamburgh Castle (Dave Head/S)

Dunstanburgh, however, Bamburgh has been restored since its Anglo-Saxon roots under King Oswald, one of England's earliest Christian pilgrims. With its state rooms still sumptuously furnished, the castle gives a powerful impression of the dramatic history it has lived through – despite being the first to fall to gunpowder bombardment in the Wars of the Roses.

Coming into Bamburgh, the road bears left and past the castle on your right – also passing what must be the most picturesque cricket pitch in the world. Then take the next right-hand turning on to the Wynding. Follow this road down towards the beach and shortly on your right is Bamburgh Beach car park. It's an ideal stopping point for the village, with a handful of pubs and cafés (see **The Copper Kettle**, below) facing the village green, but also only about 15 minutes' walk to the castle.

## THE ESSENTIALS

**GETTING THERE** By road, Amble is just over 50km north of Newcastle upon Tyne via the A1, or for a more scenic coastal route via Tynemouth, Whitley Bay and Blyth on the A1058, A189 and A1068, it's just over 58km. The nearest train station is at Alnmouth, 14km to the south, which has regular trains from Newcastle on the East Coast Main Line (⊘ crosscountrytrains.co.uk; ⊘ lner.co.uk) taking 25–45 minutes, plus around 30 minutes on the X20 or X18 bus with Arriva North East (⊘ arrivabus.co.uk/north-east).

**FACILITIES** There are public toilets in Amble, Seahouses and Bamburgh, and cafés en route have toilets for customers.

### WHERE TO EAT

✕ **The Old School Gallery Café** Foxton Rd, Alnmouth NE66 3NH; ⊘ 01665 850554; ⊘ theoldschoolgallery.co.uk. On the edge of town, this gallery/café sits nicely on our route to Bamburgh: perfect for refuelling before the long hill coming up. It serves snacks, pizzas (from mobile van, Thu–Sun), cakes, tray bakes, tea & coffee, and has tables outdoors in the playground. **£**

✕ **Saltwater Café** The Wynding, Beadnell NE67 5AS; ⊘ 01665 720333; ⊘ northcoastcollective.uk/saltwatercafe. This great little gastro-bistro opposite the village church offers a tempting range of b/fasts, afternoon teas & a contemporary dinner menu focusing on local produce, including fish & shellfish. It's tucked away in the heart of this quiet village, but well worth going out of the way for. **££**

✖ **The Copper Kettle** 21 Front St, Bamburgh NE69 7BW; ✆ 01668 214315; ⌁ copperkettlebamburgh.co.uk. Overlooking the village green in the centre of Bamburgh, this traditional tearoom serves delicious homemade cakes, fresh-baked scones & savoury snacks, including haggis & locally caught 'kipper in a bun'; it has several snug dining rooms & a patio garden (with back alley for locking up bikes). It's very popular, so worth booking ahead. **££**

## FURTHER INFORMATION

ℹ **Tourist Information Centre** Quarry car park, Craster NE66 3TW; ✆ 01665 576007. The nearest tourist information centre to Bamburgh is here in Craster, with staff available for local advice & booking facilities (ie: for coastal castles & birdwatching boat trips), as well as guidebooks & maps for sale.

# 18 WOOLER TO LINDISFARNE

| | |
|---|---|
| **START/FINISH** | Wooler/Lindisfarne |
| **DISTANCE/TIME** | 33.3km/3–3½hrs |
| **DIFFICULTY/TERRAIN** | ② Mostly on B-roads and back lanes, apart from a short off-road detour to St Cuthbert's Cave; undulating terrain, mostly downhill to the coast makes it suitable for moderately fit cyclists, including families with older children |
| **SCENIC RATING** | ⑥ Tranquil countryside, from the Cheviot Hills and moorland to the coast; historic St Cuthbert's Cave and the Holy Island of Lindisfarne |
| **SUITABLE FOR** | Gravel bike or hybrid |
| **NCN ROUTE** | Partly on Sandstone Way and NCN1 |
| **MAPS** | OS Explorer 340 (1:25 000) |
| **KOMOOT REF** | 945650742 |

↑ Lindisfarne Castle (Michael Conrad/S)

T his scenic route from countryside to coast is like a 'Best of Northumbria' package; with its combination of river valley, moorland, forest and coastline, sprinkled with some stunning historic monuments.

From the traditional market town of Wooler, at the foot of the Cheviots, we wind northeast across the lush valley of the River Till, down to the coast and the Holy Island of Lindisfarne, one of the earliest Christian sites in the British Isles. En route, we climb off-road briefly (on to St Cuthbert's Way) to visit St Cuthbert's Cave: an age-worn grotto high on the moors, where monks were said to have brought the saint's body in AD875, before taking it to his final resting place on Lindisfarne.

Meandering cross-country, we soak up stunning views over the valley to the rounded Cheviot Hills, and as we descend to the coast we're drawn on by the magical sight of Lindisfarne Castle, perched on its crag on Holy Island, one of the most important pilgrimage sites in early English Christianity.

Note that this ride partly follows the Sandstone Way & the NCN1 (Coast & Castles Cycle Route), both of which are well signposted, but with directions given below where we detour off the set routes.

Finally, a pedantic point: the names Holy Island and Lindisfarne are both used for the island; sometimes, as above, both together. For the sake of brevity, I have stuck to Lindisfarne (mostly!)

## THE ROUTE

Start at ❶ **Padgepool Place car park**, next to the Tourist Information Centre/Library in the centre of Wooler. It's a vibrant and traditional market town at the foot of the Cheviot Hills, popular as a base for adventurous off-road cycling and walking routes. Turn right and downhill through the High Street, then at the bottom, on Market Place, turn left on to Church Street, which winds steeply downhill to the Wooler Water River. Cross over the A697 and then take a right–left dogleg to cross the iron bridge over the river.

Continue along the B6348, on the level now and out into the countryside, with open moorland on your right and the rounded Cheviot Hills on the horizon to your left. Go straight on for about 2.7km then, just before the B6348 starts climbing up over the fell, turn left and over an old stone bridge across the River Till, with literally dazzling views over the water towards the Cheviots. The 16th-century ❷ **Weetwood Bridge** is a Grade II-listed monument, commemorated as a stopping place of the English army on 9 September 1513, the day before the historic Battle of Flodden.

As the road bears left, 300m after the bridge, carry on straight ahead to a smaller lane, signposted Hortons and Lowick. We climb quite steeply for a short way but the road then levels out, rolling gently through the valley. Carry on for around 1km, with the road then winding around to the right for another couple of kilometres, through ❸ **West Horton** and **East Horton**, farming hamlets on opposite banks of a little stream, Horton Burn. After a nice downhill stretch for 2km we come to a T-junction, where we turn left on to the B6349 (a continuation of the B6348 that we took out of Wooler), signposted Belford.

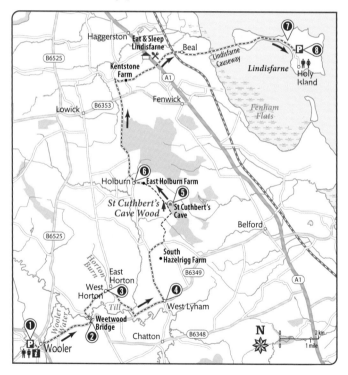

At a crossroads by the hamlet of ❹ **West Lyham**, about 1km after the T-junction, turn left again on to a smaller road, signposted Holburn. Carry on up this road for around 2.5km and, about 500m after passing **South Hazelrigg Farm** on your right, we come to a side road on the right – opposite a statue of St Cuthbert – signposted Belford. This is our off-road 5km detour to St Cuthbert's Cave: well worth it, by the way, not just because of the history of this early Christian saint, but also for the fun of rambling across unspoilt moorland and getting even more stunning views of the Cheviots. (If you don't fancy the uphill off-road challenge, however, carry straight on here and rejoin our main route after 3.7km in Holburn.)

About 1km up the Belford road, as it winds uphill to the right, turn left on to a gravel track. The gravel track soon turns into a wide, grassy path, continuing straight ahead then winding uphill towards a pine forest plantation. After 900m, at a crossroads in the path between two fields, we turn right, back on to a gravel track and then a grassy path, climbing gradually towards the trees. In about another 800m, we go through a gate and turn left along the edge of the forest.

The tree-side path here is grassy, levelling out after the long climb up from the valley, but with a few bumps and dips. Look out too for wildlife here in this remote spot: on my recent ride I was startled first by a hare bounding across a field, and then a roe deer fawn, tiptoeing shyly towards me then bounding silently into the undergrowth.

Reaching the edge of the plantation, in about 800m, we go through a gate into St Cuthbert's Cave Wood, an airy pine grove, with ❺ **St Cuthbert's Cave** itself up a short path signposted on the right. The sandstone overhang is worn and blackened with campfire ashes on the sandy floor, left perhaps by modern-day pilgrims. From up here you can see over the trees and back towards the Cheviots. It's a lonely but peaceful spot, and it's not difficult to imagine the monks braving the elements to seek shelter here nearly 1,400 years ago (see box, page 181).

Go back to the main path below, and turn right to leave the woods through another gate. At the fork in the path go straight on, winding left downhill through the bracken (with St Cuthbert's Way continuing up over the moor to the right). After about 1km, through a couple of gated fields and over Poplar Burn, the path becomes narrower, more overgrown with prickly gorse and bumpier too. If you get sidetracked, though, the path winds left generally, and downhill overall, heading towards Holburn. Coming at last to one final gate, go through and carry on ahead (leaving the Sandstone Way, signposted right here) on to a gravel road, passing **East Holburn Farm** on your right.

Coming out of ❻ **Holburn** at a T-junction, turn right and, after all that slogging through the gorse and bracken, enjoy a lovely long downhill run through fields and farms (note this is where you rejoin our main route if you gave St Cuthbert's Cave a miss and went straight on instead at South Hazelrigg Farm, above).

After about 3km, at a crossroads with the B6353, carry straight on, signposted Haggerston, then 500m later turn right, signposted Kentstone and Beal. Climb uphill for a few hundred metres until you come to **Kentstone Farm** on the right, with a glorious wide panorama of the coast spreading out below. Follow the road downhill again now for another 1km or so, coming to the A1, the main arterial route through Northumberland. It's a single carriageway here, with filter lanes, but it's flat and straight in either direction to see oncoming traffic. Nevertheless, cross over carefully – safer to dismount – and carry on to Holy Island Road opposite.

Follow the cycle path down the right of the road, as it can get busy here during the summer holiday season. And before whizzing down for a final downhill spree, check the tide tables for crossing the Causeway over to Lindisfarne (⌖holyislandcrossingtimes.northumberland.gov.uk). There are two crossings a day, but at high tide it is not safe for any vehicle to cross (although I met three Norwegians who waded across up to their waists, following the Pilgrims Way marker posts, it is definitely not safe for cycling!). If you're too late or early, though, there's the Lindisfarne Inn, here at the A1 crossing, or the **Eat & Sleep Lindisfarne** hostel and café, just behind the pub (see below).

Otherwise, carry on down through Beal and over the level crossing, with the path running parallel to either the left- or right-hand side of the road; then after the Barn at Beal (see below) continuing on a rough gravel

## ST CUTHBERT OF LINDISFARNE – A THIN PLACE

There are certain places around the world which are revered for their special spiritual aura and a perceived proximity between Heaven and Earth. Lindisfarne is one of these so-called 'Thin Places', attracting pilgrims for more than 1,500 years to this end-of-the-Earth outpost.

Perhaps in response to Roman Catholics making spiritual journeys to saints' shrines, the Anglo-Saxon world also introduced its own shrines, one of the first and most important being on Lindisfarne to honour St Cuthbert. During his period as a hermit on one of the Farne Islands, Cuthbert's piety gained widespread fame: ironic perhaps, for someone in search of solitude. Nevertheless, Cuthbert reluctantly accepted his appointment as Bishop of Lindisfarne, from AD684 to AD686. He then spent a year travelling and preaching the Gospel, but finally returned to the Farne Islands, where he died in AD687. When his body was exhumed and found to be uncorrupted, 11 years after burial, Cuthbert was canonised and his remains eventually brought back to his final place of rest on Lindisfarne.

St Cuthbert's Way is now a firmly established pilgrimage, drawing Christians from across the UK and beyond. Starting in Melrose, in the Scottish Borders, the path runs for 100km across Northumberland to Lindisfarne, following the eight-year journey taken by monks carrying the saint's body with them.

↑ Statue of St Cuthbert, near South Hazelrigg Farm (Huw Hennessy)

track. (Note that, if you're not planning to go on to Holy Island but instead continue northwards to the Scottish border then, shortly after passing the Barn at Beal, the NCN1 turns left and leads north to Berwick-upon-Tweed, which is also our next route; see page 184.)

❼ **Lindisfarne** is a hugely popular landmark and historic destination, both for tourists and pilgrims, so be prepared for queues of traffic heading over to the island. And go carefully on the **Lindisfarne Causeway**: it is paved but immersed by the sea twice a day, so it can be wet and slippery.

Follow the road winding to the north end of the island, where the priory and castle face each other across the sheltered harbour – one of the most spectacular sights in Northumberland, if not the whole of the UK. Before we reach the harbour, though, we come to ❽ **Chare Ends car park**, which is the end of the ride.

Tide times permitting, a longer stay at Lindisfarne is a must. Besides its medieval priory (⊘ english-heritage.org.uk) and 16th-century Lindisfarne Castle (⊘ nationaltrust.org.uk/lindisfarne-castle), the island boasts long sandy beaches which are perfect for walking, and also wildlife watching, from roe deer grazing in the sand dunes to wading birds massing on the mudbanks by the Causeway.

## THE ESSENTIALS

**GETTING THERE** By road, Wooler is 75km north of Newcastle upon Tyne via the A1 and A697, or 98km southeast of Edinburgh via the A68. By train, the nearest station is at Alnmouth, around 25 minutes from Newcastle (⊘ crosscountrytrains.co.uk; ⊘ lner.co.uk), with the onward Arriva North East X20 MAX bus (⊘ arrivabus.co.uk/north-east) taking around 1½ hours.

**FACILITIES** There are public toilets in Wooler at the bus station, just off the High Street, and in Lindisfarne near the harbour, on Green Lane.

### WHERE TO EAT

✗ **Ramblers Café** 48 High St, Wooler NE71 6BG; ✆ 07514 413650; ⓕ Ramblers. This corner café at the bottom end of Wooler High St has a loyal local following for its great-value

& hearty fodder, including all-day b/fasts, bangers & mash, homemade soups, jacket potatoes, & home-baked cakes & pastries. Open daytime only, 09.00–15.00; closed Sun. **£**

**✕ Eat & Sleep Lindisfarne** West Mains Hse, Beal TD15 2PD; ✆ 01289 381827; ⊗ eatandsleeplindisfarne.co.uk. Tucked down a lane off the A1/Holy Island Road junction, this laid-back café is a popular pit stop with bikers (hence piles of motorbike magazines in the lobby). It offers a good-value menu, from all-day b/fasts to locally caught lobster and crab from Holy Island, as well as freshly made sandwiches, cakes & tray bakes. It's also a budget bunkhouse (see page 218), recently renovated after Storm Arwen damage in 2021. **£**

**✕ Pilgrims Coffee House** Marygate, Holy Island TD15 2SJ; ✆ 01289 389109; ⊗ pilgrimscoffee.com. In the centre of the village a couple of minutes' walk from Lindisfarne Priory, this little café roasts its own ethically sourced coffee beans &, in addition to a range of coffee, teas & other hot drinks, has homemade cakes, scones & a range of tempting sweet snacks. With a bright and airy walled garden it's very cosy on sunny days – or sheltered from winter winds too. **£**

## FURTHER INFORMATION

**🛈 Wooler Tourist Information Centre** Padgepool Pl, Wooler NE71 6BL; ✆ 01668 282123. Housed inside Wooler Library, behind the car park at the start of the ride, this excellent visitor centre has lots of local information, with helpful & knowledgeable staff on hand for advice. There's even a local produce stand & book swap, so you can feed your body & mind before setting off.

# 19 LINDISFARNE TO BERWICK-UPON-TWEED

| | |
|---|---|
| **START/FINISH** | Lindisfarne/Berwick-upon-Tweed |
| **DISTANCE/TIME** | 23.7km/2½hrs |
| **DIFFICULTY/TERRAIN** | ② Mostly off-road, on grassy paths and gravel tracks, with just a few road junctions at the end through Berwick-upon-Tweed (with optional road detour from Cocklawburns to Berwick) |
| **SCENIC RATING** | ⑧ With the Cheviots on the western horizon, head northwards up the coastal path, past wide sandy beaches and dunes to Berwick-upon-Tweed, near the Scottish border |
| **SUITABLE FOR** | Gravel or hybrid bike |
| **NCN ROUTE** | NCN1 and Sandstone Way |
| **MAPS** | OS Explorer 340 & 346 (1:25 000) |
| **KOMOOT REF** | 948726217 |

↑ Lindisfarne Causeway and refuge (Helen Hotson/S)

From the Holy Island of Lindisfarne to Berwick-upon-Tweed, the most northerly town in England, this coastal route winds up through the dunes, overlooking wide sandy beaches and craggy headlands, with the ever-present Cheviots straddling the horizon in the west. It's a wild and windswept route, mostly off-road or on minor B-roads and with no busy road crossings, so an ideal ride for novice riders looking to step up a gear. It's also a great ride for wildlife watching, from wading birds in the intertidal mudflats of Lindisfarne to possible sightings of dolphins and seals along the coast.

As the route starts on the tidal island, which is cut off by the sea twice a day, be sure to check the tide tables when you plan your ride (⌖ holyislandcrossingtimes. northumberland.gov.uk), as it is impassable at other times.

Note also that this ride is either on the NCN1 (Coast & Castles Cycle Route) or the Sandstone Way (sometimes both) until we reach Berwick. Both cycle paths are well signposted throughout, so directions are given below where we deviate on to other routes.

## THE ROUTE

Start from ❶ **Chare Ends car park** on the outskirts of Holy Island village. Turn right and cross over **Lindisfarne Causeway** to the mainland. As the road is flooded by the sea twice daily, it can be wet and slippery, so go carefully! With the windswept sand dunes on your right and coastal mudflats on your left, this is a great area for spotting wading shore birds, including turnstones, curlews and oystercatchers. If you're lucky, you might even spot a shy roe deer grazing in the dunes.

Coming on to the mainland, just as the road starts climbing up towards **Beal**, turn right on to the cycle path, signposted Berwick, on NCN1 (Coast & Castles Cycle Route) and the Sandstone Way. The track is smooth gravel at first but, after about 1km when you cross a small bridge over a stream, it narrows to a grassy path, with the tufts of grass and dunes on your right and the sea beyond. You might care to cast a farewell glance behind you over the sandbanks back to Lindisfarne, one of the most iconic images of Northumberland.

The grassy path continues on to a gravel trail, which passes Goswick Farm on your left after about 3km. This trail then becomes a paved road as we start looping inland away from the coast and skirting **Goswick Golf**

**Course** on our right. Follow the road turning left past the golf clubhouse and over a **level crossing**.

Meandering inland and gently up and down, after a couple of kilometres, as the road bears left towards Cheswick, turn right. Pass a Georgian hall,

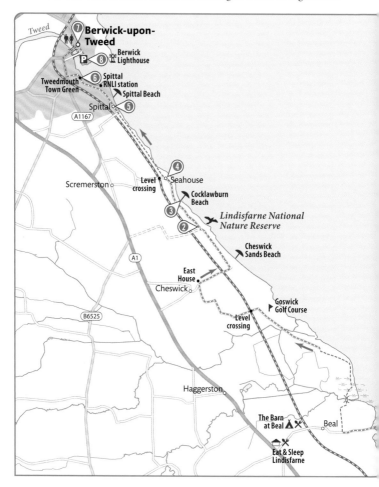

**East House**, and the adjacent Cheswick Farm on your left, with the sea coming into view again now, a short way ahead. Cross a humpbacked railway bridge and turn left on to a gravel path, alongside **Cheswick Sands Beach**. This beachside area is part of ❷ **Lindisfarne National Nature Reserve**, also including much of Lindisfarne itself. It comprises dunes, saltmarsh and mudflats; it's rich in wildlife, with 11 species of orchid as well as huge numbers of migratory birds, including rare light-bellied brent geese. With occasional glimpses of the sea from between the dune banks, you may also spot seals, dolphins and even whales offshore.

Continuing through the dunes, after just over 1km go straight on at an angled fork by the car park for ❸ **Cocklawburn Beach**. The road climbs slowly uphill now to the end of the beach, and from the top of the hill there are magnificent long-distance views back over the wide sands, down to Lindisfarne and even the hazy outline of Bamburgh Castle beyond.

Just beyond Cocklawburn Beach, at ❹ **Seahouse**, the road bears left. Follow this road if you want a smoother alternative to the off-road coastal path, which includes one steep downhill section on rough gravel. The road alternative heads inland, over a **level crossing**, right

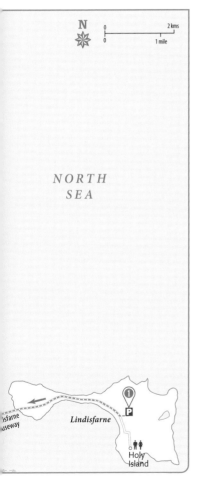

at the next T-junction, then winding around **Scremerston**, before turning right on to Sunnyside Cut – Northumberland Road (A1167). This road rejoins our main route just before crossing the bridge over the River Tweed into Berwick.

Otherwise, take the right-hand fork at Seahouse, then left on to a grassy path, through a gate and across a field. Now our nostalgic views back south are replaced by similarly splendid vistas northwards up the coast. Beyond the rocky headlands is sandy **Spittal Beach** and the Tweed Estuary, with the red-and-white **Berwick Lighthouse** at the mouth of the river. And beyond that: bonny Scotland!

Continue along this windy path for another 2km or so, over some muddy bumps and dips, until we go through another gate and into the residential outskirts of ❺ **Spittal**, on the south bank of the Tweed overlooking Berwick.

Carry on steeply downhill – take care here on steep and loose rubbly gravel – and into Spittal, almost at sea level now and with the East Coast Main Line behind tall fencing on the left. At a crossroads with Princes Street, go straight on along riverside Dock Road, past an RNLI lifeboat station and ❻ **Tweedmouth Town Green** on the right.

Continue along Dock Road for another 700m, approaching the two road bridges over the Tweed into ❼ **Berwick-upon-Tweed**. Turn left on Union Brae and immediately right on Prince Edward Road. At the mini-roundabout, join the shared cycle lane/footpath on the left over the Royal Tweed Bridge/A1167. (This is where the road detour from **Seahouse**, above, rejoins the main route.)

Once across over the Tweed Bridge, the cycle path turns left on to Bank Hill, which winds right and narrows alongside the old city wall (where cyclists have to dismount for the last few metres), leading up to a T-junction. Turn right on to Marygate, and right again on Hide Hill – Sandgate. Dismount again to go back under the old city wall and into ❽ **Quayside car park**, our final destination. We're right by the riverside here, with the **Lowry Café** adjacent (see below); Berwick Boat Trips ( berwickboattrips.co.uk) also start from here.

## LOWRY AND TURNER – THE ART ON TWEEDSIDE

Manchester-born artist L S Lowry is best known for his grim cityscapes, populated usually with downtrodden matchstick people, while J M W Turner is famous as one of England's greatest landscape artists, renowned for moody skies such as that depicted in his 1842 *Steamer in a Snowstorm*.

Both artists were also frequent visitors to the Tweedside border region, with Lowry coming to Berwick-upon-Tweed many times from the 1930s. For his part, Turner was drawn by the romantic ruins of Norham Castle, overlooking the river 13km upstream from Berwick.

With his genius for light and shade, Turner produced three paintings of Norham Castle, which he revisited several times in 1797, 1801 and 1831. *Norham Castle Sunrise*, in which he almost immerses the subject into the landscape, is still one of the artist's most popular works. Visitors to Norham today can stand on the village green and see how little the castle, overlooking the far end of the village, has changed since Turner's visits, as demonstrated by an information plaque illustrated with another of his paintings, *Norham Village and Castle* (1797). Critics have even asserted that, as Turner first visited Norham as a young man of 21 and then became obsessed with making many studies of the local landscape, this was the inspiration that made his name.

In recognition of the many visits that L S Lowry made to Berwick, meanwhile, the town has created a Lowry Trail, picking out the various sites in Berwick that featured in his paintings and drawings. In contrast to his famous but dark artworks, however, Lowry's paintings here were lighter and brighter, such as *On the Sands*, where his normally hunched characters now play happily on the beach. For details of the Lowry Trail, visit ⌖ berwickpreservationtrust.co.uk/lowry-trail/.

All in all, here's a good place to end our ride, with a few things to see and do in this attractive, historic town. Over the centuries, **Berwick** bounced to and fro between Scotland and England, like pass-the-parcel, and only officially settled on the English side in 1746. Surviving stretches of Elizabethan walls are reminders of its embattled past; there's also a

thriving market (Marygate, on Wednesday and Sunday) and a network of cobblestoned lanes to explore.

(See page 192 for **Route 20, Berwick to Norham**, if you want to link two rides together.)

## THE ESSENTIALS

**GETTING THERE** By road, Lindisfarne is almost equidistant between Edinburgh (113km to the north) and Newcastle (96km to the south), both via the A1 and Lindisfarne Causeway. The nearest station is at Berwick-upon-Tweed, with trains from Edinburgh taking approximately 40 minutes (⊘ crosscountrytrains.co.uk; ⊘ lner.co.uk), connecting with the 477 bus (Borders Buses, ⊘ bordersbuses.co.uk) which takes around half an hour.

**FACILITIES** There are public toilets in Lindisfarne on Green Lane, near the harbour, and in Berwick on Castlegate.

↑ Completed in 1850, the 28 arches of the Royal Border Bridge carry rail traffic across the River Tweed (BBA Photography/S)

## WHERE TO EAT

✕ **The Barn at Beal** Beal Farm TD15 2PB; ✆ 01289 540044; ⬙ barnatbeal.com. Halfway along the Lindisfarne Causeway, with beautiful views overlooking Lindisfarne, this combined café, restaurant & bar (part of the adjacent campsite, see page 218), serves b/fasts, light lunches, afternoon teas & snacks, with cakes, scones & pastries baked fresh on the premises. Its dinner menu is smarter than might be expected for a campsite, typically featuring local fish, lobster, & vegetarian options (open daytime daily & Wed–Sat for evening meals: booking essential). ££

✕ **Lowry's at the Chandlery** Quayside, Berwick-upon-Tweed TD15 1HE; ✆ 01289 309327; ◼ Lowry's at the Chandlery. Nicely located by the riverside in the heart of Berwick's old quarter, this arty café is decorated with paintings by L S Lowry, the artist who visited the town many times (see box, page 189). The café serves tasty freshly made salads, crab soups, sandwiches & a delicious assortment of homemade cakes & pastries, with tables indoors or outside on the cobblestoned quayside. £

✕ **Atelier** 41–43 Bridge St, Berwick TD15 1ES; ✆ 01289 298180; ◼ Atelier. This casually hip café-deli in the centre of Berwick specialises in Mediterranean cheeses & charcuterie with good-value sharing platters, as well as Scottish mussels & homemade soups & pies. Its bar stocks a wide range of real ales, ciders & artisan gins. ££

## FURTHER INFORMATION

◼ **Berwick Visitors Centre** Walkergate, Berwick TD15 1DD; ✆ 07354 056068; ◼ Berwick Visitor Centre. This privately run tourist office in the town centre offers a little more than the average information centre, with a miniature model of Berwick, historical film show & a little café, all in addition to its friendly staff giving helpful advice, & guidebooks & maps for sale.

# 20 BERWICK-UPON-TWEED TO NORHAM

| | |
|---|---|
| **START/FINISH** | Berwick-upon-Tweed/Norham |
| **DISTANCE/TIME** | 19.2km/2hrs |
| **DIFFICULTY/TERRAIN** | ① All on road, with only a few junctions to negotiate and one or two hills to climb |
| **SCENIC RATING** | ⑧ A picturesque mix of Borders history and scenery, meandering through the beautiful Tweed Valley from Berwick-upon-Tweed upstream to Norham |
| **SUITABLE FOR** | Touring bike or road bike |
| **NCN ROUTE** | NCN1, NCN68 and NCN76 |
| **MAPS** | OS Explorer 346 and 339 (1:25 000) |
| **KOMOOT REF** | 986355984 |

This picturesque ride follows the lush valley of the River Tweed inland to Norham. Starting from Berwick-upon-Tweed we follow the north bank of the Tweed upstream, crossing over the border into Scotland near stately Paxton House. Winding down to the river, we return to Northumberland over the recently restored Union Chain Bridge, the oldest vehicular suspension bridge in the world, before reaching Norham. This pretty riverside village seems a sleepy sort of place today but it endured a tempestuous past during the Anglo-Scottish wars, with its castle besieged by the Scots nine times. Latterly, the castle's romantic ruins provided a long-standing inspiration to landscape artist J M W Turner (see box, page 189).

It's not a long ride, with no dauntingly steep or long hills, so it's suitable for reasonably fit riders with some cycling experience. It largely follows several National Cycle Network routes, including NCN1 (Coast & Castles Cycle Route), NCN68 (Pennines Cycleway) and briefly the NCN76 (Round to the Forth), with directions given when we leave and rejoin these cycle routes. The ride also ties in with our Route 19, up the coast from Lindisfarne (see page 184, with some tips about what to do in Berwick).

## THE ROUTE

Start from ❶ **Bridge Street car park**, one block inland from Berwick Quayside. Turn right out of the car park and right again on to Bridge Street, then left up Hide Hill and left again on Marygate, through Berwick's main shopping district (keep alert for pedestrians crossing and give parked

← The Union Chain Bridge (Norham Bike Yard)

cars a clear berth). Continue up Marygate, which runs into Castlegate and over the railway bridge, with the station on your left.

At a forked junction in front of an old toll house, take the left fork on to Castle Terrace (A6105). Still climbing gradually, go through one of Berwick's swankier suburbs, with large houses overlooking a bend in the Tweed below and hazy outlines of the Cheviot Hills on the horizon to the south.

Coming to the top of the hill, leaving the last of the houses behind, turn left on to Paxton Road. Follow the cycle-path signs through a **gate** at the end of this no-through road, then after around 400m go through another **gate** on the right on to a cycle path which then continues left, alongside the A1. Cross over the A1 after around 250m, via a cycle-path crossing which then turns left and joins a side road on the right, the B6461/Paxton Road, signposted Paxton and Norham. If this stretch of zigzagging over the A1 sounds fiddly, rest assured it's all clearly signposted and with safe cycle crossings. We're also starting to descend now, after the climb out of Berwick.

Shortly after joining this side road, cross the bridge over ❷ **Whiteadder Water**. There are beautiful views up- and downstream from the bridge,

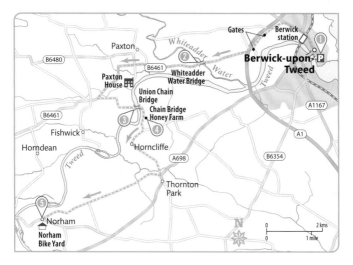

perhaps with mallards and swans bobbing along the drifting current. After 1km, just beyond a former toll house, note the cheery 'Scotland Welcomes You' sign on the left as we cross the border.

After another 1km into Scotland, soon after the road bears left, we pass **Paxton House** on our left with the road winding around to the left, with the estate's high stone perimeter walls running alongside us. This impressive 18th-century stately home sits at the end of a driveway, overlooking the Tweed. It is open to visitors, with tours of the house and river trips by canoe, kayak or paddle board also available (⌂ paxtonhouse. co.uk). Oh, and there's also a café here, the Stables Tearoom (see below).

A couple of kilometres after Paxton House, as the road bends right just before **Fishwick**, turn sharp left by a small pine grove on to a smaller road. Carry on down this quiet country lane for around 1.5km, until we come to the ❸ **Union Chain Bridge**, straddling the border between Scotland and England. Completed in 1820, this historic bridge over the Tweed is the oldest surviving suspension bridge in Europe (see box, page 196).

Crossing over the bridge, turn right and climb uphill, coming to the entrance to ❹ **Chain Bridge Honey Farm** on your left. There's a fascinating

↑ The picture gallery in Paxton House (Jim Gibson/A)

museum of honey here (free entry), including a live 'slice' of hive – safely behind glass! They also have an eclectic mix of vintage farm machinery and other old vehicles dotted around the grounds, including a café in a double-decker bus (see below). There's also a great viewpoint from opposite the driveway to the honey farm, looking back down the steep valley to the bridge.

## THE UNION CHAIN BRIDGE

Hailed as a major engineering achievement when it opened in 1820, with a single span of 137m the Union Chain Bridge was the longest suspension bridge in the world. Until this time, the only other river crossing over the River Tweed between Horncliffe and Paxton was at New Water Ford, which was prone to dangerous flooding and high tides. With the growing demand for coal and lime to be brought over from Northumberland to Berwickshire in Scotland, the need for a purpose-built bridge became urgent. A naval officer, Capt Samuel Brown, solved the problem with a pioneering new design using flexible chain links, based on systems he had invented for ships' rigging and anchor chains. Brown's bridge was completed in a year, and at a cost of £7,700 was considerably less expensive than a traditional stone bridge.

In order to show its strength when the bridge first opened to the public, Brown drove across it in a two-wheeled carriage, followed by a convoy of 12 loaded carts weighing 20 tonnes. There were 600 eager spectators, some of whom had travelled across Europe to witness the historic event.

Now the oldest vehicular suspension bridge in the world, it was closed in October 2020 for restoration work due to be completed by summer 2023, but this was still to be confirmed at the time of writing so it's advisable to check before setting off: e ucb@museumsnorthumberland.org.uk. The major project involved the complete dismantling of the structure, leaving only the two masonry towers in place. It is expected to extend the bridge's life for a further 120 years, by which time the original wrought-iron parts (many of which were renovated and re-used) will be 320 years old.

From the honey farm, continue up the road for another 600m, coming to a T-junction with the entrance to Horncliffe House, a stately Georgian hall, on your right. Turn right here, signposted Norham, bypassing the village of **Horncliffe** on your right and continuing for another 1.5km until you come to a T-junction, just before the A698. Turn right here and follow the undulating road through arable fields for around 4km, leading finally to ⑤ **Norham**. The road winds steeply downhill into this quiet but welcoming little village, around the foot of historic **Norham Castle** (see box, page 189). At the bottom of the road, we come to the village green and the end of our ride, with plenty of parking spaces here and on adjacent roads.

While many villages across the UK have sadly lost their local shops, Norham can still boast a thriving bakery and butcher's shop. Just beyond the village green, on the right, is the Mason's Arms, a great little local pub (see below), and just around the corner is **Norham Bike Yard**, one of the best cycling hubs in Northumberland, as well as a B&B (see page 217).

↑ Some of the old machinery on display at Chain Bridge Honey Farm, with the Café Bus in the background (Huw Hennessy)

# THE ESSENTIALS

**GETTING THERE** By road, Berwick-upon-Tweed is 91km south of Edinburgh via the A1 and A1167. By train, the town's station is on the East Coast Main Line, with regular trains from Edinburgh on LNER (⌀lner. co.uk) taking around 40 minutes.

**FACILITIES** There are public toilets in Berwick on Castlegate, and customer toilets in cafés en route as well as at the Mason's Arms in Norham.

## WHERE TO EAT

✕ **Northern Soul Kitchen** 19 West St, Berwick TD15 1NG; ✐ 01289 298160; ⌀ northernsoulkitchen.co.uk. This commendable food-waste initiative café in the centre of Berwick offers a great range of hot & cold meals, from steaks to falafel burgers & salads, using good, healthy food destined for landfill & with a pay-what-you-can-afford pricing policy (at the time of writing, it's only open 10.00–16.30 Wed–Sat). £

✕ **The Stables Tearoom** Paxton Hse TD15 1SZ; ✐ 01289 386291; ⌀ paxtonhouse.co.uk. Based in the grand Georgian Paxton House, just over the Scottish border on our route to Norham, this café serves freshly made snacks, soups & sandwiches (with bread from Norham's bakery), afternoon teas, with gluten-free, vegetarian & vegan options (on request); there's also Pilgrims Coffee from Lindisfarne & locally made Doddington Dairy ice cream from the Cheviots. It has cosy tables indoors, or you can sit out in the stable courtyard. £

✕ **Café Bus** Chain Bridge Honey Farm, Horncliffe TD15 2XT; ✐ 01289 282362; ⌀ chainbridgehoney.co.uk. Housed in a well-loved, olive-green double-decker bus in the grounds of the honey farm up the hill from the Union Chain Bridge, this cute little café offers a range of freshly made cakes, sandwiches, pastries, teas, coffees & cold drinks, with tables upstairs in the bus or outside in the farmyard. The shop in the adjacent visitor centre sells a huge range of honey & beeswax products, also available online. £

## FURTHER INFORMATION

ℹ️ **Berwick Visitors Centre** Walkergate, Berwick TD15 1DD; ✐ 07354 056068; f Berwick Visitor Centre. This privately run tourist office in the town centre offers a little more than the average information centre, with a miniature model of Berwick, historical film show & a little café, all in addition to its friendly staff giving helpful advice, & guidebooks & maps for sale.

# NORHAM BIKE YARD

*A family run Bed & Breakfast in the pretty village of Norham*

Come and explore the fantastic cycling that Northumberland and the neighbouring Scottish Borders have to offer where our warm welcome awaits

*For more information visit*
**www.norhambikeyard.com**
**email: norhambikeyard@gmail.com**
**or find us on Facebook, Twitter and Instagram**

# 21 TWEED TO TILL RIVERS LOOP

| | |
|---|---|
| **START/FINISH** | Norham |
| **DISTANCE/TIME** | 37.3km/3½hrs |
| **DIFFICULTY/TERRAIN** | ① Through undulating rural valleys, mostly on minor B-roads and back lanes, with one short stretch on the A698 and a short off-road track |
| **SCENIC RATING** | ⑧ Tweed and Till river valleys, with lush, wooded riverbanks and farm meadows, and peppered with historic sites from battle-scarred Norham Castle to the Union Chain Bridge, and a detour to a Neolithic stone circle |
| **SUITABLE FOR** | Road bike, touring bike or hybrid |
| **NCN ROUTE** | NCN68, NCN1 and NCN72 |
| **MAPS** | OS Explorer 339 and 346 (1:25 000) |
| **KOMOOT REF** | 947816154 |

↑ Canoeing on the tranquil River Tweed, near Norham (Huw Hennessy)

tarting from Norham, by the River Tweed, this leisurely cross-country ride traverses the Tweed Valley southwards to Etal, on the historic Ford and Etal Estate by the River Till. Looping back north, we cross the Tweed on the newly restored Union Chain Bridge and over the Scottish border into Berwickshire. Following the Tweed upstream we loop south again, through Ladykirk, and back over the Tweed to Norham, now a sleepy village but with battle-scarred Norham Castle as a reminder of its war-torn history.

It's a relatively long but undulating route, with a couple of very short A-road junctions to deal with and a pleasant off-road trail by the River Till. All in all, it's suitable for reasonably fit riders with some road cycling experience.

## THE ROUTE

Start from the village green in the centre of ❶ **Norham**, with the hilltop castle on your left, at the top end of the village. Turn right up Castle Street, with the clock and village hall on your left. At the T-junction turn left, joining the NCN68, and follow the road out of the village.

After about 1km, turn right, passing the former ❷ **Norham Station** on your right. Now a private house, the station was on a branch of the North Eastern Railway line, with trains running from 1851 until it closed in 1965. The new owners have preserved many of the station buildings; it's not open to the public, but if you're interested in its history, visit ⌀ norhamstation. co.uk.

At the brow of the hill, after about another 1km, we come to a left–right dogleg crossing over the ❸ **A698**, signposted Grindon and Felkington: we're only on the A-road for a few metres and it's not a busy road here, but if you'd rather avoid the junction, just dismount and walk across the verge to the side road. Carry on, generally southwards, through **Grindon**, with its neat row of cottages on your left. The road then meanders right, left and right, then across the Till Valley with wide, flat arable fields and the rounded Cheviot Hills on the horizon further south.

Climbing up to a crossroads, 2.6km after Grindon, carry on straight ahead towards Etal, then wind around the foot of the bare-topped ❹ **Duddo Hill** on our right. Just as we start to descend after the previous crossroads, turn right, signposted Tindal House, on to a narrower back road. Levelling out now, the road then bears left through an avenue of slender plane trees between the fields. Just before reaching **❺ Tindal House**, turn left on to a track (NCN68 sign half-buried in the hedgerow).

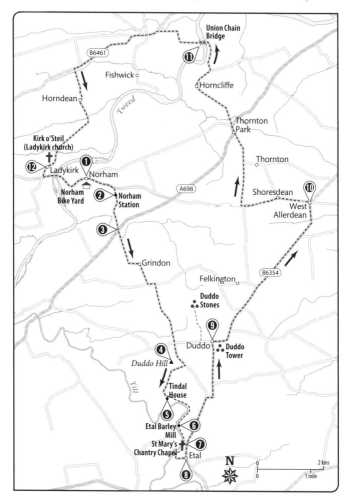

This track winds right and towards the River Till, a tributary of the Tweed, fringed with overhanging trees. It's gently downhill at first, then zigzagging steeply down to the riverbank, the rubbly path becoming rougher, so go carefully. Turn left at the bottom, with the gently flowing water sparkling between the trees, and a high-banked meadow across the opposite bank.

Follow the beautiful shady trail under the trees for a couple more kilometres, until we reach Etal. Along the way, you might notice a couple of ruined remains by the riverside. First, after about 750m, the site of a former watermill, the ❻ **Etal Barley Mill**. Now in ruins and overgrown with ivy, the watermill dates from the 18th century, when the miller and his family lived on the site, producing high-quality flour for Etal village. About another 1km further along are the remains of ❼ **St Mary's Chantry Chapel**, also now in ruins. Built in 1345 by Sir Robert Manners, of Etal Castle, the chapel survived until the 19th century before succumbing to the passage of time, and was replaced with the current St Mary's Chapel in Etal village.

Shortly after the chapel, we reach ❽ **Etal** itself (pronounced 'eet-ll', to rhyme with 'beetle'), a pretty and beautifully kept village on the banks of the Till. It's part of the Ford and Etal Estate, an extensive site which also includes Etal Castle, Heatherslaw Light Railway and the nearby memorial at Branxton to the 1513 Battle of Flodden (the bloodiest conflict in the Anglo-Scottish wars and where 10,000 Scots, including King James I of Scotland, were killed). A huge range of activities on offer in the area, including local walks and bike rides, makes it well worth a return visit (for details, visit ⌖ ford-and-etal.co.uk).

Coming in to Etal, at the T-junction turn sharp left uphill. Pass the entrance to the estate, with Etal Castle on your right. Continue through the village, with its manicured grass verges and the **Black Bull Inn**, opposite the old post office which is now home to the **Lavender Tearooms** (see below). We're at our southernmost point here and around a third of the way through the ride, so this might be a good place for a refreshment break.

Otherwise, carry on up to the crossroads, and turn left on to the B6354 (leaving the NCN68), heading north again now, back towards the Tweed.

Continue on a nice, level and straight road for around 3km from here all the way to the hamlet of ❾ **Duddo**. The broad river valley has uninterrupted views across the fields, east to the sea and west to the Cheviots. At Duddo, pass the ruined **Duddo Tower** peeking over a pine grove on the right. The castle was a 16th-century pele tower (see box, page 95), but there are also much older historical remains near here: a Neolithic stone circle, some 4,000 years old. The **Duddo Stones** are about 1km north of the village. To get there, turn left into the village, where the B6354 winds around to the right, and take the footpath about 300m along on the right. A permissive path leads across a field up to the circle of five weathered sandstone blocks, each about 2m tall, on a grassy knoll overlooking the valley.

Continuing north through Duddo, carry straight on at the crossroads at the top of the hill. Enjoy a nice long downhill run from here for about 6km, until we climb up to another hill crest at ❿ **West Allerdean**, with the Plough on the Hill inn on your left. At the crossroads, shortly after the pub (temporarily closed at the time of writing), turn left, signposted Shoresdean. A couple of kilometres later take the right-hand turn, signposted Horncliffe, a narrow back lane rolling gently downhill. About 1km along this lane, continue straight ahead at a right-hand fork.

After another 1km we come back to the A698 at a T-junction opposite **Thornton Park**. Turn right here, briefly following the road downhill for around 400m before turning left on to a smaller road, signposted Horncliffe. Turn right almost immediately, also signposted Horncliffe (rejoining the NCN68).

In about 1.5km, climbing at first, then down again, the road winds right around **Horncliffe**. Shortly after passing a Georgian hall called Horncliffe House on your left, turn left, signposted Union Chain Bridge (and NCN1 joining the NCN68 here).

We're approaching the south bank of the Tweed now, gently descending to the river, its steep banks fringed with trees, bracken and reeds. After about 300m, pass the entrance to the **Chain Bridge Honey Farm and Café** (see page 195) on your right, a perfect spot for a tea-break, plus there's an impressive view of the ⓫ **Union Chain Bridge** below, opposite the driveway. Continue downhill from here for around another 450m, to

## DESTINATION TWEED

From its source, high in Scotland's Lowther Hills, to its mouth 156km downstream at Berwick-upon-Tweed, the River Tweed is one of the longest and arguably most beautiful rivers in the British Isles. It is one of the UK's most prized salmon-fishing rivers, and was known for its historic mills powering the region's textile industry, giving its name to the world-famous tweed cloth. Most of the Tweed is in Scotland, forming the main river of the Scottish Borders, but some of its course also forms the border between Scotland and England.

Now, a major new project, 'Destination Tweed', funded by the National Lottery Heritage Fund, has been launched to 'celebrate and share the nature, history and stories of the River Tweed'. The five-year project will include the Tweed Trail, stretching from Moffat, near the river source, to Berwick-upon-Tweed, and featuring walking and cycling paths to take visitors on journeys of discovery to its diverse attractions, including landscapes, wildlife habitats and local communities' historic sites, such as castles and ancient monuments. There is already an existing cycle route along the Tweed, the Tweed Cycleway, so it is expected that the new project's route will be based on this. The Tweed Cycleway, part of the National Cycle Network, runs for just over 100km through the Scottish Borders from Berwick-upon-Tweed through Melrose, Galashiels, Innerleithen and Dewar. Its first section, from Berwick to Norham, is the same as our Route 20. Check the Bradt website at ⭤ bradtguides.com/updates for any Tweed Trail news as it becomes available.

↑ The River Tweed near Peebles (AngieC333/S)

the historic bridge spanning the border with Scotland, recently restored in a three-year project (see box, page 196). It's a single carriageway across the bridge, so check for oncoming vehicles before crossing; there are also paved sidewalks, which might be preferable if they are clear.

Across the other side of the Tweed, now in Scotland, with a friendly 'Welcome' sign after the bridge, continue up the road, mostly uphill. After about 1.5km, at an angled T-junction, continue straight ahead, on to the B6461, signposted Kelso (leaving the NCN1 and NCN68 here). After 3km, turn left, signposted Horndean, on to a smaller back lane. Winding, mostly downhill now, through the hamlet of **Horndean**, after about 3km we come to ⓬ **Ladykirk**. Dominating this sleepy farming hamlet is the distinguished **Kirk o'Steil**, an early 16th-century church with a tall dome, looking as if it might be more at home in Andalucía than the Scottish Borders, to this uninformed writer at least. It does have an impressive history, in fact: having nearly drowned in the nearby Tweed, King James IV had the church built in solid stone as a lasting symbol of his gratitude. Which it now is, as the oldest surviving church in Berwickshire still in use. A peek inside reveals some fine Victorian stained glass, stone sculptures (including a bust of James IV) and a carved wooden parish chest, dated 1651.

Take the left fork on the outskirts of Ladykirk, shortly followed by a sharp left-hand turn on to the B6470, by an age-worn stone fountain on the right-hand corner. Heading eastwards now back towards the Tweed, the road winds steeply downhill through the trees before opening out by the river. Cross the 19th-century stone bridge over the Tweed, with lovely views up and down the valley. Looking right upstream, the river has split in two, with an island in the middle offering safe haven for swans, ducks and other waterbirds.

Across the bridge, a sign on the right proclaims England (no 'Welcome', unlike Scotland). To counter any accusations of bias, though, I should also mention a friendlier sign opposite, welcoming us to 'Northumberland, England's Border Country'. The road winds around to the left (rejoining the NCN1) into Norham and back to the village green, where our river loop ride comes to an end. A welcoming pint or a hot cuppa awaits tired cyclists in the **Mason's Arms**, which we just passed on the left (see below).

## THE ESSENTIALS

**GETTING THERE** By road, Norham is just over 84km south of Edinburgh via the A68 and A697. The nearest train station is at Berwick-upon-Tweed, 12km east of Norham, with trains on LNER (⟡lner.co.uk) taking around 45 minutes; the connecting 67 bus (⟡bordersbuses.co.uk) takes a further 20 minutes or so.

**FACILITIES** There are no public toilets en route, but the eateries listed below have customer toilets.

## WHERE TO EAT

✕ **The Black Bull Inn** Etal Village TD12 4TL ⟡ 01890 820200; ⟡ theblackbulletal.co.uk. In the heart of the pretty riverside village, this equally pretty, thatch-roofed pub has an all-day menu featuring reliable traditional British favourites, including fish'n'chips, steak-and-ale pie & bangers & mash, as well as salads, burgers & one or two local specialities, such as haggis fritters (with homemade Irn Bru jam!). Indoor tables or gardens front & back. **££**

✕ **Lavender Tearooms** Etal Village TD12 4TL; ⟡ 01890 820761; ⟡ lavendertearooms. org.uk. Across the road from the Black Bull Inn in delightful Etal, this family-owned post office, shop & café serves light lunches, with delicious soups, sandwiches & quiches.

Afternoon teas feature a selection of tray bakes, cakes – including lavender cake, of course – & a speciality called a 'Singing Hinnie' – a scone that is griddled until it sings! **£**

✕ **The Mason's Arms** West St, Norham TD15 2LB; ⟡ 01289 382326; ⟡ themasonsarmsnorham.co.uk. A former coaching inn, this friendly village local has a snug bar in front, with a cosy dining room & modern extension in the back. The menu offers an interesting mix of pub classics & international favourites, from 'Pie of the Week' to 'Bangkok Bad Boy veggie burger' & chicken & chorizo paella. It's the only eatery in the village & gets very busy, so advance booking is strongly advisable. **££**

## FURTHER INFORMATION

ℹ️ **Berwick Visitors Centre** Walkergate, Berwick TD15 1DD; ⟡ 07354 056068; ⬛ Berwick Visitor Centre. The nearest tourist office is in Berwick, around 12km from Norham. It's a highly rated information centre with friendly staff on hand for advice, & guidebooks & maps for sale. Otherwise, try the Norham Bike Yard (see page 217), whose owners know the area inside out.

# ACCOMMODATION

These hotels, B&Bs, self-catering cottages, holiday parks and campsites have been chosen for their character, value for money and location close to the cycle routes (numbered circles show the closest route/s). Accommodation is listed by area, in descending price order. Price codes are based on room rates per night during the summer high season, although most places also have cheaper off-season rates:

**£** up to £70    **££** £70–150    **£££** £150+

## COUNTY DURHAM

**Farnley Towers** The Avenue, Durham DH1 4DX; ☏ 0191 3750011; ⬦ farnley-tower.co.uk; ❶ ❷. This imposing Victorian town house, a short walk from the historic centre of Durham, has 17 en-suite rooms, including sgls, dbls & family-sized, with TV & Wi-Fi. It also has a restaurant specialising in Indian cuisine, & a bar. There is limited on-site parking available & secure cycle-storage facilities. Rates include b/fast, with a range of choices including vegan & gluten-free options. **£££**

**South Causey Inn** Beamish Burn Rd, Stanley DH9 0LS; ☏ 01207 23555; ⬦ southcausey. co.uk; ❷. This upmarket contemporary hotel close to Durham Cathedral has 39 stylishly luxurious rooms, including 1 eccentric suite in a converted double-decker bus; some rooms have twin bathtubs, hot tubs or whirlpool bath. The adjoining restaurant serves refined British cuisine & the cocktail bar is housed in a repurposed 1960s fire engine. Also has secure cycle store & private parking. **££–£££**

**Edge Knoll Holiday Cottages** Edge Farm, Hamsterley DL13 3PF; ☏ 07971 883431; ⬦ edgeknollfarm.co.uk; ❶. These 2 holiday cottages are based in a converted 17th-century milking byre on a former farm only 10mins' drive from Hamsterley Forest. Each sleep up to 4 people with 1 dbl & 1 twin-bedded room, comfortable lounge (1 has a wood burner) with TV & Wi-Fi, & a fully equipped kitchen. Cycle storage is available in a lockable outbuilding with work bench & outside washing facilities. Available for weekly bookings only. **££**

**The Victoria Inn** Witton-le-Wear, Bishop Auckland DL14 0AS; ☏ 01388 488058; ⬦ thevicwlw.co.uk; ❶. This brilliant B&B above the pub has 5 comfortable en-suite rooms with TV, Wi-Fi & tea- & coffee-making facilities. The homemade b/fast is delicious, ample to fuel you up probably for tackling the MTB trails around nearby Hamsterley Forest, & the pub downstairs has a great local vibe, stocked with an impressive range of wines & spirits. There's secure bike storage in a locked garage. **££**

**West Hall Glamping** Norburn Lane, Witton Gilbert DH7 6TS; ☏ 07879 101497; ⏁ westhallglamping.co.uk; ❶ ❷. This luxuriously appointed glamping site in a handy location between Hamsterley Forest & Durham has 6 spacious en-suite pods, sleeping up to 4 people. Each come with kitchenette, TV, Wi-Fi & private outdoor space with hot tub, barbecue & firepit, plus secure storage for up to 8 bikes. **££**

**Langdon Beck YHA** Barnard Castle DL12 0XN; ☏ 01833 622228; ⏁ yha.org.uk/hostel/yha -langdon-beck; ❶. This rural youth hostel is set in Upper Teesdale, northwest of Hamsterley Forest, with 2 dorms & 8 private rooms. There's a kitchen, games room, Wi-Fi in shared areas & a lockable cycle shed (for up to 10 bikes). **£**

## NEWCASTLE & GATESHEAD

**Hotel du Vin** Allan Hse, City Rd, Newcastle upon Tyne NE1 2BE; ☏ 0191 389 8628; ⏁ hotelduvin.com/Newcastle; ❷ ❸. Housed in a converted Edwardian office building overlooking the Tyne, in hip Ouseburn, this chic boutique hotel has 42 rooms & suites, all individually designed, with stylish furnishings & top-quality amenities including deep baths, drench showers, plasma TV & Nespresso coffee machine. There's secure cycle storage in the locked garage. **£££**

**Hilton Newcastle Gateshead** Bottle Bank, Gateshead NE8 2AR; ☏ 0191 490 9700; ⏁ hilton.com/en/hotels/nclhihi-hilton -newcastle-gateshead; ❷ ❸. With a stunning location on Gateshead Quayside overlooking the Tyne Bridge, this large, modern hotel has all the creature comforts expected from the Hilton group including heated pool, sauna & gym. Its 254 rooms are spacious & smart, some with great riverside views. They also do a very good buffet b/fast & there's a large car park beneath the hotel & secure indoor bike storage. Best of all, good-value room rates are often available via online booking portals. **££**

**YHA Newcastle** 17 Carliol Sq, Newcastle upon Tyne NE1 6UQ; ☏ 0345 260 2583; ⏁ yha. org.uk/hostel/yha-newcastle-central; ❷ ❸. Housed in a former prison, this is a great hostel close to Grey's Quarter & High Bridge St, two of the city's buzziest nightlife neighbourhoods. 52 rooms including dorms, private rooms & suites, plus café, bar, lounge area, free Wi-Fi & secure cycle store. **£**

## NORTH PENNINES & NORTHUMBERLAND NATIONAL PARK

**Hesleyside Huts** Hesleyside, Bellingham NE48 2LA; ☏ 01434 220068; ⏁ hesleysidehuts. co.uk; ❽–⓫. This glamping site in the grounds of Hesleyside Hall has 7 individually designed log cabins, shepherd's huts, tree-house & tower. All are en suite & luxuriously furnished, with king-sized beds, log burner & cooking facilities. There's secure indoor cycle storage. **£££**

**Lord Crewe Arms** The Square, Blanchland DH8 9SP; ✆ 01434 677100; ⬧ lordcrewearmsblanchland.co.uk; ❶ ❹ ❺. This luxury country house hotel dates from the 12th century as a guesthouse to nearby Blanchland Abbey. The 21 rooms & 5 suites are all lavishly furnished, with king-sized beds, Wi-Fi, flat-screen TV, DAB radio & tea- & coffee-making facilities. There's an on-site restaurant & secure indoor cycle storage (& the nearby village shop sells cycling accessories). **£££**

**Wallington Hall cottages** Cambo, nr Morpeth NE61 4AR; ✆ 0344 800 20790; ⬧ nationaltrust.org.uk/wallington; ❸. National Trust's Wallington Hall has 4 holiday cottages in & around the estate (sleeping 4–16 people). All are comfortably furnished with kitchen, sitting room, garden & private parking, & 1, Laundry Cottage, has a locked shed for bikes. 3-night min stay; bike hire is available at Wallington Hall (see page 221). **£££**

**Battlesteads Hotel** Wark on Tyne NE48 3LS; ✆ 01434 230209; ⬧ battlesteads.com; ❽–⓫. By the B6320 as you enter the village from the south, this 18th-century former farmhouse has been tastefully converted into a luxury hotel with pub & restaurant. It has 22 en-suite individually styled bedrooms, including twin & family rooms, all with flat-screen TV, free Wi-Fi & tea- & coffee-making facilities. B&B rates. **££**

**The Buteland Stop** Bellingham NE48 2HR; ✆ 07966 429140; ⬧ thebutelandstop.co.uk; ⓫. With a beautiful location overlooking the meadows & moors of Buteland Fell, right on Route 11, these 2 converted shepherd's huts are luxuriously furnished, each sleeping 2, with dbl bed, cooking facilities, TV, en-suite shower & toilet & wood-burning stove. **££**

**Capheaton Hall** Capheaton, nr Morpeth NE19 2AB; ✆ 0191 375 8152; ⬧ capheatonhall. co.uk; ❸. This impressive 17th-century country hall, conveniently located right on Route 13 in the rural hamlet of Capheaton, offers luxurious accommodation in a range of cottages or the west wing of the house, sleeping 2–8 people. All are beautifully furnished with comfortable living areas & fully equipped kitchen, as well as private parking & secure cycle storage. Bookings for 7 nights min in peak summer season. **££**

**Crackin' View B&B** Lanehead NE48 1NT; ✆ 01434 240057; ⬧ crackinview.com; ❽–⓫. These holiday cottages & guesthouse live up to their name, with stunning hilltop views over the moor & fens of Northumberland National Park. There are 4 en-suite B&B rooms with tea- & coffee-making facilities, flat-screen TV & free Wi-Fi, & the cottage (sleeping 2) comes with kitchen, lounge & wet room. **££**

**Kellah Farm** Haltwhistle NE49 0JL; ✆ 01434 320816; ⬧ kellah.co.uk; ❹ ❺. This family-run B&B in the heart of the Pennines Valley has 4 cosy en-suite rooms, each with plasma TV & tea- & coffee-making facilities. The spacious downstairs lounge is packed with games, books & local information, & the b/fasts (range of choices, including vegetarian options) are superb, using the farm's own freshly laid eggs. There is ample bike storage in a secure outhouse. 3 self-catering cottages also available, sleeping 2–6. **££**

**Kielder Village Campsite** Kielder NE48 1EJ; 01434 239257; kieldercampsite.co.uk; ❻ ❼. With its handy & peaceful forest location (ie: no phone signal!) near Kielder Castle & the starting points for our Kielder routes, this well-equipped campsite has a couple of camping fields for 40 tents plus 28 electric hook-ups & 2 pods, sleeping up to 4 adults. On-site shower block, dry room, shop & children's play area. **££**

**Knoppingsholme Farmhouse & Stable** Lanehead NE48 1JZ; 01434 240345; tarsetholidaycottages.co.uk; ❾ ❿. Set on a farm overlooking Northumberland National Park near Lanehead, this luxurious holiday cottage in a converted stable sleeps 4 people, with 1 dbl & 1 twin. It has a spacious open-plan living room/kitchen/dining room, with log burner, TV & DVD player, & private parking space. **££**

**Landal Kielder Waterside** Hexham NE48 1BT; 01434 251000; kielderwaterside.com; ❻ ❼. With a range of 32 lodges & 17 log cabins on the banks of Kielder Water in Northumberland National Park, this site makes an ideal base for cycling & many other activities on offer. The spacious, comfortable lodges (some with lakeside views) are fully equipped, with 2 bedrooms sleeping up to 3 people, kitchen, lounge with flat-screen TV & PlayStation, & an outdoor deck area with hot tub – great for stargazing in this Dark Sky Reserve. The family-friendly site also has children's play

areas, games cabin, crazy golf & indoor pool, plus a restaurant, café & shop. **££**

**Newcastle House** Front St, Rothbury NE65 7UT; 01669 620334; rothburynewcastlehouse. co.uk; ⓬. This traditional B&B in the centre of Rothbury has 3 dbl/twin rooms above its restaurant (page 127). They're all nicely furnished, with smart TV, free Wi-Fi & tea- & coffee-making facilities. It also has a 13-bed bunkhouse in the main building & with secure bike storage in the yard (which is locked overnight). **££**

**The Old Repeater Station** Military Rd, Haydon Bridge NE47 6NQ; 01434 688668; hadrians-wall-bedandbreakfast.co.uk; ❹ ❺. This warm & friendly family-run B&B near Hadrian's Wall & Vindolanda has 4 en-suite rooms & 1 self-contained apt, with guest sitting room & garden. The b/fasts are very good (including full English or veggie options) & evening meals are also available. There's secure cycle storage in a garden shed. In case you're wondering, the name comes from the building's original use as a telephone signal booster station. **££**

**Overland Adventures** Whalton, Morpeth NE61 3XD; 07860 280477; overland -adventures.co.uk/overland-adventure-routes; ⓭. This alternative adventure outfit offers a Land Rover Defender that is fully equipped with a safari-style tent, cooker, solar-powered shower & a host of camping kit, so that you can literally pitch up in campsites anywhere across Northumberland. There are also different Land

Rover models available, sleeping 3–5; bike racks included. Readers of this book can get a 10% discount voucher by emailing the code 'CYCLE10' to **e** hello@overland-adventures.co.uk. Vehicle pick-up from their base in Whalton or from Newcastle Airport, regional stations & ferry terminals. **££**

**Riverdale Hall Hotel** Bellingham NE48 2JT; ✆ 01434 220254; ⌖ riverdalehallhotel.co.uk; **❽–⓫**. On the edge of Bellingham by the River North Tyne, this luxurious country house hotel in a former Victorian mansion has 28 rooms & 4 self-catering apts. The hotel retains much of its original features, with a restaurant overlooking the grounds leading down to the river, as well as indoor swimming pool & sauna. Cyclists are welcomed, with secure indoor storage for bikes. **££**

**Tosson Tower Farm** Great Tosson, Rothbury NE65 7NW; ✆ 01669 620228; ⌖ tossontowerfarm.com; **⓬**. Traditional B&B rooms or self-catering cottages are offered at this lovely 19th-century farmhouse at the foot of the Simonside Hills, a few kilometres south of Rothbury. The farmhouse has 3 en-suite bedrooms (2 dbl & 1 twin), all beautifully furnished & with smart TV, hospitality tray, shared fridge & guest lounge. The 3 cottages sleep 6–10, all luxuriously furnished & with kitchen, washing machine & lounge with TV & DVD player. Secure cycle storage. 2-night min stay. **££**

**Bellingham Camping & Caravan Club** Bellingham NE47 7JT; ✆ 01434 344427; ⌖ campingandcaravanningclub.co.uk; **❽–⓫**. This excellent campsite on a level, tree-lined field about 1km outside Bellingham has 70 camping pitches (plus hook-ups) & 4 cosy glamping pods. There's also a shop, information office (very knowledgeable & helpful staff), kitchen, TV lounge, games room, washroom & drying room, all spotlessly clean & well maintained. New for 2023 is a purpose-built cycle store, with room for 12 bikes, CCTV protection & bike-wash facilities. **£**

**The Blackcock Inn** Falstone NE47 7JT; ✆ 01434 240200; ⌖ theblackcockinnatfalstone.com; **❻–❽**. This beautifully preserved 16th-century coaching inn in this sleepy riverside village has 5 recently refurbished dbl & twin rooms (4 en suite). A choice of hearty b/fasts are included in B&B rates, & behind the pub's beer garden is a self-catering cottage sleeping 2. There's secure storage for guests' bikes in their garage. **£**

**The Boe Rigg** Charlton NE48 1PE; ✆ 01434 240663; ⌖ theboerigg.co.uk; **❾–⓫**. Set on the edge of the moor just inside Northumberland National Park, between Bellingham & Lanehead, this lovely little campsite has 30 grassy pitches & electric hook-ups. On-site washroom, laundry, shop, licensed restaurant & children's playroom. **£**

**Brockalee Farm Caravan Site** Bardon Mill NE47 7JT; ✆ 01434 344427; ⌖ brockaleefarm.wixsite.com/campatbrockaleefarm; **❹ ❺**. A member of the Camping & Caravanning Club, this small, family-run site set on a farm to the north of Bardon Mill has 4 tent pitches & hook-ups for c/vans, plus washroom, shared kitchen & secure bike storage (cycle racks & garage). **£**

**Brownrigg Lodges** Bellingham NE48 2HR; ✆ 01434 220390; ⬙ brownrigglodges.com; ❽–⓫. These self-catering lodges & private rooms (in a former 1930s camp school) are a short walk from Bellingham, on the edge of the Northumberland National Park. 4 lodges sleep up to 6, with communal kitchen, laundry & lounge, & the 6 en-suite rooms come with TV & tea- & coffee-making facilities. There's secure cycle storage, free Wi-Fi, games room & outdoor sports facilities. **£**

**Demesne Farm Bunkhouse & Campsite** Bellingham NE48 2BS; ✆ 01434 220258; ⬙ demesnefarmcampsite.co.uk; ❽–⓫. This no-frills but clean & well-run campsite on a working farm is just on the outskirts of Bellingham. It has 30 tent pitches on a level grassy field, as well as 12 electric hook-ups, plus toilet, shower cubicle & washing-up facilities. **£**

**Fountain Cottage B&B** Bellingham NE48 2DE; ✆ 01434 239224; ⬙ fountain-cottage.com; ❽–⓫. Set in a former Victorian workhouse in the centre of Bellingham, this friendly B&B is bursting with character. It has 6 comfortable en-suite rooms with smart TV, free Wi-Fi & tea- & coffee-making facilities. Downstairs is an excellent café (page 99), with secure bike storage in an outbuilding; it also offers a 10% discount for cyclists (ditto for the café menu too). **£**

**Hollybush Inn** Greenhaugh NE48 1PW; ✆ 01434 240391; ⬙ hollybushinn.net; ❽–⓫. This 18th-century inn sits in a quiet moorland village in the heart of Northumberland National Park. It has 7 en-suite B&B rooms (6 upstairs & 1 on the ground floor), with a restaurant & bar by a roaring log fire downstairs adding to its cosy welcome. It also has a storage shed for up to 4 bikes. **£**

**Ninebanks YHA** Mohope, Hexham NE47 8DQ; ✆ 01434 345288; ⬙ ninebanks.org.uk; ❹ ❺. This family-run hostel based in an 18th-century cottage in the North Pennines has 6 en-suite rooms (with shared living & dining room) & 2 en-suite chalets (sleeping 2) with kitchenette & log burner. There's also a small shed with racks for bike storage. **£**

**The Sill YHA** Military Rd, Bardon Mill NE47 7AN; ✆ 0345 260 2702; ⬙ yha.org.uk/hostel/yha-the-sill-at-hadrians-wall; ❹ ❺. Based at the Sill – National Landscape Discovery Centre, near Vindolanda & Hadrian's Wall, this purpose-built modern hostel has 26 rooms, including dorms for 8 people & 18 en-suite private rooms for 2–4. Free Wi-Fi, kitchen & dining area, café & bar, shop, secure cycle store & spacious outdoor area. **£**

**Snabdough Farm** Tarset NE48 1LB; ✆ 01434 240239; ⬙ snabdoughfarmbedandbreakfast-kielder.co.uk; 🕒 May–Oct only; ❾ ❿. One of the former bastles (historic fortified farms), this 16th-century farmhouse B&B between Bellingham & Kielder Forest has 2 en-suite twin rooms, with TV & tea- & coffee-making facilities. B/fasts are made with fresh produce from the farm, & there's secure cycle storage in the garage. **£**

**Westfield House Farm** Thropton, Rothbury NE65 7LB; ✆ 01669 640089; ⊘ westfieldhousefarm.com; **⑫**. This small, family-run glamping site to the west of Rothbury, overlooking the Simonside Hills, has 3 shepherd's huts (with 4 more coming later in 2023) on a hay-meadow near the farmhouse. Each sleep 2, with dbl bed, toilet, kitchen, wood-fired hot tub outside & welcome hamper pack for your first b/fast. They also run a B&B, with 2 dbl/twin en-suite bedrooms – 1 is roomy & plush, the other more cosy, in a converted tractor shed! There's secure bike storage inside the farm's garage, & to prove their green credentials they plant a tree or 3 hedging plants on the farm for every direct booking. **££**

**Wild Northumbrian** Thorneyburn, Tarset NE48 1NA; ✆ 01669 650166; ⊘ wildnorthumbrian. co.uk; **⑨ ⑩**. Perched on high moorland in Northumberland National Park, this family-run glamping site between Bellingham & Kielder Forest has 4 Mongolian yurts, a shepherd's hut &, coolest of all, a tree-house yurt, all with a communal kitchen/shower/washing-up block. With its peaceful, remote location, the site also lies inside the International Dark Sky Park, so it makes a great spot for stargazing. **£**

## NORTHUMBERLAND COAST & SCOTTISH BORDERS

**Budle Hall** Budle Bay, Bamburgh NE69 7AJ; ✆ 01668 214297; ⊘ budlehall.com; **⑰**. This family-run B&B is housed in a beautiful early 19th-century stately home, set in spacious grounds 5mins by bike up the coast from Bamburgh. There are 4 comfortable, tastefully appointed dbl/twin rooms, guest lounge with log fire, honesty bar & 2 grand pianos. Camping & holiday lodges also available. Very friendly & knowledgeable owners (one of whom is a keen cyclist), & secure cycle storage. **£££**

**The Fishing Boat Inn** Boulmer NE65 0XP; ✆ 01665 577750; ⊘ thefishingboatinn. com; **⑰**. With 3 luxuriously furnished en-suite rooms, this modern boutique hotel right on the seafront in Boulmer offers idyllic pampering for saddle-sore cyclists. All rooms have private balconies & come with complimentary bottle of wine, bathrobes & slippers. There's a seaview restaurant too, a bar with an outdoor deck, and a secure area at the back of the pub for locking up bikes. **£££**

**Bamburgh Under Canvas** Glororum, Bamburgh, NE69 7AW; what3words ///flinch.space.besotted; ✆ 07791 963926; ⊘ bamburghundercanvas.co.uk, **⑰**. This glamping site is in the tiny hamlet of Glororum, around 15mins' walk inland from Bamburgh, with local shops & a range of eateries. It has 5 bell tents on a level field, each sleeping 2 people, with double bed & kitted out with gas stove, table & chairs, table lamp & a fire pit/barbecue in its private fenced enclosure (1 deluxe tent also has a wood-fired hot tub);

there are 2 shared bathrooms with hot showers. It's an adults-only site; minimum 2-night stay during the week, 3 nights over w/ends (check-in Mon, Wed & Fri). **££**

**The Blue Bell Inn** Pallinsburn TD12 4SH; ✆ 01890 820789; ♂ bluebellcrookham. co.uk; ⓴ ㉑. Just off the A697 near Etal, this pub/B&B has 4 en-suite rooms & a self-catering 2-bed cottage sleeping up to 5. The restaurant downstairs serves good traditional pub grub & there's a well-stocked bar including malt whiskies, 25 different gins & real ales from local breweries in Northumberland & Berwickshire. **££**

**Crastercarr B&B** 22 South Acres, Craster NE66 3TN; ✆ 07885 704865; ⓰ ⓱. Right on the seafront in Craster, so an ideal choice for cyclists on our 2 routes, this little B&B has 2 beautifully furnished rooms, 1 with sea view & both with king-sized beds & free Wi-Fi. There's free parking & a great b/fast too, including the option of Craster kippers, of course. Note that they don't have a website, but are usually booked via online agencies. **££**

**Fairfield Guesthouse** 16 Station Rd, Warkworth NE65 0XP; ✆ 01665 714455; ♂ fairfield-guesthouse.com; ⓮ ⓯. This plush B&B on the outskirts of Warkworth is in a well-preserved Victorian town house with 4 en-suite rooms (3 dbl & 1 twin), each individually styled & furnished with smart TV, radio & tea- & coffee-making facilities. There's a spacious guest lounge & terrace garden, & they also have a self-catering, open-plan garden apt,

sleeping 2 (minimum 1 week booking). Off-road parking & secure storage available for bikes. **££**

**Greycroft B&B** Croft Pl, Alnwick NE66 1XU; ✆ 01665 602127; ♂ greycroftalnwick. co.uk; ⓮ ⓯. Based in a beautiful Victorian town house in a quiet side street only a couple of minutes' walk from the town centre, this superb, family-run guesthouse has 6 spacious & comfortable en-suite rooms, with smart TV, radio, tea- & coffee-making facilities, Wi-Fi & shared fridge. There's a cosy guest lounge, library, honesty bar & walled garden, & the extremely friendly owners know the area inside out. B/fast is excellent too (from veggie options to full English) & there is indoor storage space for up to 3 bikes. **££**

**Hay Farm House B&B** Cornhill-on-Tweed TD12 4TR; ✆ 01890 820647; ♂ hayfarm. co.uk; ㉑. Based in a solid old farmhouse in the heart of the Etal Valley countryside, this welcoming, family-run B&B has 3 rooms, all beautifully furnished & with smart TV, fridge, electric blankets & tea- & coffee-making kit. The guest room downstairs is very cosy, with log fire & deep sofas to sink into, & the b/fasts offer a delicious range of local produce, including sausages, bacon, black pudding & their own farm eggs. There's secure cycle storage in the garage behind the farmhouse. Min 2-night stay. **££**

**Humbleton Falls Holiday Cottage** Highburn Hse Country Holiday Park, Wooler NE71 6EE; ✆ 01668 281344; ♂ highburn-house.co.uk; ⓲. This traditional stone cottage is just outside

# ORIGINAL COTTAGES

From *cycling-breaks-full-of-action-and-sports* Cottages
To *clearing-your-head-and-getting-lost-in-your-thoughts* Cottages

Let with us or book with us at
**originalcottages.co.uk**

The Shambles
*Ref: GD1889*

Wooler, close to local beauty spot Humbleton Hill. There are 3 dbl/twin bedrooms (1 en suite), lounge with TV & radio, kitchen with microwave oven, washing machine & dishwasher, safe cycle storage & enclosed back garden & patio. Weekly rates only. **££** (**£** for camping in adjacent holiday park)

**Norham Bike Yard** West St, Norham TD15 2LB; ✆ 01289 382442; ⏏ norhambikeyard.com; ❷⓿ ❷❶. This brilliant little family-run B&B just up the road from Norham's village green is one of the most cycle-friendly hubs in Northumberland, with on-site bike shop, workshop, cleaning station & cycling club, & decorated inside with cycling photos & knick knacks. There are 4 comfortable & spotlessly clean en-suite rooms with tea- & coffee-making facilities, & excellent b/fasts too – try the overnight oats & bacon/ sausage bap. Its guest lounge has an extensive library of cycling books for sale, & the friendly owners are local cycling experts. There's off-road parking in the pretty garden & indoor lockable cycle storage. **££**

**The Old Rectory** Howick NE66 3LE; ✆ 01665 577590; ⏏ oldrectoryhowick.co.uk; ⓰. This well-preserved Georgian country house in the little hamlet of Howick has 4 dbl/twin en-suite rooms, each with tea- & coffee-making kit & free Wi-Fi, or for a glamping-lite experience there's a bell tent in the back garden (available Apr–Sep). There's a guest lounge & garden, & plus 4 cats to complete the cosy welcome. Besides including a range of b/fasts, they also do evening meals (except on Sat). **££**

**The Shambles** The Haven, Beadnell NE67 5AT; ✆ 01665 721790; ⏏ originalcottages.co.uk (booking ref GD1889); ⓰ ⓱. This luxurious cottage, 3mins' walk from Beadnell seafront, sleeps 4, with dbl bedrooms, fully equipped kitchen including microwave, dishwasher & washer-drier, spacious open-plan lounge with wood burner, TV den/games room, Alexa audio, smart TV, terraced patio garden, secure indoor storage for up to 3 bikes & private parking space. **££**

**Shoreside Camping Huts** The Old School Gallery, Foxton Rd, Alnmouth NE66 3NH; ✆ 01665 830554; ⏏ alnmouthhuts.com; ⓴ ⓯. With the same owners as the Old School Gallery (page 174), these 4 modern glamping pods sit pretty overlooking Alnmouth beach, around 15mins' walk from Alnmouth village (no access by car). Each pod has a dbl bed (children's sofa bed available), kitchenette & toilet; the front porch is big enough for a couple of bikes, & there's an outdoor picnic bench & shared shower block. Min 2-night stay (3 during summer w/ends). **££**

**Alnwick YHA** 34–48 Green Batt, Alnwick NE66 1TU; ✆ 01665 660800; ⏏ alnwickyouthhostel. co.uk; ⓴ ⓯. This really bike-friendly hostel in the centre of town is housed in the former courtroom (complete with bars on the windows!). It has 15 en-suite rooms (sleeping 1–6) as well as a dining room, lounge, games room, self-catering kitchen & courtyard. It also has a restaurant, serving particularly tasty b/fasts, & a recently built secure 'Cycle Hub' store & meeting room. Plus, you don't have to be a YHA member to stay here. **£**

**The Barn at Beal** Beal Farm, Beal TD15 2PB; ✆ 01289 540044; ⟨⟩ barnatbeal.com; ⑲. With a stunning setting overlooking Lindisfarne (& next to the Lindisfarne Causeway & NCN1), this small campsite on a working farm has 11 pitches as well as hook-ups for c/vans, with good facilities such as kitchen, washroom, restaurant, bar & shop. **£**

**Berwick YHA** Dewar's Lane, Berwick-upon-Tweed TD15 1HJ; ✆ 0345 3719676; ⟨⟩ yha. org.uk/hostel/yha-berwick; ⑲ ⑳. This cyclist-friendly hostel is ideally located just around the corner from the start of our ride to Norham, & opposite Berwick Cycles (page 220). Based in a converted 18th-century granary (with a 'Tower of Pisa-like lean!'), it has 5 private rooms as well as 2 single-sex dorms (sleeping 6) with shared bathroom. Its wide range of facilities includes kitchen, laundry, lounge, dining room, café & secure cycle storage. **£**

**The Byre** Birling, Warkworth NE65 0XS; ✆ 07794 896960; ⟨⟩ thebyrewarkworth northumberland.co.uk; ⑭ ⑮. Conveniently located on 2 of our routes, near the seafront just outside Warkworth, this holiday cottage is a tastefully converted 100-year-old dairy & cattle byre, decorated with a nautical theme. It has 1 dbl & 1 twin room, with shared bathroom, kitchen, lounge & dining room, & private, enclosed patio garden (with storage space for bikes under the roof overhang or inside the garage). **£**

**Coast & Castles Camping** Boulmer Rd, Longhoughton NE66 3NU; ⟨⟩ coastandcastles. com; ⑯ ⑰. Recently opened (in 2021), this eco-glamping site is just a few kilometres inland near Boulmer, repurposed from a former admin base of the adjacent RAF Boulmer. It has 15 camping pitches, 7 safari-style glamping tents (kitted out with dbl bed, stove, kitchen facilities, table & chairs & outdoor yard with firepit) & 15 pitches with hook-ups, plus showers & washing-up block, bar kiosk & take-away barbecue van on summer w/ends. They're rewilding the site by planting native trees, hedges & plants, with solar-powered lighting & recycled gravel pathways. **£**

**Eat & Sleep Lindisfarne** West Mains Hse, Beal TD15 2PD; ✆ 01289 381827; ⟨⟩ eatandsleeplindisfarne.co.uk; ⑱ ⑲. Conveniently located by the junction of the A1/Holy Island Road to Lindisfarne, this friendly hostel-style accommodation has 3 basic but clean mixed dorms each sleeping 6 (2 dorms sharing a communal bathroom & 1 en-suite), communal kitchen & dining area, outdoor terrace & secure indoor cycle store. Its good-value café (page 183) serves all-day b/fasts, local fish & seafood. **£**

**Walkmill Campsite** nr Guyzance, Warkworth NE65 9AJ; ✆ 01665 710155; ⟨⟩ walkmillcampsite.co.uk; ⑭ ⑮. In a tranquil meadow by the River Coquet a few kilometres inland from Warkworth, this simple but quiet & clean campsite has 10 pitches for tents, plus hook-ups for motorhomes & c/vans, a shower

& toilet block, & kitchen & indoor sitting area (with digital radio). The on-site shop sells a good range of produce including local bacon, sausages, cheese, ice cream, & Pilgrims Coffee from Holy Island. **£**

**Waren Caravan Park** Waren Mill, Bamburgh NE70 7EE; 📞 01668 214366; 🖥 meadowhead. co.uk/parks/waren/; **⑰**. With a hillside setting giving great views over Budle Bay to Bamburgh Castle, this extensive, family-friendly holiday park offers static c/vans, wigwams, glamping pods, c/van hook-ups & 43 tent pitches. Its many amenities include shop, pub, playground & nature trail. **£**

**Wooler Youth Hostel** 30 Cheviot St, Wooler NE71 6LW; 📞 01668 281365; 🖥 woolerhostel. co.uk; **⑱**. This excellent little hostel has a range of accommodation including an 8-bed dorm, 10 private rooms & 4 shepherd's huts, as well as kitchen, lounge, drying room, café, garden & private car park. It also has a secure cycle store with electric recharging points for e-bikes. **£**

↑ Preparing for the downhill detour to Allen Banks (Route 5, page 59) (Huw Hennessy)

# CYCLE HIRE AND REPAIRS

## BIKE HIRE

Most shops will include a helmet, pump, tools & lock in the bike hire.

**Berwick Cycles** 17a Bridge St, Berwick-upon-Tweed TD15 1ES; ✆ 01289 331476; 🖰 berwickcycles.co.uk; **⑲**–**㉑**. Based in the historic heart of Berwick near the YHA (page 218), this versatile bike shop has a small selection of hybrids, mountain bikes & e-bikes for hire, as well as bike sales, accessories, guided bike tours & local route guides.

**The Bike Place** Kielder Water NE48 1EG; ✆ 01434 250457/250144; 🖰 thebikeplace. co.uk; **❻ ❼**. Has 2 outlets on Kielder Water: 1 opposite the visitor centre at Kielder Castle, the other at Kielder Waterside (page 211). Adults' & kids' MTBs, trailers & infants' buggies for hire, as well as accessories, bike-training courses & workshop.

**Coquet Cycles** Willowburn Industrial Estate, Alnwick NE66 2PF; ✆ 07599 350000; 🖰 coquetcycles.co.uk; **⑭**–**⑰**. This shop has a large fleet of bikes for sale, as well as adults' & children's bikes for hire (including e-bikes). Handy location, close to the Aln Valley Railway on Route 14. They will deliver hire bikes locally, and also have a workshop & offer roadside repairs.

**The Cycle Hub** Quayside, Newcastle upon Tyne NE6 1BU; ✆ 0191 276 7250; 🖰 thecyclehub. org; **❶**–**❸**. This great cycling hub has a wide selection of hybrids, road bikes, fold-ups & tandems for hire, as well as kids' tagalongs & trailers. Also has a workshop, offers 'Posh Parks' & the 'Toon' cycling tours, & has a café. Adjacent is cycling holiday specialist Saddle Skedaddle (🖰 skedaddle.com). City cycling tours with Newcastle Tour Company (🖰 newcastletourcompany.com) leave from here.

**Eco Cycle Adventures** Haugh Lane Industrial Estate, Hexham NE46 3PU; ✆ 01434 6006500; 🖰 ecocycleadventures.co.uk; **❹ ❺**. This highly recommended outfit has a range of quality mountain bikes, hybrids & e-bikes for hire. They also run cycling tours, holidays & bike transportation across the UK & Europe.

**Go Electric** The Harbour, Seahouses NE68 7RL; ✆ 07912 370800; The Common, Wooler NE71 6RL; ✆ 07912 370900; 🖰 goelectrichire.co.uk; **⑭**–**⑱**. With branches in Seahouses & Wooler, this e-bike hire specialist is handy both for coast & inland, with a fleet of Specialized e-bikes & e-MTBs (electric mountain bikes) for adults. Local delivery available & they also offer an 'Ultimate Challenge' local tour trail, following cryptic clues.

**Hadrian Cycling Ltd** 5 Greencroft, Haltwhistle NE49 9AY; ✆ 07456 953114; 🖰 hadriancyclingltd.co.uk; **❹ ❺**. Based in Haltwhistle in the North Pennines, this small family-run business has a fleet of high-quality

Cube e-bikes for hire, & also runs local e-bike tours. Hire bikes can be picked up locally or delivered (for min 2-day hire).

**Pedal Power** Coquet Enterprise Park, Amble NE65 0PE; ✆ 01665 713448; ⌂ pedal-power. co.uk/cycle-hire/; **⑭**–**⑰**. Based in Amble & well located for several of our coastal rides, this hire company has a large fleet of Dawes, Giant & Merida bikes for adults & kids. It also has e-bikes, tandems, tagalongs & kids' seats & will deliver hire bikes locally. Can transport bikes & run cycling holidays across the north of England & Scotland.

**Ride Hamsterley** Bedburn DL13 3NL; ✆ 0333 444 0629; ⌂ hamsterley.bike; ⏱ Sat–Sun only; **❶**. Based at the visitor centre in Hamsterley Forest, this specialist outfit has a range of locally made Bird MTBs plus Frog MTBs for children, & also offers servicing, repairs & accessories.

**Wallington Hall** Cambo, nr Morpeth NE61 4AR; ✆ 01670 773606; ⌂ nationaltrust. org.uk/wallington; **⑫**. Based at the National Trust Wallington estate between Bellingham & Morpeth, this bike hire centre has adults' hybrids & e-bikes as well as children's bikes & trailers. No advance booking, but it has a large fleet available. Note, though, that its bikes are only for use on the cycle trails around the grounds.

## CYCLE SHOPS

**North Pennine Cycles** Nenthead, Alston, Cumbria CA9 3PF; ✆ 01434 381324; ⌂ northpenninecycles.co.uk; **❶**–**❸** **❺**. Based just over the county border in Cumbria, this shop sells a good range of bikes & accessories & has a workshop for servicing & repairs.

**Recyke y'Bike** 164 Brinkburn St, Byker, Newcastle upon Tyne NE6 2AR; ✆ 0191 265 4197; Ropery Lane, Chester-le-Street, DH3 3NN; ✆ 0191 406 4485; ⌂ recyke.bike; 🇫 Recyke y'Bike. This commendable 're-cycling' charity refurbishes & sells donated bikes from across northeast England. Has a range of bikes for adults & children; they also do repairs, servicing & bike maintenance training courses.

**Twelfth City Cyclery** 318 Hexham Rd, Heddon-on-the-Wall NE15 9QX; ✆ 07862 355274; ⌂ twelfthcitycyclery.com; **❷**–**❺**. This bike shop & cycling community hub in the Tyne Valley has an expert team who can fit, service & repair a huge range of bike brands, with spares & accessories for sale.

**WATBike** Thorneyford Farm, Kirkley, Ponteland NE20 0AJ; ✆ 01661 825599; ⌂ watbike.co.uk; **❹** **❺** **⑬**. Another worthy community-based cycling hub, northwest of Newcastle, with organised tours & weekly rides. Also offers bike transportation, refurbished cycle sales, parts & repairs.

# FURTHER INFORMATION

## CYCLING ORGANISATIONS

**Cycling Minds** ⚲ cyclingminds.org. This inspiring local cycling charity based in Hexham helps disadvantaged people in West Northumberland by getting more people involved in cycling, as well as providing professional training & workshops.

**Cycling UK** ⚲ cyclinguk.org. One of the largest & oldest cycling membership organisations in the UK. Its bimonthly *Cycle* magazine is worth the membership alone, packed with the latest bike news, routes & readers' tips.

**Euro Velo** ⚲ en.eurovelo.com. A Europe-wide cycling network, with more than 90,000km of cycle routes covering 36 countries, including the UK.

**Sustrans** ⚲ sustrans.org.uk. The cycling charity behind the National Cycle Network, with its superb cycle paths around the UK. Its website has detailed maps & routes, including the long-distance C2C Coast-to-Coast route from Cumbria to Tyneside.

## APPS

These are a few of the best-known navigation apps (with offline maps to use where internet signal is unavailable). Useful in conjunction with this book, of course!

**Gmap Pedometer** ⚲ gmap-pedometer. com. Useful for planning routes in advance, for cyclists & walkers. Covers footpaths & gives details of overall ascent/descent.

**komoot** ⚲ komoot.com. Ready-made routes worldwide for cyclists, runners & walkers, with downloadable route maps & handy offline facility. Its impressive network of active members creates great community interaction, with up-to-date feedback. As used in this book, so unsurprisingly it's my favourite.

**Strava** ⚲ strava.com. One of the big worldwide route trackers for runners & cyclists, with lots of buttons & bells that particularly appeal to competitive athletes (or those who want to be one).

## USEFUL WEBSITES

**English Heritage** ⚲ english-heritage.org. uk. Many of Northumberland's more than 70 historic castles and ancient sites are in the care of English Heritage, magnificent monuments of the region's turbulent history from Warkworth (⓮ ⓯) & Dunstanburgh (⓱) to Lindisfarne (⓲ ⓳) & Norham (⓴ ㉑).

**Forestry England** ⚲ forestryengland.uk. The UK's forestry management service, which includes Hamsterley, Harwood & Kielder among its forest parks in Northumbria, with details of local activities & facilities. Check in advance if you're planning to visit the forests, for updates on closures during seasonal work.

**The National Trust** ⚲ nationaltrust.org.uk. The national conservation charity, with dozens of stately homes, castles & nature reserves across the Northeast, including many on our routes such as Gibside (**❸**), Cragside (**⓬**) & the Farne Islands (**⓱**).

**NewcastleGateshead** ⚲ newcastle gateshead.com. The official tourist office for the twin cities facing each other across the Tyne, with masses of info on attractions & activities In & around Tyneside, including cycle routes, route maps & bike shops.

**Northumberland National Park** ⚲ northumberlandnationalpark.org.uk. Spanning the heartland of Northumbria, from the North Pennines to the Scottish Borders, the national park offers spectacular cycling territory, with details here of recommended routes.

**This is Durham** ⚲ thisisdurham.com. The official visitor information authority, with heaps of handy tips, including a dedicated cycling section covering local routes & more.

**Visit Northumberland** ⚲ visit northumberland.com. The official visitor website for Northumberland, with an abundance of listings for what to do & where to go, including cycling-friendly places to eat & stay.

## FURTHER READING

### Books on Northumbria

**Slow Travel Northumberland** (Bradt Guides, 2019, 320pp). Part of Bradt's Slow Travel series, written by local expert Gemma Hall, this comprehensive guide is packed with details about the best of this diverse county, plus personal favourite tips including lesser-known walks, waterfalls & beaches.

**Slow Travel Durham** (Bradt Guides, 2023, 320pp). Another of Bradt's Slow Travel series, recently published, and also written by Gemma Hall. The book covers Durham city as well as the wider countryside and Coast Path. The author's expert inside tips include exploring old railway routes by bike and discovering lesser-known

sites, such as abandoned collieries, secluded bathing pools and hidden places to spot the rare black grouse.

**The Northumbrians** by Dan Jackson (Hurst & Co, 2019, 315pp). From the Venerable Bede to *Viz* magazine, Lord Armstrong to Paul Gascoigne, this book lifts the lid on what Geordies are really like, behind the hard-working, heavy drinking stereotypes. Unashamedly proud Northumbrian Jackson brings the region to life in his highly readable history, from the Viking invasions to its post-industrial regeneration.

**The Anglo-Saxon Age** by Martin Wall (Amberley Publishing, 2016, 256pp). Fought over by successive waves of invaders, northeast

England saw some of the bloodiest conflicts in the British Isles. This compact but detailed history explains how the ancient kingdom of Northumbria was formed, & the Anglo Saxons' role in shaping today's UK.

**The Borders** by Alistair Moffat (Birlinn Ltd, 2018, 602pp). If you visit the Border bastles & are interested in learning more about the Reiver raiders (see page 95), you might want to read this impressive book. In gripping detail, Moffat demystifies the complexities of the Anglo-Scottish borderlands, from the earliest hunter-gatherers to the Celtic warlords & the Romans.

## Bike books

**The Big Book of Cycling for Beginners** by Tori Bortmann (Rodale Books, 2014, 290pp). Although it was published back in 2014 (predating e-bikes – ancient history!), this comprehensive book covers everything from safe cycling to the best nutrition for cyclists. US cycling consultant Bortmann also gives confidence-boosting insights on the benefits of cycling to our physical & mental health.

**Bike Repair Manual** by Chris Sidwells (Dorling Kindersley, 2021, 176pp). A handy, pocket-sized manual with detailed illustrations. Full of tips on practical maintenance, accessible to the complete beginner, it also includes an overview of different types of bike & accessory, for adults & children.

# ACKNOWLEDGEMENTS

First, many thanks to Bradt for letting me loose on my bike again for another cycling guide; in particular to my editor Chris, who did a superb job, particularly in picking up my errant ramblings; also to Anna, Claire, Hugh, Sue and all the team, not to forget cartographer David McCutcheon for his maps, superb as always.

Huge thanks once again to komoot for supporting us on another cycling guide, and to Rob Marshall, for untying my navigational knots when I got stuck and for writing the Foreword.

I'm deeply grateful to Jordan Matthews (Cycling UK's development officer for northeast England) for all his help and advice, for writing his expert overview in the Introduction, and for keeping me company on the Durham to Newcastle Cathedrals route.

During my research for this book I was helped by many people, so I'd like to give a Big Geordie shout-out to the following, for their time and generosity: Ted Liddle, of Cycle Northumberland – some of the rides here are based on his routes; Chris Follwell at Big Local Gateshead; Halina Figon for the Newcastle Highlights Tour, and Anna Unger, of Newcastle's Posh Parks Cycling Tour; Jane Bower and Shaun Cutler for the Cathedrals Cycle Route; Toby Price at Cycling Minds; Claire Blake at WATBike; Sue Bolam of Alnwick Cycling Club; Adam Walker at Saddle Skedaddle; Michael Mountney of Saint Oswald's Way Management Group; Simon Rudman from Northumberland County Council and Edward Cawthorn of the Friends of the Union Chain Bridge; and Celia and Ralph Cresswell of Budle Hall for local cycling tips and for the 'Thin Place' idea. You all gave me loads of insider's tips, some of which I didn't have room for. Apologies for my ingratitude – next time we'll have to fit in twice as many rides.

My partner and sometime fellow cyclist Caitlin and I gratefully received generous hospitality, from Hamsterley to Norham, so we'd like to thank the following: Cris Brown, Jennie Meikle, Ruth Tweedie and colleagues at Visit Northumberland and Hayley Quarmby at NGI (NewcastleGateshead Initiative), whose fantastic support made us feel so welcome; also, to Carolyne Hall of the Victoria Inn, Witton-le-Wear; Andrew Robson of the Camping & Caravanning Club; Stacey Turnbull and Lauren Maltas, of Original Cottages; Audrey and Tom Bowes, of Greycroft B&B, Alnwick; and Mary-Rose and Jim Blyth, of Norham Bike Yard (plus, Jim's local cycling knowledge and not to mention his scrumptious flapjacks, the ultimate cycling fuel).

Special thanks to my dear friend Kevin for the generous loan of his mountain bike – without which I'd probably still be lost somewhere in Harwood Forest.

And finally, but most of all, my deepest thanks to Caitlin, my ever-patient partner, meticulous fact-checker, and cycling soulmate: for keeping me going to the last full stop.

# INDEX

Page numbers in **bold** indicate main entries; those in *italics* indicate maps.

accommodation 21, **208–19**
Aln Valley 139–42
Alnwick 11, 145–7
Alnwick to Warkworth Loop 4, 8,
   **138–47**, *140*
   accommodation 215, 217–18
   food and drink 146–7
   getting there 145
   tourist information 147
Amble to Bamburgh 4, 8, **164–75**, *166*
   accommodation 215, 217–18
   food and drink 174–5
   getting there 174
   tourist information 175
*Angel of the North* 33, **34–5**
Anglo-Scottish wars 95, 104, 106, 135,
   153, 165, 172, 193, 203, 224
Armstrong, Lord William 95, **124–5**,
   126, 223

B&Bs *see* accommodation
bastles 91, 94, 95
beaches 182
   Cheswick Sands 187
   Cocklawburn 187
   Howdiemont Sands 160
   Lindisfarne 182
   Spittal 188
   Sugar Sands 160
Bellingham 11, 21, 83–4, **87–9**
Bellingham Bastles Loop 5, 7, **90–9**, *92*
   accommodation 209–14
   food and drink 99
   getting there 98
   tourist information 99
Bellingham to Greenhaugh Loop 5, 7,
   **100–7**, *102*
   accommodation 209–14
   food and drink 107
   getting there 106

   tourist information 107
Bellingham to Rothbury 5, 7, **118–27**,
   *120–1*
   accommodation 211–12, 214
   food and drink 127
   getting there 126
   tourist information 127
Bellingham to Wark Loop 5, 7, **108–17**,
   *110*
   accommodation 209–10, 212–13
   food and drink 117
   getting there 116
   tourist information 117
Berwick-upon-Tweed 188–91
Berwick-upon-Tweed to Norham 4, 9,
   **192–8**, *194*
   accommodation 214–15, 217
   food and drink 198
   getting there 198
   tourist information 198
bikes
   equipment and accessories 15
   hire 22, 220–1
   maintenance 14–15
   on public transport 16
   shops 221
   types of 13–14
Border Reivers 93, **95**, 104, 224
Brown, Lancelot 'Capability' 87, 92,
   130, 132

cafes *see* food and drink *under individual
   trails*
camping *see* accommodation
castles
   Alnwick 145, 153
   Bamburgh 171, 173–4, 187
   Belsay 128
   Dally 87
   Dunstanburgh 157
   Lindisfarne 134, 177, 182

Norham 189, 197, 201
Warkworth 153, 154, 165, 167
cathedrals and churches
Durham Cathedral 31
Kirk o'Steil 206
St Aidan's Thorneyburn 103
St Andrew's, Bolam 135
St Giles', Birtley 112–13
St Nicholas Cathedral Church of
Newcastle 36
Cathedrals Cycle Route 12, 19, 31–7
Cheviot Hills 104, 177, 184
Coast & Castles Cycle Route (NCN1)
139, 141–2, 152–4, 165–74, 177–83,
185–91, 193–8
Coquet Island 142, 143, 150
Craster 157, 161–3
Craster to Howick Loop 4, 8, **156–63**, 158
accommodation 214, 217–18
food and drink 163
getting there 162–3
tourist information 163
cycling
Cycling UK Community Cycling
Club 12
Dragon Cycle Trail, Wallington Hall
132
further reading 223–4
mountain biking 18
National Cycle Routes (NCN) 20
organisations 222
route apps 222
safety 16–18
trail routes 4–5, 20
Tweed Cycleway 205
what to wear 16

Dark Sky Discovery Sites 68, **69**, 93,
104, 105
Darling, Grace 143
Derwent Valley 19, 43–5
dry stone walls 112
Durham Cathedral to Newcastle
Cathedral 5, 6, **30–7**, 32
accommodation 208–9
food and drink 37

getting there 37
tourist information 37

Falstone to Bellingham 5, 7, **82–9**, 84
accommodation 210–12
food and drink 89
getting there 88
tourist information 89
Farne Islands 143, 171, 172, 181
food and drink see entries under
individual trails
price codes 21
forests
Hamsterley 24–9
Harwood 119, 122–5
Kielder 65–73
further reading 223–4

Gateshead 31, 34–6, 40, 46
Gormley, Sir Antony 33, 34
Greenhaugh 93–4

Hadrian's Cycleway 39–42
Hamsterley Forest MTB Trail 5, 6, 22,
**24–9**, 26
accommodation 208–9
food and drink 29
getting there 29
tourist information 29
Haydon Bridge 56–7
Haydon Bridge to Vindolanda Loop 5,
6, **50–7**, 52
accommodation 210–12
food and drink 57
getting there 56
tourist information 57
historic homes, monuments and sites
Belsay Hall and Castle 128, 132–3
Black Middens Bastle 94
Cragside 124–5, 126
Craster Tower Gateway 157
Dunston Staiths 41, 44–6
Gibside 39, 43, 45
Hadrian's Wall 51, 54–6, 104
Hesleyside Hall 91–2, 106
Highgreen Manor 95–6

Howick Hall 157, 158–9
Paxton House 193, 195
Snabdough Farm (Bastle) 92–3
Stublick Chimney 60–1
Vindolanda 51, 54–5, 56
Wallington Hall 22, 129–30, 132, 136
Weetwood Bridge 178
Whalton Manor 128, 129, 134
Holy Island *see* Lindisfarne
hotels *see* accommodation

International Dark Sky Park 10, **69**

Jekyll, Gertrude 134

Kielder Forest 65–73
Kielder Water 22, 64–73, 75–81, 84, 86
komoot **3**, 20–1

Lakeside Way Trail, Kielder Forest 5, 7,
    **64–73**, *66*
    accommodation 211–12
    food and drink 72–3
    getting there 72
    tourist information 73
Lindisfarne 160, 171, 176, 177, 180, **181**,
    **182–3**
    Lindisfarne Causeway 180, 182
Lindisfarne to Berwick-upon-Tweed 4, 9,
    **184–91**, *186–7*
    accommodation 217–18
    food and drink 191
    getting there 190
    tourist information 191
Lowry, L S 189
Lucas, David 94
Lutyens, Sir Edwin 134

Mountain Bike trails
    Hamsterley Forest 25–9
    Osprey Chick, Kielder Forest 28–35
museums and galleries
    Baltic Centre for Contemporary Art
        40, 46
    Bellingham Heritage Centre 88

National Landscape Discovery Centre
    (The Sill) 55

Newcastle upon Tyne 22, 36–7, 39–41
    Quayside 39
Newcastle upon Tyne to Derwent Valley
    Loop 5, 6, **38–48**, *40*
    accommodation 209
    food and drink 47–8
    getting there 47
    tourist information 48
Norham 197–8
North Pennines 11, 25–9, 51–7, 58–63
North Tyne Valley 83, 87, 101–7, 109–17
Northumberland National Park 10, 11,
    17, 55, 69, 83, 90–9, 101–3, **104–5**,
    118–27
Northumbria 10

Osprey Chick MTB Trail, Kielder Forest
    4, 7, **74–81**, *76*
    accommodation 211–12
    food and drink 80–1
    getting there 80
    tourist information 81

parks, gardens and nature reserves
    Allen Banks and Staward Gorge 61
    Bakethin Nature Reserve, Kielder
        Water 72
    Bolam Lake and Country Park 135–6
    Derwent Country Park 39, 43–4
    International Dark Sky Park 10, 69,
        104, 105
    Lindisfarne National Nature Reserve
        187
    Muckle Moss National Nature
        Reserve 53, 56
    Northumberland Wildlife Trust,
        Kielder Water 78
    RSPB Coquet Island 142
    Saltwell Park 35
Pennine Cycleway 104, 116, 119–26
Pennine Way 83
Pennines Panorama Loop 5, 6, **58–63**, *60*
    accommodation 210–13

food and drink 63
getting there 62
tourist information 63
pubs *see* food and drink *under individual
trails*

railways
Aln Valley Railway 139–41
Derwent Valley Railway 45
restaurants *see* food and drink *under
individual trails*
River Tyne 36, 40–6, 86
Rothbury 118, 126

St Aidan
St Cuthbert 33, 167, 179, **181**
St Cuthbert's Cave 177, 179
St Cuthbert's Way 33, 179–81
St Oswald 123
St Oswald's Way 123–4, 152
Sandstone Way 19, 118–26, 176–83,
184–91
Scotland 11, 87, 95, 112, 114, 181, 189,
193–5, 203, 205, 206
Shaw, Richard Norman 125
Simonside Hills 123–5

Turner, J M W 19, **189**, 193
Tweed to Till Rivers Loop 4, 9, **200–7**, *202*
accommodation 214–15

food and drink 207
getting there 207
tourist information 207
Tyne Valleys (South and North Tyne)
53–63, 83–9

Union Chain Bridge 193, 195, **196**
useful websites 222–3

Wallington to Belsay Loop 5, 8, **128–37**,
*130*
accommodation 210–11
food and drink 136–7
getting there 136
tourist information 137
Ward, Gilbert 160
Wark (on Tyne) 109, 113, **114–15**
Warkworth West Loop 4, 8, **148–55**, *150*
accommodation 215, 217
food and drink 154–5
getting there 154
tourist information 155
where to stay *see* accommodation
Wilbourn, Colin 84
Wooler 177, 182–3
Wooler to Lindisfarne 4, 9, **176–83**, *178*
accommodation 215, 219
food and drink 183
getting there 182
tourist information 183

## INDEX OF ADVERTISERS

Camping & Caravanning Club 226
Greycroft 147
Hotel du Vin 48

Norham Bike Yard 199
Original Cottages 216

Published in association with komoot
First edition published April 2023

komoot

Bradt Guides Ltd
31a High Street, Chesham, Buckinghamshire, HP5 1BW, England
www.bradtguides.com
Print edition published in the USA by The Globe Pequot Press Inc,
PO Box 480, Guilford, Connecticut 06437–0480

Text copyright © 2023 Bradt Guides Ltd
Maps copyright © 2023 Bradt Guides Ltd; includes map data © OpenStreetMap
contributors
Photographs copyright © 2023 Individual photographers (see below)
Project Manager: Chris Reed
Cover research: Ian Spick, Bradt Guides

ISBN: 9781804690956

**British Library Cataloguing in Publication Data**
A catalogue record for this book is available from the British Library

**Photographs** Photographers credited beside images & also those from libraries
credited as follows: Alamy.com (A); Shutterstock.com (S)
*Front cover* Top: View towards Bamburgh Castle (Sara Winter/S); Bottom: Cycling
through Chopwell Woods, Gateshead (Graeme Peacock/NewcastleGateshead
Initiative)
*Back cover* Cycling the high moorland overlooking Bellingham (Caitlin Hennessy)
*Title page* Cyclists on the Lakeside Way trail in Kielder Water and Forest Park
(Jon Sparks/A)

**Maps** David McCutcheon FBCart.S

Typeset by BBR Design, Sheffield
Production managed by Zenith Media; printed in the UK
Digital conversion by www.dataworks.co.in

# THE BRADT STORY

## In the beginning

It all began in 1974 on an Amazon river barge. During an 18-month trip through South America, two adventurous young backpackers – Hilary Bradt and her then husband, George – decided to write about the hiking trails they had discovered through the Andes. *Backpacking Along Ancient Ways in Peru and Bolivia* included the very first descriptions of the Inca Trail. It was the start of a colourful journey to becoming one of the best-loved travel publishers in the world; you can read the full story on our website (bradtguides. com/ourstory).

## Getting there first

Hilary quickly gained a reputation for being a true travel pioneer, and in the 1980s she started to focus on guides to places overlooked by other publishers. The Bradt Guides list became a roll call of guidebook 'firsts'. We published the first guide to Madagascar, followed by Mauritius, Czechoslovakia and Vietnam. The 1990s saw the beginning of our extensive coverage of Africa: Tanzania, Uganda, South Africa, and Eritrea. Later, post-conflict guides became a feature: Rwanda, Mozambique, Angola, and Sierra Leone, as well as the first standalone guides to the Baltic States following the fall of the Iron Curtain, and the first post-war guides to Bosnia, Kosovo and Albania.

## Comprehensive – and with a conscience

Today, we are the world's largest independently owned travel publisher, with more than 200 titles. However, our ethos remains unchanged. Hilary is still keenly involved, and **we still get there first**: two-thirds of Bradt guides have no direct competition.

But we don't just get there first. Our guides are also known for being **more comprehensive** than any other series. We avoid templates and tick-lists. Each guide is a one-of-a-kind expression of an expert author's interests, knowledge and enthusiasm for telling it how it really is.

And a commitment to wildlife, conservation and respect for local communities has always been at the heart of our books. Bradt Guides was **championing sustainable travel** before any other guidebook publisher. We even have a series dedicated to Slow Travel in the UK, award-winning books that explore the country with a passion and depth you'll find nowhere else.

## Thank you!

We can only do what we do because of the support of readers like you – people who value less-obvious experiences, less-visited places and a more thoughtful approach to travel. Those who, like us, take travel seriously.

**Bradt** GUIDES

### TRAVEL TAKEN SERIOUSLY